Presented To:

_____

By:

_____

Date:

_____

QUIET MOMENTS
WITH GOD

DEVOTIONAL JOURNAL

for Women

HONOR **HB** BOOKS

An Imprint of Cook Communications Ministries • Colorado Springs, CO

2 3 4 5 6 7 8 9 10 11 Printing/Year 08 07 06 05 04

Quiet Moments with God Devotional Journal for Women
ISBN 1-56292-984-4
Copyright © 2001 by Honor Books, an imprint of
Cook Communications Ministries, Colorado Springs, CO 80918
Cook Communications, Paris, Ontario
Kingsway Communications, Eastbourne, England

Developed by Bordon Book
Compiled by Snapdragon Editorial Group, Tulsa, Oklahoma

QUIET MOMENTS WITH GOD

DEVOTIONAL JOURNAL

for Women

Introduction

Life is so busy at times that we lose track of what is going on inside where the most important activities take place—our thoughts. We know that what we think influences what we do, but we are doing so much for everyone else at such a rapid rate that to stop and think about our own life, our own walk with God, our relationships with others, and the many blessings we have been given can feel very hard to do.

Quiet Moments with God Devotional Journal for Women is a tool that you can use to slow down, read a scripture and a reflection on life, and write what you really think about it all. Getting it down on paper will make your desire to grow and be the kind of person God meant you to be turn into reality. Each reflection will give you something to think about. There is an entry for each day of the year. Each journal entry has a prompt that helps get you started writing what you really want out of life, what you really care about, what you are really determined to do to become your best. There is even a thought-provoking quotation to consider as you move through your day.

Quiet Moments with God Devotional Journal for Women may just be the catalyst to some of the most creative and productive times of your life. And it only takes a little bit of time each day. So take a quiet moment and get to know two very important people in your life: God, of course, and—someone He loves very much—yourself.

Hidden Beauty

O LORD, our LORD, how majestic is
your name in all the earth!
PSALM 8:9

Shortly after the New Year arrived, Brenda noticed the clutter on her dining room table. She thought of the Christmas celebration just a few weeks earlier and how beautiful her table had been as she welcomed friends and family into her home.

Now life was back to normal. The tree was packed up, and the nativity scene had been put away. The elegant setting had been removed from her table and replaced with several bills that needed to be paid. Contributing to the jumble was a box of tissues (the remnant of a post-holiday bout of pneumonia) and an address book.

Brenda picked up the address book and flipped through the pages. Each page was filled with names, addresses, and telephone numbers. She realized that this book represented her family and friends, and she thought about how fortunate she was to have so many people who loved her. As she read the names, she offered up a prayer for each one. She prayed for their special needs and asked God to walk with them daily.

She picked up the tissues and thanked God for her health. Then she looked over the bills and thanked God for her career and the opportunity to provide for her family. One by one, she counted her many blessings.

At first glance, the things on Brenda's table seemed to invade the beauty of her home, but as she looked at each item, she realized that every one served as a reminder of God's presence in her life.

If men thanked God for good things,
they wouldn't have time to
complain about the bad.

What ITEM DO I SEE BEFORE ME THAT REMINDS ME OF GOD'S BLESSINGS?

Apple Pie Problems

He who was seated on the throne said,
"I am making everything new!"
REVELATION 21:5

Lord, I NEED
TO TALK TO
YOU TODAY
ABOUT . . .

Marilyn's favorite apple pie rolled from her fingertips without a pause. The pie crust lay trimmed and ready in the pie pan, awaiting the seasoned filling. Everything looked just fine. Yet as she added a sprinkling of walnuts and placed the top crust in position, a heavy sigh escaped from her lips. Her mind was not on the pie but rather on a troubled relationship with a close friend.

As she slid the pie into the oven, Marilyn remembered hearing a speaker who encouraged her listeners to keep a prayer journal. The speaker said she usually prayed aloud as she wrote her concerns in a journal. She felt it helped her clarify her problems and keep track of God's answers.

Marilyn picked up a blank book she had been given for Christmas. Sitting at the kitchen table, she began to write a letter to God, pouring out her heart and her hurt about this troubled relationship. Before she knew it, the oven timer sounded, and she sniffed the familiar warm scent of apples filling the room.

Surprisingly, her heart felt lighter. She was struck by the similarity between the pie and the prayer journal. Wrapped between two piecrusts and left to time and the work of the oven, the apples had changed from tart and crisp to sweet and smooth. In the same way, Marilyn had wrapped her concerns between the covers of prayer. God needed time to work. She knew He would change that soured relationship and make things sweet again.

Friendship is in loving rather
than in being loved.

A Leather-Bound Cover

Man looketh on the outward appearance,
but the LORD looketh on the heart.

1 SAMUEL 16:7 KJV

Some OF
GOD'S GREAT-
EST TREASURES
I'VE RECENTLY
ENJOYED
ARE . . .

Dodie Gadient, a schoolteacher, decided to see the sights she had taught about. Traveling alone in a truck with camper in tow, she launched out. One afternoon in California's rush-hour traffic, the water pump on her truck blew. In spite of the traffic jam she caused, no one seemed interested in helping.

Leaning up against the trailer, she prayed, "Please, God, send me an angel . . . preferably one with mechanical experience." Within four minutes, a huge Harley drove up, ridden by an enormous man sporting long hair, a beard, and tattooed arms. He jumped off and went to work. A little while later, he flagged down a larger truck, attached a tow chain to the disabled truck, and whisked the whole fifty-six-foot rig off the freeway onto a side street, where he worked on the water pump.

The schoolteacher was too dumbfounded to talk—especially when she read the back of his leather jacket: "Hell's Angels—California." As he finished the task, she finally got up the courage to say, "Thanks so much."

Noticing her surprise, he looked her straight in the eye, "Don't judge a book by its cover. You may not know who you're talking to." With that he smiled, closed the hood of the truck, and with a wave, he was gone.[1]

God has a way of opening our eyes and showing us His greatest treasures—people—if we will look beyond our prejudices. Allow Him to show you a few of His treasures today!

Don't judge any man until you have
walked two moons in his moccasins.

Accepting Substitutes

Unto him that is able to do exceeding abundantly above all that we ask or think, according to the power that worketh in us.
EPHESIANS 3:20 KJV

Some OF GOD'S SUBSTI-TUTES I CAN LOOK AT IN A DIFFERENT WAY ARE . . .

A woman moved to Wyoming. Clothing stores were in short supply, and her busy ranch life left little time for trips to larger cities to shop. Her situation was more difficult because she was a hard-to-fit size. She began relying on a major store catalog, which carried her size. The printed order forms sent by the store had this sentence at the bottom: "If we do not have the article you ordered in stock, may we substitute?"

She was hesitant to trust strangers to make an appropriate substitution, but she replied, "Yes," hoping it wouldn't be necessary.

One day she opened a package and found a letter, which read in part, "We are sorry that the article you ordered is out of stock, but we have substituted . . . " Then she found an article of greater quality worth double the price she paid!

After that, the woman wrote YES in large red letters at the bottom of the order form by the substitution question. She knew the store would provide her with the best they had.

When we pray, we can trust God to send us the perfect answer because, as our Maker, He knows what will fit us better than we do. Because He knows the future, He can answer in a way that goes beyond our highest expectations. Every time He sends "substitutes," we can be sure He is sending something much better than we could have ever imagined.

*When life isn't the way you like,
like it the way it is.*

The "To Be" List

*When the Holy Spirit controls our lives
he will produce this kind of fruit in us: love,
joy, peace, patience, kindness, goodness,
faithfulness, gentleness and self-control.*
GALATIANS 5:22-23 TLB

Nearly all of us write a "to do" list. The Scriptures compel us, however, to have a *"to be"* list.

From a "to do" perspective, we tend to come before the Lord and say, "This is my list, and this is my schedule. Please be with me, help me, and bless me."

From a *"to be"* perspective, we might pray:

- Help me to reflect Your love today.
- Help me to display Your joy.
- Help me to manifest Your peace.
- Help me to practice Your patience.
- Help me to express Your kindness.
- Help me to make known Your goodness.
- Help me to reveal Your faithfulness.
- Help me to show Your gentleness.
- Help me to exhibit Your self-control.

However, these traits are the distinguishing marks of God's presence in our lives. Our "to be" list, should begin with time spent with Him.

In order to express the Lord's kindness, for example, we first must *receive* the Lord's kindness. In receiving His kindness, we become much more attuned to opportunities in which we might show His kindness to others. "Being kind" becomes a part of everything we do. The way we do our chores, hold our meetings, run our errands, and engage in our projects display His kindness to those around us.

When we make our "to be" list our top priority, the things we have "to do" become much more obvious—and far less burdensome!

*He who labors as he prays lifts
his heart to God with his hands.*

Some ITEMS ON MY "TO BE LIST" THAT ARE MOST IMPOR-TANT TO ME ARE . . .

Everyday Benefits

Blessed be the Lord,
Who daily loads us with benefits.
PSALM 68:19 NKJV

What
ARE SOME
ADDITIONAL
BLESSINGS
THAT I CAN
ADD TO
THIS LIST?

Blessings we take for granted are often forgotten. Yet every day God "loads us with benefits." This morning think of some common things you may have taken for granted—and thank God for them:

- Lungs that work well and steadily—ten to fifteen times each minute.
- Bones that protect vital organs and the muscles that hold them in their place.
- A healthy disease-fighting immune system.
- An untiring heart that pumps nine pints of blood through a sixty-thousand-mile network of vessels.
- Our five senses—eyes to see the dawn, ears to hear your loved one's voice, a nose to smell the freshness of the early dew, the sense of touch to enjoy a hug, and the sense of taste to savor breakfast.
- Nerve cells that send messages to other parts of the body.
- The ability—and desire—to get up and out of bed in the morning.
- A place to live and a place to work.
- Loving and supportive family, friends, and colleagues and the opportunities to let them know you care about them.
- An intimate relationship with God through Jesus Christ.
- Each day's unique beauty—the angle of the sun, white clouds stretched out across the blue afternoon sky, the gold and pink sunset.
- The rotation of the earth that gives us day and night.
- Times for quiet reflection and grateful remembrances.
- The gift of laughter—and the ability to laugh at our mistakes.

Reflect upon your present blessings,
of which everyone has many.

Explore the Scenery

The earth is full of the goodness of the LORD.
PSALM 33:5 NKJV

How CAN
I SHARE
SOME OF
THE SIMPLE
THINGS IN
LIFE WITH
THOSE
AROUND ME?

Every day has moments worth savoring and enjoying to the fullest. It may take some effort to search out those moments, but the reward is a sense of enriched meaning in life, which is in turn motivating and satisfying.

Watch your children scamper for the school bus. Play freely in a warm spring rain shower. Take your brown-bag lunch to the park and watch the geese circle on the pond or the elderly men bowl on the green. Gaze out a window and watch the birds making their nest on a ledge or the careful balancing act of window washers at work on the building across the boulevard. Enjoy a steaming cup of cappuccino in a garden-room cafe while a string ensemble plays in the background. Watch puppies tumble about in their play or kittens toying with a ball of yarn. Linger at a balcony rail with a glass of tangy lemonade and watch the sun set in golden glory.

Harold V. Melchert once said: "Live your life each day as you would climb a mountain. An occasional glance toward the summit keeps the goal in mind, but many beautiful scenes are to be observed from each new vantage point. Climb slowly, steadily, enjoying each passing moment; and the view from the summit will serve as a fitting climax for the journey."

God's creation is all around us. Take time today to enjoy what God has done and is doing! You'll enjoy what *you* are doing more.

❧

The kiss of the sun for pardon,
The song of the birds for mirth,
One is nearer God's heart in a garden
Than anywhere else on earth.

With Attitude

Whatever you do, do all to the glory of God.
1 CORINTHIANS 10:31 RSV

I can
FIND MORE
SATISFACTION
IN MY WORK
BY . . .

"To love what you do and feel that it matters—how could anything be more fun?" asks Katharine Graham. No matter what work we do, our attitude toward our work is vital to our sense of self-worth. The ideal is to love the work we do and feel that it has significance. While no job is pleasant all the time, it is possible to derive satisfaction from what we bring to a job—the attitude with which we perform our tasks.

For example, Brother Lawrence, the seventeenth-century Carmelite, found joy in his job washing dishes at the monastery. In the monotony of his routine work, he found the opportunity to focus on God and feel His presence.

Modern-day entrepreneurs Ben Cohen and Jerry Greenfield make and sell ice cream with a purpose. The bottom line of Ben & Jerry's Homemade, Inc. is "How much money is left over at the end of the year?" and "How have we improved life in the community?"

"Leftover money" funds Ben & Jerry's Foundation, which distributes funds to worthy nonprofit causes. These are charities that help needy children, preserve the Amazonian rain forest, provide safe shelter for emotionally or psychologically distressed people, and fund a business staffed by unemployed homeless people. By helping others with their profits, Ben and Jerry put more *meaning* into their ice cream business.

If you feel your work is insignificant, ask God to open your eyes! When you do all for Him and are willing to serve others, no task is unimportant!

People who make room in their hearts for others will themselves find accommodation everywhere.

Starry, Starry Night

*The heavens declare the glory of God; and
the firmament sheweth his handywork.*

PSALM 19:1 KJV

How WOULD
BEING GOD'S
FRIEND
CHANGE
THE WAY I
FEEL ABOUT
MYSELF . . .

Remember when you were a child, lying on your back outdoors, staring up at the celestial stream of stars and moon? All was peaceful and still. How relaxing it was to quietly gaze at the shimmering lights and simply dream! Even as an adult, you are not too old for that. Everyone needs a quiet time to be alone with God, without television, radio, or teaching tapes. If you can't find quiet time, perhaps you've given it away. You can take it back now.

God created you more special than all other things, even the stars in the heavens. The psalmist wrote in Psalms 8:3-5 KJV, *"When I consider thy heavens, the work of thy fingers, the moon and the stars, which thou hast ordained; What is man, that thou art mindful of him? and the son of man that thou visitest him? For thou hast made him a little lower than the angels, and hast crowned him with glory and honour."*

God has a special place in His heart just for you and wants you to know Him in a more intimate way. The Lord desires this relationship even more than you do. Your friendship pleases Him.

As you spend time with God, you will be strengthened. This strength will keep you from throwing in the towel when times get tough. Make your quiet time top priority. Consider it an appointment with God. Plan to spend time with God each day and give it first place.

*So necessary is our friendship to
God that He approaches us and
asks us to be His friends.*

I Can See Clearly Now

We know that, when He appears, we shall be like Him, because we shall see Him just as He is.
1 JOHN 3:2 NASB

How CAN
I BETTER
USE THE
RESOURCES
GOD HAS
GIVEN ME TO
HELP ME
ALONG
LIFE'S WAY?

Between Macon and Valdosta, Georgia, lies a stretch of Interstate 75, known for heavy fog that causes massive pileups of cars, vans, trucks, and campers. Several times each year horrible accidents happen as drivers enter the thick fog. Many can't even see the front of their own vehicles, much less beyond.

The result is a disaster waiting to happen—and often it does. Many are injured, vehicles are destroyed, and motorists are delayed for hours. The costs to personal property, the city, and the state, as well as the increase in insurance rates, are astronomical. The worst tragedy is the loss of human life.

People often come to Christ in a fog. The fog lifts and we can perceive life in a whole new realm. Even more exciting is the knowledge that the day will come when we can stand before Christ, when we will see Him clearly just as He is, in all His glory. Nothing will be able to cloud the true and living Christ from our vision. For now, we must trust Him to see for us, then guide and direct us through His Word and prayer.

Heaven is the place where questions and answers become one.

Downhill from Here

*Ye are a chosen generation, a royal priesthood,
an holy nation, a peculiar people; that ye should
shew forth the praises of him who hath called
you out of darkness into His marvellous light.*

1 PETER 2:9 KJV

Jean-Claude Killy, the French ski champion, did more than just work hard at his sport.

When he made his nation's ski team in the early 1960s, he was determined to be the best. He decided vigorous training was the key. However, other team members were working just as hard. In the end, it was a change in style, not conditioning, that set Killy apart.

The goal in ski racing is to ski down a prescribed mountain course faster than anyone else. Killy began experimenting and found that skiing with his legs apart gave him better balance. He also found that if he sat back on his skis when executing a turn, instead of leaning forward as was customary, he had better control, which also resulted in faster times. Rather than regarding his ski poles as an accessory for balance, Killy tried using them to propel himself forward.

Killy's style was unorthodox. But when he won most of the major ski events in 1966 and 1967, including three gold medals at the Winter Olympics, skiers around the world took notice. Today, the Killy style is the norm among downhill and slalom racers.[2]

As Christians we are not called to conform to the world's standards, but to God's standards. Our lifestyle should challenge people to come to Jesus Christ and live according to His higher ways and purposes. The Christian "style" may seem odd to the unbeliever, but in the end, it is the style that will prevail!

Are THERE AREAS IN MY LIFE THAT HAVE BEEN CONFORMED TO THE WORLD'S STANDARD RATHER THAN THAT OF CHRIST?

*If you want to be original,
just try being yourself,
because God has never made
two people exactly alike.*

19

Prepare to Dare

Every prudent man acts out of knowledge,
but a fool exposes his folly.
PROVERBS 13:16

What CIR-
CUMSTANCES
IN MY LIFE
COULD BE
CLUES TO
GOD'S PLAN
FOR ME?

Charles Lindbergh took a calculated risk when he decided to fly across the Atlantic, alone, in a single-engine plane. He certainly might have been fearful if he had never flown before or had known nothing about planes. He might have been anxious if he hadn't trusted the builder of his plane or his mechanics. And he certainly would have been labeled foolish if he had decided to make the trip on a whim, without advance planning.

But none of those factors were true in Lindbergh's case. He was an experienced pilot and mechanic who personally spent months overseeing the construction of his plane. He participated in the planning of every detail of his historic flight. The end result was a safe trip, finished ahead of schedule with fuel to spare.[3]

Likewise, heroic spiritual moments are nearly always grounded in advance preparation. Moses grew up in Pharaoh's court, unknowingly preparing for the day he would demand that Pharaoh let the Hebrew people leave Egypt.

Esther prepared herself for a year before she won the "contest" to be queen. She prepared herself again before boldly going to the king to expose the enemy of her people.

You may not see clearly what God's purpose is for your life, but you can trust in the fact that He is preparing you for it. He will not waste a moment of your life. So make every relationship and experience count today because He is grooming you for future greatness!

I would rather walk with God in
the dark than go alone in the light.

Serendipity Moments

We are his workmanship, created in Christ Jesus unto good works.
EPHESIANS 2:10 KJV

I will ASK GOD TO INSPIRE ME CREATIVELY IN THE FOLLOWING AREAS . . .

Serendipity, according to Merriam-Webster's Collegiate Dictionary, is "the faculty or phenomenon of finding valuable or agreeable things not sought for." We sometimes call it an "accident, dumb luck, or fate," but serendipity has given us new products and better ways of doing things. Consider this example . . .

While George Ballas was driving his car through a car wash, he had a moment of serendipity that made him a millionaire. As he watched the strings of the brushes cleaning his car, he turned his mind to his list of things to do, among them edging his lawn.

Suddenly an idea "popped" into his head. He took another long look at the strings on the rotating brush. The strings straightened out when turning at high speed but were still flexible enough to reach into every nook and cranny of his car to get it clean. He asked himself, *Why not use a nylon cord, whirling at high speed, to trim the grass and weeds around the trees and the house?* His idea—his serendipity—led to the invention of the Weedeater.

Where do we get new ideas? God is the Master behind serendipity! He may not always give you a million-dollar idea, but He will make you more creative. One expert gives this advice: Capture the ideas, jot them down quickly before they are gone, and evaluate them later. Take time to daydream with the Lord. Seek new challenges. Expand your perspective. Learn and do new things.[4]

Whatever is worth doing at all is worth doing well.

Take a Breather

*The Lord God formed man of the dust
of the ground, and breathed into
his nostrils the breath of life.*
GENESIS 2:7 NKJV

The AREAS OF
MY LIFE IN
WHICH I NEED
A BREATHER
ARE . . .

The fast-paced, relentless duties of life often cause us to declare with a sigh, "I need a breather." We may be voicing more truth than we realize! Medical researchers have discovered that for virtually every person who *works*—whether at physically demanding manual labor or intellectually demanding white-collar labor—performance level improves when a person breathes properly.

Good breathing is defined as regular, deep, and slow. The opposite—uneven, shallow, and rapid—is a sure sign to most physicians that something is seriously wrong. Good breathing is essential for good health. It supplies oxygen to the bloodstream, which is vital for the functioning of all bodily organs, especially the heart and brain.

The Scriptures tell us God breathes His life into us both physically and spiritually. Jesus breathed upon His disciples to impart the Holy Spirit to them. (See John 20:22.) The early church experienced the Holy Spirit as a rushing mighty wind—a manifestation of the breath of God. (See Acts 2:1-2.)

Today in our personal lives, an awareness of the Spirit of God working in us is often experienced as a fresh breeze, one that cleanses and revives us in every part of our being. The word *inspiration* literally means to have the things of the Spirit put *into us*.

We do well to take a periodic "breather" in the Lord's presence. When we do, we find our spirits are refreshed and renewed at a level deeper than the superficiality of our daily routine.

Rest is the sweet sauce of labor.

Editing Your Life

Seeing we also are compassed about with so great a
cloud of witnesses, let us lay aside every weight,
and the sin which doth so easily beset us.
HEBREWS 12:1 KJV

Disney films are known the world over as the best in animation, but the studio didn't earn that reputation easily. One of the reasons for the level of excellence achieved was the filmmaker himself. Walt Disney was ruthless about cutting anything that got in the way of the unfolding story.

Ward Kimball, one of the animators for *Snow White,* recalls working 240 days on a four-minute sequence. In this scene, the dwarfs made soup for Snow White, almost destroying the kitchen in the process. Disney thought it was funny, but he decided that it interrupted the flow of the picture, so it was edited out.

Often we find ourselves doing "good" things, which are not only unnecessary but also a distraction from the unfolding story of our lives. Like the soup scene, many of these things are worthwhile or entertaining, but they lack the essential element of being the best use of the time and talents God has given us.

The next time you're asked to take on another "good scene," ask yourself the following questions:

- Does this fit in with the plan God has set before me—do I have a lasting inner peace about it?
- Will this task help me or others grow closer to the Lord?
- Can I do this without taking away from the time I've already committed to my family, church, job, or friends?

Be diligent concerning the multitude of *good* things you edit out of your life in favor of the *great* things God wants to do through you!

◦◦◦

The wisest thing is Time,
for it brings everything to light.

How CAN I DO A BETTER JOB OF EDITING MY LIFE?

Faulty Assumptions

The pride of thine heart hath deceived thee,
thou that dwellest in the clefts of the rock,
whose habitation is high; that saith in his heart,
who shall bring me down to the ground?
OBADIAH 1:3 KJV

What STEPS
CAN I TAKE
TO AVOID
PRIDEFUL
ASSUMPTIONS
ABOUT
OTHERS?

A traveler at an airport went to a lounge and bought a small package of cookies to eat while reading a newspaper. Gradually, she became aware of a rustling noise. Looking from behind her paper, she was flabbergasted to see a neatly dressed man helping himself to her cookies. Not wanting to make a scene, she leaned over and took a cookie herself.

A minute or two passed, and then she heard more rustling. He was helping himself to another cookie! By this time, they had come to the end of the package. She was angry but didn't dare allow herself to say anything. Then, as if to add insult to injury, the man broke the remaining cookie in two, pushed half across to her, ate the other half, and left.

Still fuming later when her flight was announced, the woman opened her handbag to get her ticket. To her shock and embarrassment, there was her pack of unopened cookies!

It's so easy to make assumptions about what is happening around us. They are not always wrong, but they are never to be trusted.

Pride caused the woman in this story to assume she was right and the gentleman was wrong. Instead of seeing him through God's eyes and praying for wisdom to handle the situation, she ignored the man. She was completely blind to his kindness toward her.

When you find yourself in a conflict with others, avoid prideful assumptions by walking in God's love.

Pride is spiritual cancer; it eats the very possibility of Love, or contentment, or even common sense.

The Guide

The Lord shall guide thee continually, and satisfy thy soul in drought, and make fat thy bones: and thou shalt be like a watered garden, and like a spring of water, whose waters fail not.

ISAIAH 58:11 KJV

I need TO ALLOW GOD TO LEAD AND GUIDE ME EACH DAY BECAUSE . . .

In *A Slow and Certain Light,* missionary Elisabeth Elliot tells of two adventurers who stopped by to see her at her mission station. Loaded heavily with equipment for the rain forest, they sought no advice. They merely asked her to teach them a few phrases of the language so they might converse a bit with the Indians.

Amazed at their temerity, she saw a parallel between these travelers and Christians. She writes: "Sometimes we come to God as the two adventurers came to me—confident and, we think, well-informed and well-equipped. But has it occurred to us that with all our accumulation of stuff, something is missing?"

She suggests that we often ask God for far too little. "We know what we need—a yes or no answer, please, to a simple question. Or perhaps a road sign. Something quick and easy to point the way. What we really ought to have is the Guide himself. Maps, road signs, a few useful phrases are good things, but infinitely better is having Someone who has been there before and knows the way."[5]

In the midst of your day, you may face unexpected situations. Trust God to be your Guide and pray, "Lord, I know this didn't take You by surprise! You knew it was coming and have already made a way for me. I thank You for taking me where I need to go and giving me everything I need to get over the rough spots along the way."

Relying on God has to begin all over again every day as if nothing had yet been done.

Praise Break

Give thanks to the Lord, for he is good;
his lovingkindness continues forever.
PSALM 136:1 TLB

Lord,
I WILL
PRAISE YOU
TODAY FOR . . .

Rather than take a coffee break today, take a praise break! Take a pause in your day to acknowledge all the specific ways in which the Lord has been good to you. Thank Him for what He is doing in your life, right now, where you are.

Nothing is too large or too small to be worthy of your praise. Every good thing you have and experience in life ultimately comes from the Lord. Sometimes blessings come directly and sometimes through the talents or skills of others who are inspired or empowered by Him. Give praise for the things you see at hand! Your praise list may include the following:

- Help with writing that important memo
- A good, kind, and thorough secretary
- The invention of paper clips and staplers
- A window through which to view the world
- Vacuum cleaners
- Microwave ovens
- Walking shoes
- Budding trees
- Ready access to vital data
- Computer repair people
- An unfailing copy machine
- The postal worker being five minutes late, which gave you time to find a stamp
- A cordial interview
- Willing colleagues
- Doormats and children who remember to use them
- A cake that survived a slammed back door
- A completed phone call
- Spell-check
- Good health
- Fulfilling work
- A loving family and circle of friends

Remember the day's blessings;
forget the day's troubles.

Look around, look down, and look up. You'll never run out of things to be thankful for!

Take Cover

He will cover you with His pinions, and under His wings you may seek refuge; His faithfulness is a shield and bulwark.

PSALM 91:4 NASB

Bouncing back from disappointment, loss, or an irritating situation can take time. When you're hurting, the thing you need to do is nurse your wounds for a little while, regroup, then go back out and face the world. What a relief it would be if angry words, dirty looks, and cruel actions had no power to hurt us.

Many of us have frying pans coated with Teflon because food doesn't stick to it. The scientists at Dow Chemical have come up with what might be called the next generation of Teflon: a fluorocarbon formula that can be sprayed or brushed onto a surface. It's been suggested it might be used to repel graffiti on subway walls, barnacles on ships, dirt on wallpaper, and ice on aircraft. Its "base" sticks to whatever it's applied to, but its "surface" repels moisture.

This is a little like being in the world, but not of it. "I pray not that thou shouldest take them out of the world, but that thou shouldest keep them from the evil," Jesus prayed for His disciples in John 17:15 KJV. "As thou has sent me into the world, even so have I also sent them into the world" (v. 18).

We have to come into contact with a lot of negatives throughout our lives, but we don't have to absorb them or let them become part of us. With the help of the Holy Spirit, we can stick to God.

Kind words don't wear out the tongue.

What CAN I DO TO REPEL THE NEGATIVES THAT COME MY WAY EACH DAY?

Good will come to him who is generous and lends freely, who conducts his affairs with justice.
PSALM 112:5

I can MAKE
A DIFFERENCE
IN MY WORLD
BY . . .

Marian Wright Edelman, attorney and founding president of the Children's Defense Fund, often speaks of how Martin Luther King had a profound impact on her life. All Americans have been affected by Dr. King's life in some way, and most have heard his famous comment, "I have a dream." But it was not his public persona that had an impact upon her; it was his willingness to admit his fears.

She writes, "I remember him as someone able to admit how often he was afraid and unsure about his next step. It was his human vulnerability and his ability to rise above it that I most remember."

She should know about rising above fear and uncertainty because her life was not an easy one, and one wonders just how often she drew strength from the self-honesty and candor of Dr. King.

Ms. Edelman grew up during the days of segregation, one of five children, the daughter of a Baptist minister. She graduated from Spelman College and Yale University Law School and was the first black woman to pass the bar in the state of Mississippi. She is a prolific and gifted writer and has devoted her life to serving as an activist for disadvantaged Americans, especially children.

She has an incredible testimony. She never doubted that she could make a difference. "I have always believed that I could help change the world because I have been lucky to have adults around me who did—in small and large ways."

He who gives to me teaches me to give.

Such as I Have, I Give

Stir up the gift of God which is in you.
2 TIMOTHY 1:6 NKJV

The word *talent* usually evokes images of great musicians, actors, and artists. But the truth is that talent comes in as many shapes and sizes as there are people, and God has given talent to each one of us.

What are some of the "not so obvious" talents? Compassion is one. Do you feel kindness toward someone in a distressing situation? Then you have been given a talent! Use that feeling to write a letter of encouragement to someone you know who is in need. Do you like to plan surprises for people who may otherwise feel forgotten or left out? Then you are gifted! Don't bury that talent— use it instead to bring joy to another person.

Perhaps you have the gift of seeing something good in every individual. Affirm the good in someone, and then spread the "good news" about them. Do you have a calm spirit in the midst of calamity? Can you think clearly when surrounded by turmoil? Then you are gifted—and your talent is very much in need. That was a talent Jesus demonstrated when He slept through the storm on a boat, didn't lose sight of His purpose when facing the angry crowd, and faced His death sentence on the Cross.

Do you have a cup of cold water to offer another person? Then you have a gift. Use it in the name of Jesus and for the glory of God.

Talent is something God gives you;
experience is something you give yourself.

What TALENTS DO I HAVE THAT I HAVE NOT CONSIDERED BEFORE?

Moments of Contentment

I have learned how to be content (satisfied to the point where I am not disturbed or disquieted) in whatever state I am.
PHILIPPIANS 4:11 AMP

What SIMPLE GIFTS IN LIFE HAVE I BEEN TAKING FOR GRANTED?

If anyone knew about "tornado days"—those days when projects and deadlines fly around you in a flurry—it was the apostle Paul. He wrote to the Corinthians that in the course of his life he was beaten to the point of death with whips and rods; stoned and left for dead; shipwrecked; in peril from rivers, bandits, and seas; sleepless and hungry; cold and without adequate clothing; and persecuted virtually everywhere he went. Yet he was able to say to the Philippians, in essence, "I have learned to be in peace, no matter what happens."

When we encounter stressful situations, we need to ask the Lord for inner contentment. This prayer by Louis Bromfield seems to have been written for just those times:

"Oh, Lord, I thank you for the privilege and gift of living in a world filled with beauty and excitement and variety.

I thank you for the gift of loving and being loved, for the friendliness and understanding and beauty of the animals on the farm and in the forest and marshes, for the green of the trees, the sound of a waterfall, the darting beauty of the trout in the brook.

I thank you for the delights of music and children, of other men's thoughts and conversation, and their books to read by the fireside or in bed with the rain falling on the roof or the snow blowing past the window."

Make the secret chamber of your heart your place to experience contentment.

The secret of contentment is knowing how to enjoy what you have.

"Fussing" Away Time

> *"Do not worry about tomorrow,*
> *for tomorrow will worry about itself."*
> MATTHEW 6:34

An older woman was taking a railway journey for the first time. She was to travel fifty miles through an interesting and beautiful region and had long looked forward to the trip. However, once on the train it took her so long to get her baskets and parcels put away, her seat comfortably arranged, the shades and shutters adjusted, the anxious questions answered, that she was just settling down to enjoy the trip when they called out the name of her station!

"Oh my!" she said. "If I had only known that we would be here so soon, I wouldn't have wasted my time in fussing. I hardly saw the scenery!"

Fussing with things left behind yesterday and things yet to do tomorrow robs us of the joys God brings to us today. If you've said, "I'm too busy to . . . " several times today, it might be time to review your priorities.

Too Busy
Too busy to read the Bible
Too busy to wait and pray!
Too busy to speak out kindly
To someone by the way!
Too busy to care and struggle,
To think of the life to come!
Too busy building mansions,
To plan for the Heavenly Home.
Too busy to help a brother
Who faces the winter blast!
Too busy to share his burden
When self in the balance is cast.
Too busy for all that is holy
On earth beneath the sky.
Too busy to serve the Master
But not too busy to die.

—Author Unknown

What RECENT BLESS- INGS DID I ENJOY BECAUSE I WAS <u>NOT</u> TOO BUSY?

Contentment comes not from having
more, but from desiring less.

So Send I You

I heard the voice of the Lord, saying,
Whom shall I send, and who will go
for us? Then said I, Here am I; send me.
ISAIAH 6:8 KJV

DO I BELIEVE
THAT GOD
SENT ME TO
THE PLACE I
AM IN NOW?
WHAT DOES HE
WANT ME
TO DO HERE?

Margaret Clarkson was a young schoolteacher in a gold-mining town in northern Ontario, Canada—far from friends and family. As she meditated on John 20:21 one evening, God spoke to her through the phrase "So send I you." She realized that this lonely area was the place to which God had sent her—her mission field. As she wrote down her thoughts in verse, one of the most popular missionary hymns of the twentieth century was born.

> So send I you to labor unrewarded,
> To serve unpaid, unloved, unsought, unknown,
> To bear rebuke, to suffer scorn and scoffing—
> So send I you to suffer for My sake.
>
> So send I you to bind the bruised and broken,
> O'er wand'ring souls to work, to weep,
>   to wake,
> To bear the burdens of a world a-weary—
> So send I you to suffer for My sake.
>
> So send I you to loneliness and longing,
> With heart ahung'ring for the loved
>   and known,
> Forsaking home and kindred, friend and
>   dear one—
> So send I you to know My love alone.
>
> So send I you to leave your life's ambition,
> To die to dear desire, self-will resign,
> To labor long and love where men revile you—
> So send I you to lose your life in Mine.
>
> So send I you to hearts made hard by hatred,
> To eyes made blind because they will not see,
> To spend—tho' it be blood—to spend and
>   spare not—
> So send I you to taste of Calvary.[6]

Nothing is impossible to the willing heart.

Living Beyond the Thunder

In all things God works for the good of those who love him, who have been called according to his purpose.

ROMANS 8:28

In *The Diary of a Young Girl,* Anne Frank wrote, "I simply can't build up my hopes on a foundation consisting of confusion, misery, and death."[7] She understood that hope originates somewhere beyond our immediate circumstances. In fact, hope—real hope—often stands alone in the darkness.

How was this young girl capable of courage and faith far beyond her years? She refused to allow the devastation of her times to shape her view of life. In her words, "It's really a wonder that I haven't dropped all my ideals. Yet I keep them. I hear the ever-approaching thunder. I can feel the sufferings of millions and yet, if I look up into the heavens, I think that it will all come right."[8]

We can't know what horrors Anne Frank and her family suffered in the Holocaust, but we do know only her father emerged alive. Yet her words live on. Decades later, several generations have read and been touched by the diary of a young girl facing one of the darkest periods in world history—a girl who chose hope in the midst of hopelessness.

Life sometimes includes hardship. When tests come, we have the same choice Anne Frank had: hold on to our ideals or drop them. When life's circumstances sound like "approaching thunder," remember the simple truth in the life of a young Jewish girl. A foundation made of the right ingredients makes for an overcoming life.

*Our hope is ever livelier than despair,
our joy livelier and more abiding
than our sorrows are.*

What RAYS OF HOPE CAN I SEE FROM THIS POINT IN MY JOURNEY?

The Good Life

Whom have I in heaven but Thee? And besides Thee, I desire nothing on earth. My flesh and my heart may fail, but God is the strength of my heart and my portion forever.
PSALMS 73:25-26 NASB

Some OF THE BEST "THINGS" IN MY WORLD ARE . . .

A popular Internet joke goes something like this:

A secretary, a paralegal, and a partner in a big law firm are walking to lunch when they find an antique oil lamp. They rub it, and a genie comes out in a puff of smoke. The genie says, "I usually grant only three wishes, so I'll give each of you just one."

"Me first!" says the secretary. "I want to be in the Bahamas, driving a speedboat, without a care in the world." Poof! She's gone.

"Me next!" says the paralegal. "I want to be in Hawaii, relaxing on the beach with my personal masseuse, an endless supply of piña coladas, and the love of my life." Poof! He's gone.

"You're next," the genie says to the partner.

The partner says, "I want those two back in the office right after lunch."

We've been told that we can "have it all." But there's too much to do, not enough time—and no magic lamp to do it for us. And we wouldn't even want it all if we didn't think it would make us happy.

However, those in the know say there's an easier path to a happy life. These three simple thoughts are cited as the keys to happiness:

1. Fret not—He loves you. (See John 13:1.)
2. Faint not—He holds you. (See Psalm 139:10.)
3. Fret not—He keeps you. (See Psalm 121:5.)

It's possible to have it all by making God your "All."

∽≫∾

Happiness grows at our own firesides, and is not to be picked in a stranger's garden.

Morning Praise!

Come before Him with joyful singing.
PSALM 100:2 NASB

Some WAYS I
CAN PRAISE
GOD WHOLE-
HEARTEDLY
ARE . . .

A young career woman moved away from her home to New York City. She rented a room from an elderly lady who had migrated to the United States years before from Sweden. The landlady offered a clean room, a shared bathroom, and use of the kitchen at a reasonable rate.

The little white-haired Swedish woman made the rules of the house very clear. There would be no smoking or drinking, no food in the bedrooms, etc. Pausing mid-sentence, the landlady asked, "Do you sing? Do you play? Music is good! I used to play the piano at the church, but not now. I'm too old. My hearing isn't good, but I love to praise God with music. God loves music."

Later that evening, after a full day of moving into her new room, the young tenant heard horrible noises coming from somewhere downstairs.

Cautiously making her way down the stairway, she followed the sounds to the kitchen door. There she discovered her new landlady standing at the stove, joyfully "singing" at the top of her lungs!

Never had the young woman heard such a horrible voice. Yet she heard that voice, precious to God, every day for as long as she rented the room just over the kitchen.

The tenant moved on, married, and had her own family. Yet, every morning she stands in front of the stove and sings off key and loud, but joyful, praises to the Lord!

What a glorious way to start the day!

✧

Joy rises in me like a summer's morn.

What a Friend!

"I have called you friends."
JOHN 15:15 RSV

Jesus HAS PROVEN HIMSELF TO BE MY FRIEND BY . . .

What a Friend we have in Jesus,
All our sins and griefs to bear!
What a privilege to carry
Everything to God in prayer!
O what peace we often forfeit!
O what needless pain we bear!
All because we do not carry
Everything to God in prayer.

Joseph Scriven, the writer of the hymn "What a Friend We Have in Jesus," had a life of great sorrow. A day or two before their wedding, his fiancée drowned. This tragedy put him in a melancholy state that stayed with him the rest of his life.

In spite of his despondent temperament, the power and presence of God were evident in Scriven's life. He was a philanthropist and a devout Christian. He had a reputation as a man "who saws wood for poor widows and sick people who are unable to pay." To other people he was the friend that they had found in Jesus.

Scriven wrote this hymn to comfort his mother in a time of sorrow. He never intended that anyone else would see it, but the manuscript was discovered by a neighbor. When asked if he had written it, Scriven said, "The Lord and I did it between us."[9]

Spend your break today with your Best Friend, Jesus. He gave himself so you and He could become friends, and friends always stand by and help each other.

You need only to share your need with the Lord Jesus in prayer to find comfort!

The dearest friend on earth is a mere shadow compared with Jesus Christ.

The Invitation

"The son said unto him, 'Father, I . . . am no more worthy to be called thy son.'"

LUKE 15:21 KJV

God HAS INVITED ME TO COME OUT OF MY COMFORT ZONE AND GROW BY . . .

Rita stood on the sidewalk, peering wistfully at the beautiful home. Through the curtained windows she saw nicely dressed people chatting with one another and enjoying refreshments. In her hand she clutched an engraved, personal invitation to the dinner party given to her by her professor who was impressed with her academic abilities and wanted her to meet others at the university.

She carefully fingered the invitation, looked down at her nice "party dress" that seemed so dull and ordinary in comparison to the gowns she saw through the window, turned, and slowly walked away. Clutched between her fingers was the unused invitation.

This poignant and painful scene from the British movie *Educating Rita* demonstrates just how difficult it is for one to accept the possibility of a new life. Rita came from a lower-middle-class family, and no one had attended university before her. She struggled with feelings of inadequacy and was forever wondering how she would "fit in." It is this sense of self-doubt that caused her to fail to take action on the invitation.

However, thanks to a persistent professor, who saw more in her than she saw in herself, she eventually stepped into a new world. By the movie's end, this once modest woman excels as a scholar.

The invitation to become and then excel as a Christian is for each of us. The greatest joy, though, is in knowing that our Master Teacher always sees much more in us than we usually see in ourselves.

∽✢∾

They can conquer who believe they can.

A New Look

Happy are the people who are in such a state;
Happy are the people whose God is the Lord!
PSALM 144:15 NKJV

Who HAS
SMILED AT ME
LATELY? WHAT
MESSAGE CAME
THROUGH?

In 1998, twenty-one-year-old Se Ri Pak became the newest "wonder kid" of women's professional golf, winning the United States Open and later becoming the first woman to shoot a 61 in an LPGA event. Having played golf for only six years before turning professional, her amazing ascent was attributed not only to talent but also to a fierce mental focus based in the Asian tradition.

Onlookers are awed at the young player's ability to ignore distractions on the course. Even her caddy was asked if they were fighting because she walks alone and does not talk with him. But he explained that it's because she is intensely focused all the time.

In fact, her control is such that Se Ri broke into tears for the first time in her life upon winning the U.S. Open. Emotional display is that unusual for her. But she explains how she's working to change that habit:

I usually look very serious, but after I started playing golf at fourteen, I saw Nancy Lopez on TV. I didn't know she was a great golfer—all I knew was that she always smiled. My goal is to be that way too. Now when I sign autographs, I always put a smile by my name. . . . Even if I don't win, I want to give people a smile.[10]

It is said a smile is the best way to improve your appearance. It's also one of the nicest things you can do for others.

A smile costs nothing but creates much.

Book Me, Papaw!

Children's children are the crown of old men; and the glory of children are their fathers.

PROVERBS 17:6 KJV

I can
HELP LAY A
FOUNDATION
FOR SOMEONE
ELSE'S LIFE
BY . . .

His eyes moistened with unbidden tears as Nicole climbed into his lap and settled comfortably against his chest. Her hair, freshly shampooed and dried, smelled of lemons and touched his cheek, soft as down. With clear blue-green eyes, she looked expectantly up at his face, thrust the trusted and well-worn book of children's stories at him, and said, "Book me, Papaw, book me!"

"Papaw" James carefully adjusted his reading glasses, cleared his throat, and began the familiar story. She knew the words by heart and excitedly "read" along with him. Every now and then he missed a word, and she politely corrected him, saying, "No, Papaw, that's not what it says. Now let's do it again so that we get it right."

She had no idea how her purity of heart thrilled his soul or how her simple trust in him moved him. James had had a far different childhood—a harsh existence, made harder still by a distant and demanding father. His father ordered him to work the fields from dawn to dusk beginning at age 5. His childhood memories sometimes continue to create anger and pain.

This first grandchild, though, has brought joy and light into his life in a way that supersedes his own childhood. He returns her love and faith with a gentleness and devotion that makes her world secure and safe beyond measure. Their relationship is made for a lifetime. For Nicole, it lays a foundation for life. For James, it heals a past of pain.

The world moves forward on the feet of little children.

Dr. Simpson and Dancing

He hath put in his heart that he may teach.
EXODUS 35:34 KJV

How CAN
I BECOME A
CHANGING
FORCE IN
THE LIVES
OF THOSE
AROUND ME?

Lively music filled the air as the college students mingled with one another, shared laughs, and danced together. Just then, Dr. Simpson walked up to Rob and asked him, "Why aren't you out there dancing with everyone else?"

"I don't want anyone to laugh at me," he responded.

"What makes you think that they would be looking at you anyway?" came her quick retort with more than a hint of laughter in her voice. She was like that—quick to challenge her students' assumptions, but in a way that provoked thought and self-examination rather than pain and embarrassment.

A respected and admired professor of English, Dr. Simpson expected much from every student. She was tough, but her classes were always full. It was exchanges like this one that made it possible for Rob to see his life from a perspective other than his own, and in gaining this insight he became more self-confident and less uptight. She helped—no, she *forced* him to grow as both a student and a person.

In the words of one author, "The teacher must be able to discern when to push and when to comfort, when to chastise and when to praise, when to challenge and when to hold back, when to encourage risk and when to protect."[11] This, Dr. Simpson did on a daily basis. And this is just the type of teacher we need. God usually provides each of us with our own unique Dr. Simpson—many times with more than one.

A good word costs no more than a bad one.

His Promise of Peace

Be still, and know that I am God.
PSALM 46:10

A woman who grew up on a large farm in Pennsylvania fondly remembers some special times with her father.

"During the winter months, Dad didn't have to work as hard and long as he did the rest of the year. In fact, it seemed like there were some times when he didn't work at all as far as I could tell.

"During those long winter months, he had a habit of sitting by the fire. He never refused my bid to climb up on his lap and he rewarded my effort by holding me close for hours at a time. Often, he would read to me or invite me to read a story to him. Sometimes I would fall asleep as we talked about all the things that are important to dads and little girls. Other times, we didn't talk at all. We just gazed at the fire and enjoyed the warmth of our closeness. Oh, how I treasured those intimate moments.

"As I grew, I thought it odd that other kids dreaded the 'indoor' days of winter. For me they meant the incredible pleasure of having my father very nearly all to myself."[12]

Just as winter is God's season of rest for the earth, we sometimes experience "winter" in our spiritual lives.

If you are going through a dry, wintry time, why not snuggle close to the Heavenly Father tonight, and listen to His gentle voice? The love and comfort He wants to give you will surely warm your heart!

❧

Peace is always beautiful.

A time THAT
I RECALL BEING
CLOSE TO GOD
WAS . . .

Perfect Harmony

Do not forsake your friend.
PROVERBS 27:10

What CHAR-
ACTERISTICS
ARE MOST
IMPORTANT IN
A FRIEND?

The late Leonard Bernstein—conductor, composer, teacher, and advocate—may well be the most important figure in American music of the twentieth century. With his personality and passion for his favorite subject, he inspired generations of new musicians and taught thousands that music should be an integral part of everyone's life.

As a public figure, Bernstein was larger than life—his charm and persuasiveness infectious. While his career progressed, he was constantly sought after for performances, lectures, and other appearances.

But it's said that in his later years, one way his personal life eroded was in his friendships. There came a time when he had few close friends. After his death, a comment from one of his longest acquaintances was that "you wanted to be his friend, but so many other people sought his attention that, eventually, the friendliest thing you could do was leave him alone."[13]

Scientific evidence now shows us how important friendships are, not only to our emotional health, but to our physical and mental health as well. These most cherished relationships are a two-way street. The following are a few tips for keeping friendships on track:

- Be aware of your friends' likes and dislikes.
- Remember your friends' birthdays and anniversaries.
- Take interest in your friends' children.
- Become sensitive to their needs.
- Keep in touch with them by phone.
- Express what you like about your relationship with another person.
- Serve your friends in thoughtful, unexpected ways.[14]

*Friendship is a plant that
must often be watered.*

Say That Again?

So shall My word be that goes forth from My mouth; It shall not return to Me void, but it shall accomplish what I please, and it shall prosper in the thing for which I sent it.

ISAIAH 55:11 NKJV

In 1954, Sylvia Wright wrote a column for the *Atlantic* in which she coined the term *mondegreen,* her code word for misheard lyrics. She wrote about hearing the following Scottish folk song, "The Bonny Earl of Morray":

Ye highlands, and ye lowlands,

Oh! whair hae ye been?

They hae slaine the Earl of Murray,

And layd him on the green.

She misheard the last line as "and Lady Mondegreen." It saddened her immensely that both the Earl and the Lady had died. Of course, she was later chagrined to learn that those were not the lyrics at all. But they made so much sense at the time.

Since then, mondegreen collectors have been on the lookout for newer and more comical misunderstandings, such as the following:

- In "America the Beautiful," one young patriot heard "Oh beautiful, for spacious skies" as "Oh beautiful, for spaceship guys."

- Another considered "Away in a Manger" a little unsettling as he sang, "The cattle are blowing the baby away."

- Then there was the Mickey Mouse Club fan who, when the cast sang "Forever hold your banners high," thought they were encouraging her to "Forever hold your Pampers high!"[15]

It's no wonder that, with all our earthly static and clamor, we sometimes think we're singing the right words when we're not. But if we begin each day in quiet conversation with God, His Word comes through loud and clear. There can be no misunderstanding God's lyrics.

What HAS GOD SAID TO ME LATELY? IF I LISTEN AGAIN CLOSER CAN I HEAR MORE?

It takes a great man to make a good listener.

Night Driving

Thy word is a lamp to my feet,
and a light to my path.
PSALM 119:105 NASB

I have
TO BE BRAVE
TO FACE . . .

A woman confessed to a friend her confusion and hesitance about an important life decision she was facing. She professed to believe in God but could not bring herself to rely on her faith to help choose her path.

"How can I know I'm doing the right thing?" she asked. "How can I possibly believe my decision will be right when I can't even see tomorrow?"

Her friend thought and finally said, "Here's how I look at it. You know when you're driving down a dark country road with no streetlights to give you any notion of where you are? It's a little scary. But you rely on headlights. Now, those headlights may show you only ten yards of road in front of you, but you see where to go for that little stretch. And as you travel that ten-yard stretch of road, the headlights show you ten more yards, and ten more, until eventually you reach your destination safe and sound.

"That's how I feel about living by faith. I may not be able to see tomorrow, next week, or next year, but I know that God will give me the light to find my way when I need it."

When you come to the edge of all the light
you know and are about to step off into
the darkness of the unknown, faith is
knowing one of two things will happen:
There will be something solid to stand on,
or you will be taught how to fly.

A Work in Progress

*We are His workmanship, created in Christ
Jesus for good works, which God prepared
beforehand that we should walk in them.*

EPHESIANS 2:10 NKJV

Many centuries ago, a young Greek artist named Timanthes studied under a respected tutor. After several years of effort, Timanthes painted an exquisite work of art. Unfortunately, he was so taken with his painting that he spent days gazing at it.

One morning, he arrived to find his work blotted out with paint. His teacher admitted destroying the painting, saying, "I did it for your own good. That painting was retarding your progress. Start again and see if you can do better." Timanthes took his teacher's advice and produced *Sacrifice of Iphigenia,* now regarded as one of the finest paintings of antiquity.[16]

Timanthes's teacher knew what many great artists know—we should never consider ourselves truly finished with our work.

When the legendary Pablo Casals reached his ninety-fifth year, a reporter asked, "Mr. Casals, you are ninety-five and the greatest cellist who ever lived. Why do you still practice six hours a day?"

And Casals answered, "Because I think I'm making progress."

Maya Angelou applies that same logic to daily life. In her book *Wouldn't Take Nothin' for My Journey Now,* she writes: "Many things continue to amaze me, even well into the sixth decade of my life. I'm startled or taken aback when people walk up to me and tell me they are Christians. My first response is the question 'Already?' It seems to me a lifelong endeavor to try to live the life of a Christian."[17]

*How exciting it is to be a work in progress!
With God's help, our possibilities
are limitless! No limits but the sky.*

Today
I WANT TO
IMPROVE IN
MY . . .

Fine China

Behold, like the clay in the potter's hand,
so are you in My hand, O house of Israel.
JEREMIAH 18:6 NASB

What
ATTITUDES
SHOULD I
CHANGE TO
MAKE MY
HEART MORE
PLIABLE IN
GOD'S HANDS?

Antique hunting one day, a collector noticed a lovely teacup and saucer. The delicate set stood out from the other china pieces in the display. She picked up the cup and examined it carefully. Discovering a small imperfection on the bottom, she lovingly held it in her hands as she thought about what might have caused the cup's flaw.

A few years earlier while visiting a pottery shop, she had watched as the potter chose a lump of clay to work and began to punch and slam it over and over again until it was just right. He shaped it, painted it, and fired it into a beautiful piece of earthenware that would be looked upon admiringly and be a serviceable item as well.

The clay, useless in its original form, had become beautiful, strong, and useful in the potter's hands. The woman thought of her own life with all its flaws, yet Jesus was willing to sacrifice himself so that she could have a good life with Him. Many lumpy places had existed in her heart prior to her salvation, but Jesus Christ, the Master Craftsman, began His work of shaping and molding, lovingly concentrating on even the finest details. This human vessel was then made fit for His service as He gently filled it to overflowing with the refining work of the Holy Spirit.

Grace is the love that gives, that loves
the unlovely and the unlovable.

Morning Drive

*This is the day the LORD has made;
we will rejoice and be glad in it.*
PSALM 118:24 NKJV

I want
TO SLOW
DOWN AND
ENJOY THE
BEAUTY OF . . .

Judy could take the freeway to work each morning and arrive instantly, nerves revved, almost before she is awake. But to her, freeways are ugly. Instead she takes the scenic route around several local lakes and starts her day with mental pictures of sunrises, flowers, and people in various states of running and walking.

She feels that nature is the attraction—a chance for a city slicker to enjoy a little tranquility. The slower pace gives her the occasion to see a small group of deer or watch the ducks and geese depart for the winter and return for their spring nesting activities. She recognizes and studies the walkers and joggers who are out regularly at the crack of dawn.

"I don't know if I have a better workday because I sneak up on the job rather than race to it," she muses. "On some mornings, I don't see one thing that nature has to offer because the day ahead refuses to wait for me to get there, and I spend the entire ride making lists in my head of things to do. But I do know that when I take the time to glance at the roses along the way, I feel more fortified, just like our mothers wanted us to be with a hearty breakfast, mittens, and hats."[18]

Taking a few moments to thank God for the glories of creation will make any day start on a better note!

*Lovely flowers are the smiles
of God's goodness.*

By Your Fruit

Love, joy, peace, patience, kindness, goodness,
faithfulness, gentleness and self-control.
Against such things there is no law.
GALATIANS 5:22-23

What WAYS
CAN I GIVE
OF MYSELF
FOR THOSE
IN NEED
AROUND ME?

With these words, Mother Teresa explained a lifetime of service: I can love only one person at a time. I can feed only one person at a time. Just one, one, one. So you begin . . . I begin. I picked up one person—maybe if I didn't pick up that one person I wouldn't have picked up 42,000."[19]

When she died, an entire world mourned.

Sometime before her death, a college professor asked his students to name people they considered truly worthy of the title "world leader." Although many different names appeared on the class list, the one name most commonly agreed upon was Mother Teresa.

The students wrote the following statements about her:

She transcends normal love.

She has a capacity for giving that makes me ashamed of my own self-centered actions.

The most remarkable thing about her is that she never grows tired of her work. She never experiences "burnout" like so many other people. I just hope that I can be as satisfied with my life as she is with hers.

Although none of the students had ever met her, they acknowledged that Mother Teresa had a profound impact on each of their lives. How? By her love. She welcomed the opportunity to fulfill her duties. Can we do any less?

Next time you have a chance to be kind, remember her words: "It is not how much we do but how much love we put in the doing."[20]

Take away love and our earth is a tomb.

May I Take Your Order?

Then shall ye call upon me, and ye shall go and pray unto me, and I will hearken unto you.
JEREMIAH 29:12 KJV

Sometimes, the only solution for a difficult day is a nice double-dip ice cream cone—that is, if you love ice cream. One fan described a recent trial in ordering her treat at a drive-thru window.

She drove up to the speaker to place her order. This ice cream franchise carried too many flavors to list them all on the menu, so customers had to ask if a special flavor was in stock. The attendant answered: "May I take your order?"

"Do you have butter brickle today?" she asked. It was her favorite since childhood, and it was becoming increasingly difficult to find.

"No, I'm sorry . . . can we get you anything else?"

Oh, the frustration of drive-thru communication. "What else do you have?" she asked.

The attendant paused and said, "Well . . . what do you *want?*"

She couldn't help herself. "I *want* butter brickle!"

It was useless. But, determined to find that flavor, she drove two miles to the next franchise store. She approached the speaker with optimism. "May I take your order?" he asked.

"Yes, do you have butter brickle today?"

After a long pause, the attendant responded, "Butter brickle *what?*"

It is so disheartening to feel that no one hears our needs. How fortunate that God not only understands our every desire, but also knows them even before we do. Philippians 4:6 ASV encourages, "In nothing be anxious; but in everything by prayer and supplication with thanksgiving let your requests be made known unto God."

A special DESIRE OF MY HEART THAT I HAVE NEVER SHARED WITH ANYONE IS . . .

Those who know when they have enough are rich.

Got Change?

God has not given us a spirit of fear, but of power and of love and of a sound mind.
2 TIMOTHY 1:7 NKJV

Is THERE A CHANGE IN MY LIFE THAT I HAVE BEEN RESISTING BECAUSE OF FEAR?

A lecturer once told this story of a counseling patient who hated her job and thought it was ruining her life. But throughout her therapy, she seemed totally unwilling to improve her situation. When he suggested she hunt for a new job, she complained that there were no decent jobs in her small town. He asked if she had considered looking for a job in the next town, fifteen miles away. She said that she would need a car to travel that far, and she didn't have one. When the therapist offered a plan to purchase an inexpensive car, she countered that it would never work because there's no place to park in the neighboring town anyway!

It's said that three things in life are certain: death, taxes, and change. If you look around, you'll notice that most people can deal with the first two better than they can with change. But without it, we'll never know how wonderful the plans God has for us can be.

Fear of change comes from fear of loss, even if we are losing something that we never liked in the first place. If you are struggling with change in your life today, take a moment to bring your fears to the Lord. With faith in His guidance, change can lead to a blessing!

Our real blessings often appear to us in the shapes of pains, losses, and disappointments; but let us have patience, and we soon shall see them in their proper figures.

Penny from Heaven

Some trust in chariots and some in horses, but
we trust in the name of the LORD our God.

PSALM 20:7

I was

ENCOURAGED

BY A FRIEND

WHO . . .

Kevin brushed the sandy-colored hair from his eyes and said, "Mom, I have a chance to be president of the fourth grade!" He reached for a cinnamon roll and poured some milk into a glass.

"You know, Son, it'll be a tough race."

The boy took a swallow of milk and wiped his face with his sleeve. "I know, Mom. But I just know I can do it."

His mother reached into the pocket of her jeans and pulled out a penny. "Why don't you take my penny from Heaven to keep your spirits up?"

The boy grinned and put the penny into his pocket. He gathered his books and stuck them into his book bag, then slung the bag over his shoulder.

Adrienne busied herself with chores, wondering if her little boy would come home disappointed by failure or elated by victory. When 3:15 finally arrived, she was ready with his favorite chocolate chip cookies.

Kevin banged in the back door, his face beaming. "I did it, Mom!" he said. "I'm the new president of the fourth-grade class!" He caught his breath and settled down in front of his plate of cookies. "I just can't believe it!" he said.

"I can," said his mother.

The boy looked puzzled. "What do you mean?"

"Take out that penny I gave you, and read what it says above Abraham Lincoln's head."

A radiant smile spread over her son's face as he read out loud, "In God We Trust!"[21]

Trust God for great things; with your
five loaves and two fishes, He will
show you a way to feed thousands.

Seeing with the Heart

Give your servant a discerning heart.
1 KINGS 3:9

I see GOD'S
HAND AT
WORK IN THE
LIFE OF MY
FRIEND . . .

Maria was a kindhearted teacher's aide who simply wanted to "love the children better" in this class for emotionally disturbed students. She could tolerate much, but Danny was wearing out her patience. It had been easier to love him before, when he would try to hurt himself rather than others. And, although Danny was only seven years old, it really hurt when he would hit her.

For many months, Danny would withdraw into a private world and try to hit his head against a wall anytime he got upset. But now, he was making "progress" because instead of withdrawing, he was striking out at Maria.

"Progress?" exclaimed Maria. "How is it progress for him to want to hurt me?"

"Danny was repeatedly abused as a small child," explained the school psychologist. "He has known only adults who were mean to him or simply ignored his most basic needs. He has had no one to hold him close; no one to dry his tears when he cried or feed him when he was hungry. For the first time in his life, he trusts an adult enough to act out his anger rather than self-destruct. You are that trustworthy adult, Maria."

Maria, with tears spilling from her eyes, exclaimed, "I see!" As comprehension dawned, her anger quickly melted.

John Ruskin wrote, "When love and skill work together, expect a masterpiece."[22]

Sometimes progress seems elusive, but if we will open the eyes of our hearts, we will see God's hand at work in our midst.

*Do what you can, with what
you have, where you are.*

The First Valentine

We love, because He first loved us.
1 JOHN 4:19 NASB

How CAN I
TELL THE
PEOPLE IN MY
LIFE THAT I
LOVE THEM?

Most people would be surprised to learn that Valentine's Day was not intended to celebrate romance with gifts of flowers and chocolate. It was a day to honor a different kind of love.

Valentine was a Christian priest who lived near Rome in a period when Christians were punished for rejecting the Roman gods. During this persecution, legends say that Valentine assisted Christians in escaping from prison. He was discovered, arrested, and sent to trial, where he was asked if he believed in the Roman gods. He called their gods false. He continued to say that the only true God was He, whom Jesus called "Father."

Valentine was imprisoned, but it did not stop him from continuing his ministry. Even the prison guards began to listen to his witness. One was the adoptive father of a blind girl, whom the priest befriended as she waited at the jail while her father worked.

When the Roman emperor heard of Valentine's persistent worship of his God, he ordered his execution. In the days before his death, Valentine offered to pray for the jailer's blind daughter, and her sight was miraculously restored when he died. As a result, the jailer's entire family—forty-six people—came to believe in the one God and were baptized.

Saint Valentine knew every step of the way that his activities would endanger his life. But he continued because he loved God and people. It was a love that deserves to be honored and modeled after every day of the year.

❧

Love is like a rose, the joy of all the earth.

Love's Variety

Now these three remain: faith, hope and love.
But the greatest of these is love.
1 CORINTHIANS 13:13

I can
SHARE GOD'S
LOVE WITH
OTHERS BY . . .

There's such a variety of love in the world: the love between spouses, the love between parent and child, the love of a friend for another. In the name of love, wars have been fought, men have dueled and lost their lives, and great achievements have been accomplished. The most unassuming individual, acting out of a heart of love, has the potential to become a hero.

However, the most unselfish love is the love Jesus has for each individual. His love is the cornerstone of our lives and the foundation of our existence as we interact with others in loving ways. Love shrivels up in isolation.

Each experience we face and every person we meet add a new dimension to the way we love. And when we open ourselves up to those we fear or dislike, we usually find new opportunities to share God's love.

Love grows and thrives when it's nurtured. A man and woman who have been married for decades discover that they love each other more deeply than they could ever have imagined as newlyweds.

In your quiet time with God, ask Him for the gift of love and share it with someone else. Give your love freely, with no strings attached, just as God gives His love to us all. Become a person of faith and hope, but most of all, become a person of love.[23]

What does love look like? It has hands to
help others. It has feet to hasten to the poor
and needy. It has eyes to see misery and
want. It has ears to hear the sighs and
sorrows of men. That is what love looks like.

Basket of Love

Gray hair is a crown of splendor;
it is attained by a righteous life.
PROVERBS 16:31

What HAVE I BEEN SHARING? WHAT IS IN MY HAND THAT I COULD SHARE?

Every Thursday Jean, a senior citizen, hustled off to visit the people on her list. Some resided in nursing homes; others were lonely at home. Thankful she could still drive, Jean filled a wicker basket with bananas or flowers and sometimes included a cassette tape of her church's Sunday service. Most of all, she packed her basket with lots of love and concern for others.

Jean often sat at the bedside of one feeble lady. Although the woman did not respond, Jean treated her tenderly as though she heard and understood every word. She chatted about current happenings, read Scripture, prayed, then kissed her goodbye at the end of the visit and said, "I'll see you next week."

As Jean's friends began to pass away, she felt lonesome for them, but she never stopped serving the Lord. She just found new friends and kept sharing God's love until He called her home.

Like a sturdy basket used for a variety of practical needs, Jean filled her heart and life with love for others. With time and heavy use, baskets may wear out, but God continues to use His children to help others as long as we are willing to carry around His love. Whether we minister to others through praying, meeting physical needs, sending cards, or just calling them on the phone, we can still serve.

Jean didn't just believe in God; she lived her faith by sharing her basket of God's love with all those around her.

With every deed you are sowing a seed,
though the harvest you may not see.

On a Clear Day

*You will go out with joy, and be led forth
with peace; the mountains and the hills will
break forth into shouts of joy before you, and
all the trees of the field will clap their hands.*
ISAIAH 55:12 NASB

My FAVORITE
PLACE OUT-
DOORS IS . . .

Many people end their workday with a trip to the gym. Doing so helps them to clear their head of the day's frustrations, gives them more energy to face the evening ahead, calms them down, and improves their mood. It is also a complete departure from sitting at a desk all day.

While any exercise can be helpful, research has shown that *where* you exercise can make a big difference in the benefits derived from a workout session. A psychologist at an East Coast university tracked hormonal and mood changes in a group of runners who participated in three different jogs:

- Outdoors
- Indoors, on a treadmill, while listening to "sounds of nature" tapes
- Indoors, on a treadmill, while listening to tapes of their own heartbeats

Can you guess which jog proved to be the most beneficial? The outdoor jog. Levels of the positive mood hormones adrenaline and noradrenaline were up, while the levels of the stress hormone cortisol were down in those who had exercised outside.

It seems environment really matters. Whether you're exercising or just taking a few moments to relax with a cup of tea, where you do it can be nearly as important as why and how you do it. Find a delightful, stimulating spot for your getaway, and make the most of your break.

As children, we often asked our neighborhood friends, "Can you come out and play?" It's still a good question to ask!

⸎

*Those who do not find time for exercise
will have to find time for illness.*

Simple Pleasures

His soul shall dwell at ease.
PSALM 25:13 KJV

I love TO
SPEND TIME
WITH MY
FRIEND
BECAUSE
SHE IS . . .

There are many ways to enjoy teatime—formal, casual, business, cream teas, Christmas tea, tea served in a mug, tea presented in a fine china cup, a picnic tea outdoors in the country, a cozy, snuggled-up-beside-the-fireplace tea for two, an elegant tea on the lawn, or an hour of culinary delight in a stylish tearoom.

Briton Aubrey Franklin was appointed "Tea Ambassador" to America by the Tea Council of the U.S.A. to instruct Americans in the proper use of tea. He recollects his memories of childhood teatimes in England:

When I was a young lad, teatime was that special hour for sharing stories and having a giggle or two with my family. These everyday gatherings, enhanced by the ritual of teatime, helped us to feel united. To be able to chat about the humorous and oftimes tremulous events of the day was not only cathartic, but enabled us to know and enjoy each other. This is what is needed today, a time set aside for the specific purpose of sharing not only tea and its delicious accompaniments, but love. Instead of friends and families tuning out by immediately switching on the telly, start tuning in to one another again. Teatime is the perfect time and is a most delightfully exhilarating habit.[24]

However you choose to do it, try to set aside some casual time to spend with a friend or loved one for no other reason than to relax, enjoy a laugh, rekindle intimacy, or help soothe each other's jangled nerves.

∽∾

Friendships multiply joys
and divide griefs.

Open the Door

Behold, I stand at the door, and knock: if any man hear my voice, and open the door, I will come in to him, and will sup with him, and he with me.
REVELATION 3:20 KJV

What ROOM IN MY LIFE DO I STILL NEED TO INVITE JESUS TO SEE?

A nurse on duty in a pediatric ward often gave the children an opportunity to listen to their own hearts with her stethoscope. One day she put the stethoscope into a little boy's ears. She asked him, "Can you hear that? What do you suppose that is?"

The little boy frowned a moment, caught up in the wonder of this strange tapping inside his chest. Then he broke into a grin and responded, "Is that Jesus knocking?"

Another story is told of a group of students who went to visit a great religious teacher. The wise teacher asked the young scholars a seemingly obvious question: "Where is the dwelling place of God?"

The students laughed among themselves and replied, "What a thing to ask! Is not the whole world full of His glory?"

The learned old man smiled and replied, "God dwells wherever people let Him in."

The little boy listening to his heart through the stethoscope seemed to have more wisdom than the group of students. With his innocent, trusting faith, he had no problem believing that Jesus was knocking on his heart's door.

Like the little boy, when we hear Jesus knocking at the closed doors of our life, it is up to us to open the door and let Him in. Even those rooms that are dark and frightening are filled with light and understanding when Jesus enters.

Lord, make my life a window for Your light to shine through and a mirror to reflect Your love to all I meet. Amen.

Accessibility

A man who has friends must himself be friendly.
PROVERBS 18:24 NKJV

I can
MEET NEW
FRIENDS BY . . .

The end of a workday is a time when you may find it very pleasant and beneficial to make yourself a little more accessible to other people. If you have had a closed-door, nose-to-the-grindstone attitude all day, now may be the time to open the door. If you've been on the phone for what seems like hours, now may be the time to wander the halls and have a brief face-to-face conversation with a colleague or someone you supervise. If you have felt bogged down with paperwork or glued to a computer screen, now may be the time to walk to the cafeteria and get an energizing snack. Invite someone to go with you or meet you there for a few minutes of casual conversation. If you have been indoors with children or house chores, it might be time to call a neighborhood friend and go for a walk.

Robert Fulghum has written: "The grass is not, in fact, always greener on the other side of the fence. Fences have nothing to do with it. The grass is greenest where it is watered."

Every day, regardless of our environment or situation, we need to have human contact and communication. God built this need into us, and from the story of God's relationship with Adam and Eve in the Garden of Eden, we can assume that God enjoyed a late-in-the-day stroll with His creation— a time of sharing lives, not simply working together on tasks.

Of all the heavenly gifts that mortal men commend, what trusty treasure in the world can countervail a friend?

Brewing Good Relationships

A word fitly spoken is like apples of gold in settings of silver.
PROVERBS 25:11 NKJV

If MY BEST
FRIEND WERE
LEAVING
TOMORROW,
I WOULD
BE SURE TO
TALK TO HER
ABOUT . . .

Most tea drinkers would never consider tossing a tea bag into the nearest cup of hot water as the proper way to make a cup of tea. When one wants the best pot of tea, there are several rules for brewing that will assure the tea is a treat for the palate.

Like brewing tea, forming good relationships takes time and attention to be satisfying. Here are ten ways to show the love of Jesus to others—guaranteed to bring out the best "flavor" of each person:

1. Speak to people. There is nothing as nice as a cheerful word of greeting.
2. Smile at people. It takes seventy-two muscles to frown, fourteen to smile.
3. Call people by name. The sweetest music is the sound of one's own name.
4. Be friendly and helpful.
5. Be cordial. Speak and act as if everything you do is a pleasure.
6. Be genuinely interested in people. You can like everybody if you try.
7. Be generous with praise—cautious with criticism.
8. Be considerate of the feelings of others. It will be appreciated.
9. Be thoughtful of the opinions of others.
10. Be alert to give service. What counts most in life is what we do for others.[25]

These things take time, but like the time spent perfecting that pot of tea, it is well worth the extra effort.

*The greatest thing a man can do for
his Heavenly Father is to be kind
to some of His other children.*

Grace for Today

*All have sinned and fall short of the glory of God,
and are justified freely by his grace.*
ROMANS 3:23-24

I know
I HAVE FOR-
GIVEN WHEN I
NO LONGER
FEEL . . .

In *The Grace of Giving*, Stephen Olford gives an account of Peter Miller, a Baptist pastor who lived in Ephrata, Pennsylvania, during the American Revolution. He enjoyed the friendship of George Washington.

Michael Wittman also lived in Ephrata. He was an evil-minded man who did all he could to oppose and humiliate the pastor. One day Michael Wittman was arrested for treason and sentenced to die. Peter Miller traveled the seventy miles to Philadelphia on foot to plead for the life of the traitor.

"No, Peter," General Washington said, "I cannot grant you the life of your friend."

"My friend!" exclaimed the old preacher. "He's the bitterest enemy I have."

"What?" exclaimed Washington. "You've walked seventy miles to save the life of an enemy? That puts the matter in a different light. I'll grant your pardon."

Peter Miller took Michael Wittman back home to Ephrata—no longer an enemy, but a friend.

Miller's example of grace and forgiveness flowed from his knowledge of God's sacrifice for the human race. Because God forgave him and sacrificed His Son for him, he found the grace to sacrifice for his enemy. Although most of us know God's grace and love for us is great, sometimes we have to be reminded that His love never fails—even when we do!

At the beginning of each day, take a deep breath and say, "Even if I blow it today, my God will still love me."

A mother's love endures through all.

Life Lessons

[Speak] the truth in love.
EPHESIANS 4:15 KJV

What
WOULD MY
REACTION BE
IF A TRUSTED
FRIEND LIED
TO ME?

Sandra was a good student who had never cheated in her life. Yet, this semester was most difficult and this last assignment had been more than she could do. In a moment of desperation, she copied the work of another student.

Her instructor, Dr. Wallace, had asked her to wait after class, and Sandra knew what was coming. Still, it was a shock when Dr. Wallace asked her if it was really her work.

"Yes," she squeaked out, then wondered why she had lied.

Looking her straight in the eye, Dr. Wallace carefully said, "You know that what you did was wrong, don't you? Take tonight to think about your answer, and I will speak with you about this again tomorrow."

It was a long night for Sandra. She had never cheated before, and now she had compounded her mistake by deliberately lying—and to someone she admired and loved. The next morning she went to see Mrs. Wallace long before school started and quietly confessed her misdeed. She received the appropriate consequences, a zero on the assignment and a detention.

Years later, Sandra often thought of that experience and felt gratitude for loving correction from someone she respected. Dr. Wallace was willing to help Sandra make honest choices—even on the heels of making a dishonest one. For Sandra, this was a life lesson about taking responsibility for past mistakes and choosing honesty no matter what the consequences.

Honesty is the first chapter of the book of wisdom.

A Firm Foundation

"The rain came down, the streams rose, and the winds blew and beat against that house; yet it did not fall, because it had its foundation on the rock."

MATTHEW 7:25

Which AREA OF MY LIKE DO I ESPECIALLY NEED STABILITY?

The world's tallest tower stands in Toronto, Ontario, Canada. The first observation deck rises to 1,136 feet, and the second is even higher at 1,815 feet. Photographs and information located inside the tower help visitors comprehend the enormous undertaking of the project. Sixty-two tons of earth and shale were removed from fifty feet into the ground for laying the concrete that rises to the sky.

From 1972 to 1974, three thousand workers were at the tower site. Harnessed by safety ropes, some of the laborers dangled outside the giant for their finishing work. Remarkably, no one sustained injuries nor died on location.

Today a rapid elevator transports visitors upward for a breathtaking view of the city and all surrounding areas. Many feel it was well worth the money, time, and effort required to build the CN Tower.

We, too, need a good foundation for facing life each day. As we pray and spend time with our Heavenly Father, we are strengthening our spiritual foundation, our support base for life. We are able to see more from His point of view and not just our own. Thus we are not overwhelmed by whatever comes our way. When we feel we're hanging on the edge or suspended in midair, we can take courage in knowing He is holding us—firmly planted—in the palm of His hand. His foundation is strong and sure, and He will not crumble and fall.

Our strength grows out of our weakness.

Read the Book

Listen to counsel and receive instruction.
PROVERBS 19:20 NKJV

If I COULD
GIVE A
YOUNGER
PERSON ONE
PIECE OF
ADVICE, IT
WOULD BE . . .

Two women having lunch together in an elegant gourmet restaurant decided to end their repast with a cup of tea. The tea was poured into exquisite china teacups, but after taking the first sip one woman complained to the waiter. "Sir, this tastes like benzene. Are you sure it's tea?"

The waiter replied, "Oh, yes, it must be. The coffee tastes like turpentine."

Instructions for good brewing:

1. Rinse out the teakettle and start with fresh, cold tap water. Never boil anything but water in your teakettle.
2. Bring the water to its first rolling boil. Never overboil! Overboiling takes the oxygen out of the water, which in turn creates a flat beverage.
3. Take the teapot to the teakettle and rinse out the pot with the boiling water from the kettle. Never take the kettle to the teapot, as you lose one degree of heat per second. Water for tea must be 212 degrees.
4. Use one teabag or teaspoon of loose tea per cup. Leaves enter the warm teapot and the infusion begins when the leaf opens.
5. Pour hot water gently over the leaves. Be careful not to bruise the leaves.
6. Allow the tea to brew for three to five minutes, according to the blend of tea and how strong you like it.[26]

Following the instructions can help us make a good cup of tea. The same is true in living a good life! The Bible is God's instruction book. We are wise to follow its instructions!

A bit of the Book in the morning, to order my onward way. A bit of the Book in the evening, to hallow the end of the day.

Comfort in the Valley

Even though I walk through the valley of the shadow of death, I fear no evil; for Thou art with me; Thy rod and Thy staff, they comfort me.

PSALM 23:4 NASB

Several years ago, after the untimely death of her youngest son, Fran had to learn to trust God. Sometimes she felt forsaken, lonely, and at times even angry that God had allowed her seventeen-month-old to succumb to bacterial meningitis. Everything medically possible had been done to no avail.

With time, God comforted her with the knowledge that her son is with Him and will be reunited with her someday. The Lord had called Fran to encourage others, even in the midst of her own pain and doubt, and help them understand that while our loved ones will always be in our hearts, our focus remains on the Lord Jesus Christ.

Fran had often read Psalm 23, but she never actually understood it until she visited Israel and saw the rugged terrain traversed by David and the shepherds. Many of the crevices on the rocky hills are so narrow and deep that the sun never shines all the way to the bottom. It remains in a shadow. Certain death would result if anyone should fall in, because rescue would be virtually impossible. David's staff helped him walk with sure footing, and the rod defended him from wild animals. Most of all, he became acutely aware of God's provision.

Through the valley times in our lives, we, too, can be sure that we are not alone. His presence is real. Jesus will still be there through all the pain and the changes in our life situations. Nothing is more comforting.

God is closest to those whose hearts are broken.

What PROMISE HAS GOD MADE TO ME THAT HAS GIVEN ME GREAT COMFORT?

Tempest in a Teapot

All the promises of God in Him are Yes, and in Him Amen, to the glory of God through us.
2 CORINTHIANS 1:20 NKJV

Instead
OF PITYING
MYSELF, I WANT
TO HANDLE
DISAPPOINT-
MENT BY . . .

In her book *Diamonds in the Dust,* Joni Eareckson Tada asks, "Do you remember when you said 'yes' to Jesus? How long ago was it? A few months, maybe years? I said 'yes' to the Lord in November 1964 when I was a teenager. But I also said 'yes' to Him just the other day."

Tada describes a day when she had a quarrel with her husband, Ken. To escape the situation, she went with a friend to the shopping mall, where she burst out in sobs of self-pity. She said, "I couldn't hide my face in a tissue, and my wheelchair was too big for me to escape behind several clothes racks. All I could do was sit there, cry, and stare at the mannequins with the plastic smiles."

Then she said aloud what she had said many times before, "Yes, Jesus, I choose You. I don't choose self-pity or resentment. I say 'yes' to You!"

She felt her heart fill with peace. She said, "Nothing about my husband had changed. But *everything* was different because of my peaceful heart. Because I said 'yes' to Jesus."[27]

We can give our frustrations and unsettled emotions to God. We can pray to Him, "Lord, I don't understand this situation, but I know I want Your peace and Your grace to change me in the midst of this storm in my life. Thank You for caring enough about me that You gave me the desire to say yes to You. Amen."

It is a pity that our tears on account of our troubles should so blind our eyes that we should not see our mercies.

Above the Clouds

You have turned for me my mourning into dancing; You have loosed my sackcloth and girded me with gladness.
PSALM 30:11 NASB

Denise rested her flushed face against the cool window. It had been hours since she had left her warm bed to fight her way to the airport. Finally, she sat on the plane, which was preparing to taxi onto the runway.

This trip, unlike many others, brought none of the familiar pleasure to her heart as the plane began to move . . . no vacation . . . no friend's wedding. This trip was a somber one to visit her ailing father in a distant state.

Her father was sick; her husband was frustrated and angry as his company transitioned to a younger, more "able" staff; and her teenage son was pushing the envelope to fit in with a group of students Denise feared and disliked. Why was all of this taking place now? *Why, Lord?* She had prayed!

As the plane slowly rose into the air, Denise surveyed the land below her. Dark and dreary under a cloudy, rainy sky, the entire landscape seemed to fit her mood. Slowly, the plane began to break through the clouds. What a difference! The dark, menacing clouds were transformed into soft white blankets. The blue sky and sunshine were bright and unwavering on the other side.

It's hard to see the light in the midst of the storm. But remember, just beyond the cloud cover is an amazing sight. Today, allow God to show you life from His perspective.

He that can have patience can have what he will.

In THE DARKEST CORNER OF MY LIFE, I KEEP BELIEVING BECAUSE . . .

Touching Life

Preserve my life according to your love.
PSALM 119:88

If I TOUCHED
THE HAND OF
GOD, I THINK
IT WOULD
FEEL . . .

The sounds of the delivery room receded to a quiet murmur of post-delivery activities and near-whispered comments between the parents. The father, gowned, with a hair net and masked face, leaned forward and touched their child who was cuddled to the mother. She looked down on the baby who was scowling, eyes tightly shut. With a sense of awe, the mother stretched forth one finger to gently smooth the child's wrinkled forehead. The need to touch her daughter was urgent, yet she was careful.

Developmental psychologists who have examined the process of childbirth and witnessed thousands of deliveries inform us that the need to gently touch one's newborn is a near-universal impulse crossing all cultural boundaries. Obviously, we have been created with an innate need to physically connect with our offspring. In this sense we are very much like God.

In *The Creation of Adam*, one of Michelangelo's famous frescoes that decorate the ceiling of the Sistine Chapel, he portrays the hand of Adam outstretched with a finger pointed. Opposite to it you see the hand of God in a similar pose reaching toward man. The two fingertips are nearly touching. No image more clearly reveals the Father's heart. He is ever-reaching out His hand to touch, with gentleness and love, those who are created in His own image.

Mothers and God share a common bond then, do they not? Both yearn to touch those made in their image.

*The love of a mother is the veil of
a softer light between the heart
and the Heavenly Father.*

Best Friends

You were called into the fellowship of his Son, Jesus Christ our Lord.

1 CORINTHIANS 1:9 NRSV

A student spent a year on a reservation in the Southwest, living with a Navajo Indian family. She slept in their home, ate their food, worked with them, and generally lived their lifestyle.

The grandmother in the family did not speak English, yet she and the student were able to form a close bond of friendship. They spent much time together, forging a relationship that was meaningful to each one, yet difficult to explain to anyone else. The two shared experiences together although they could not talk with each other. In spite of the language difference, they developed a closeness of mutual understanding and affection.

Over the months each one of them worked to learn phrases in the other one's language. The student learned some Navajo phrases, and the grandmother picked up some English words.

As the student climbed into her pickup truck to leave, her dear friend, the grandmother, came to say good-bye. With tears flowing down her cheeks, the grandmother put her hands on either side of the student's face. She looked directly into the young woman's eyes and said in her newly learned words: "I like me best when I'm with you."

Good friends are the ones around whom we "like ourselves best" because they have a way of bringing out the best in us. Jesus is that kind of Friend to us. He will bring out the best in us so we can say to Him, "I like me best when I'm with You."

What is a friend?
A single soul dwelling in two bodies.

The SWEETEST THING A FRIEND EVER SAID TO ME WAS . . .

A Heart for Art

*Do good, O LORD, to those who are good, and
to those who are upright in their hearts.*
PSALM 125:4 NASB

How WOULD
I REPAY A TRUE
KINDNESS
FROM
ANOTHER'S
HEART?

Nguyen Van Lam began selling coffee from a cart in 1950. Several years later, he bought a building near an art school. Many of his customers were struggling art students who could barely afford to put food in their stomachs, much less buy art supplies. Lam, an impassioned art lover, loaned them money so they could practice their craft.

Several of the artists—who later became quite famous—repaid Lam's generosity with paintings, prints, and drawings. Over the years, his collection grew to more than a thousand pieces of art. Only a small portion of the collection is displayed in the Café Lam in Hanoi, but it covers almost every square inch of wall space.

Lam's extensive collection is a precious treasure. To protect the art during the war, he stored the art in an air-raid shelter. These days, he hopes to turn his building into a museum to permanently display his collection for future generations to enjoy.

Lam loves artists as much as he loves art. He admires their generous spirits, their ability to find beauty in everything, and the way they pour themselves into their work without demanding something back.[28]

Time with Jesus can be time spent in a lovely art gallery, where He shows you all the colors and patterns of your life. Just as Lam cared for the struggling artists, Jesus cares for you. He is your Comforter, Friend, Protector, and the Source of all creativity and beauty.

*God's love for us is proclaimed
with each sunrise.*

Pass It On

In truth I perceive that God shows no partiality.
ACTS 10:34 NKJV

I know
GOD LOVES ME
ESPECIALLY
BECAUSE OF
THE TIME
HE . . .

Through the years, kitchens have played a major role in Connie's life. When she was growing up, she lived on a farm surrounded by aunts, uncles, cousins, siblings, her mother, and her grandmother. She often remembered the hot summer days when the kitchen would be steamy because they were canning. Canning was a family affair. The men raised and harvested the crops; the children peeled, chopped, and prepared the produce; and the women cooked and did the actual canning. There was much lively discussion over recipes, techniques, and timing.

At some point during the day, Grandma would sneak Connie under the table and give her a taste of whatever was being canned. Grandma would warn her to keep this their special secret. In fact, it was such a secret that Connie didn't find out until a few years ago that Grandma did this for all her cousins and siblings.

Because of it, Connie always thought she was Grandma's favorite grandchild, and that knowledge had sustained her through many rough times. When she found out that everyone in her generation thought they were Grandma's favorite grandchild, it didn't diminish that special feeling. She was awed by the love that Grandma gave to the whole family. Her grandmother became the model for the kind of person she wanted to be.

God is the same way. He loves each one of us as if we were the only person in the universe. We are individually and personally His own special children.

*A grandma knows the art
of giving from the heart.*

Redirected Anger

A gentle answer turns away wrath,
but a harsh word stirs up anger.
PROVERBS 15:1

Someone HAS CHEATED ME, HOW COULD I TURN IT INTO A BLESSING?

A Salvation Army officer stationed in New Zealand tells of an old Maori woman who won the name Warrior Brown for her fighting ability when she was drunk or enraged. After her conversion to Christianity, she was asked to give her testimony at an open-air meeting. One of her old enemies took the opportunity to loudly make fun of her. He ended his harangue by throwing a large potato at her, which hit her with a nasty blow.

The crowd grew deadly silent. A week earlier, the cowardly insulter would have needed to sprint into hiding to salvage his teeth. But what a different response they witnessed that night!

Warrior picked up the potato without a word and put it into her pocket. No more was heard of the incident until the harvest festival came around, when she appeared with a little sack of potatoes to share. She explained she had cut up and planted the potato and was now presenting it to the Lord as part of her increase.

Warrior had learned how to live in peace with her neighbors and yet be a strong spiritual "warrior" for the Lord's cause. What a beautiful example of taking the ill people do and turning it into praise for the Father in Heaven!

The heart benevolent and
kind the most resembles God.

One Hundred Years!

My job was to plant the seed in your hearts,
and Apollos watered it, but it was God,
not we, who made it grow.
1 CORINTHIANS 3:6 NLT

While Cheryl organized her newly arrived seed order, she found a bonus seed packet containing cactus seeds. She flipped the envelope over to read the planting instructions: "Seeds will germinate in one to one hundred years."

"One hundred years!" she exclaimed aloud. "It would take a wheelbarrow full of faith to sow those seeds. But then, faith is what motivates most gardeners. Few of us live to see a tree seedling grow to its fullest potential. We cannot know if we will still be living in the same place when our biennials bloom. Yet we plan, plant, and have faith in our work."

It's been the same for Christians since Jesus gave the "Great Commission," telling us to plant seeds of faith throughout the world. We are part of a team working for God. We may be the person to plant the Gospel seed in someone's heart, or we may be the one to water it. If faith germinates in a heart and a disciple grows, the accomplishment isn't ours but the Holy Spirit's. We may not even be around to enjoy the harvest.

Cheryl planted her cactus seeds, but they still hadn't germinated when she moved two years later. She remembered them often, however, just as she often remembered to pray for the seeds of faith she'd planted in people's hearts.

The smallest seed of faith is better
than the largest fruit of happiness.

Today I NEED FAITH TO BELIEVE THAT ONE DAY . . .

Rise and Shine

"Take my yoke upon you and learn from me,
for I am gentle and humble in heart,
and you will find rest for your souls."
MATTHEW 11:29

A special
TIME I SPENT
WITH GOD
WAS . . .

Janie jolted awake at the sound of her alarm clock. This was her third day waking up in the middle of the night . . . at least it felt like the middle of the night, although it was actually early morning. Her reasons for waking herself up seemed vague and worthless, and she longed to put her head back down onto the pillow.

"No!" she said, waking up again with a start. She had promised herself she would do this, and she was going to, no matter what. Janie stumbled to the bathroom, splashed water on her face, and carefully traversed the steps. Downstairs, she started a pot of coffee and sat down at the kitchen table. She had originally started doing her devotions on the sofa, only to discover they lasted only the five minutes it took for her to fall asleep again. At the kitchen table, she took out her Bible, her notebook, and a devotional. Her attitude brightened.

Once she was up, every moment was worth it. Meeting God in the early morning hours didn't make her grumpy as she always anticipated, but instead it revitalized her and brought her peace.

God's yoke *is* light; He *is* the rest for our souls that we think sleep should bring. Taking the time with our Savior in the early morning hours is better than fine cappuccino and the smell of omelettes and bacon. It truly is the best part of our day.

Take heed of still waters,
they quick pass away.

An Open Door

I run in the path of your commands,
for you have set my heart free.
PSALM 119:32

The DOOR I
SEE OPEN
BEFORE ME
LEADS TO . . .

One afternoon, a woman was visiting a great old stone church in the English countryside. The massive doors of the church were flung wide to allow the warm sunshine into the chilly, stone structure.

As she sat enjoying the ritual, a small bird flew in through the open doors. Full of fear, it flew near the ceiling, vainly looking for a way out into the sunshine. Seeing the light coming through the dark stained glass windows, it flew to one, then the next, and finally back toward the ceiling. It continued flying about in this way for several minutes, quickly exhausting its strength in frenzied panic.

Nearly ready to fall to the floor, the bird made a final lunge for one of the large rafters. Realizing it was in no immediate danger, it hopped a little on the beam, turned around, and suddenly saw the open door. Without hesitation it flew out into the sunshine, loudly singing a joyful song as it went.

Suddenly, the woman realized that she was like the bird. She had flitted about, trying to live a "good" life of noble works without recognizing that the door of salvation had been open to her all the time. She suddenly understood that to avoid flying errantly into places that offered no hope of eternal life, she need only stop flapping and be still in the Lord's presence. From that vantage point, she could better see the door of grace that He had prepared for her.

The deepest wishes of the heart find
expression in secret prayer.

Scheduled Rest

Jesus said to them, "Come with me by yourselves to a quiet place and get some rest."
MARK 6:31

I can FIND REST IN MY DAILY CIRCUM- STANCES THIS WEEK BY . . .

Researchers say that Americans today are plagued with more stress-related health problems than any other generation in history. Stress is a contributing factor to heart disease and high blood pressure and has been linked to an increase in bad cholesterol and the worsening of arthritis.

How can we keep the daily pressures of life from becoming debilitating stress? God's solution has always been to take a day of rest. Return to the simple pleasures of the kitchen. The kitchen in our great-grandmothers' time was both the center of family activity and the center of rest. Family meals were made and shared around a common table. Conversation was the primary form of entertainment—not the television, radio, or compact disc player with headphones. Comforting aromas greeted family members throughout the day. And nothing could beat the smell of a chicken roasting in the oven for Sunday dinner.

So put your daily planner away for one day each week. Make sure everyone in the family knows that this will be a "scheduled" day of rest. Before you go to bed the night before, use your modern appliances to help give you a jump-start on the day. Pop some dough ingredients in the bread machine and set the timer on the coffeepot. You'll awaken to the smell of freshly perked coffee and freshly baked bread. Those inviting aromas will make you want to linger in the kitchen—to chat, to laugh, to love, and to rest. God—and our great-grandmothers—will be pleased.

Take rest; a field that has rested gives a bountiful crop.

Faith Moves Forward

"Men of Galilee," they said, "why do
you stand here looking into the sky?"
ACTS 1:11

I believe
GOD'S PLAN
FOR ME
INVOLVES . . .

For days Ginny tried to make some sense out of the feelings that swirled within her. Compared to someone else's problems, Ginny's concerns seemed only minor inconveniences, but for her, they were overwhelming. Finances, relationships, work, health, church—no matter where she turned, there were problems, and all of them seemed beyond her control. Tears mingled with the soapsuds as she finished the dishes. Drying her hands, she sat heavily on a kitchen chair and whispered, "Lord, what am I supposed to do?"

And quietly the answer came. When the disciples witnessed Christ's return to Heaven, they stood gazing into the sky, not knowing what to do. They were paralyzed by the overwhelming responsibility that He had placed on their shoulders to share the Gospel message with the world. It took a gentle shove from one of God's angels to get them moving down the path that had been placed before them, to turn them away from their fears and back to their faith as they followed God's plan for their lives.

Sure enough, just like those disciples, Ginny had been paralyzed by her dread. She asked forgiveness for her fearful focus, and even before she reached the "Amen," she had a direction . . . a pathway. All she needed to do was faithfully follow God's plan. He'd take care of the rest.

They can conquer who believe they can.

The Lost Ring

Godliness with contentment is great gain.
For we brought nothing into the world,
and we can take nothing out of it.
1 TIMOTHY 6:6-7

What IS MY
MOST PRIZED
POSSESSION
AND WHY?

When Ginger lost the deep-blue sapphire ring that had belonged to her mother, she was devastated. The sapphire, surrounded by twenty-three tiny diamonds, had been passed on to her after her mother died that November.

Ginger planned on having the ring sized to fit her smaller hand. For safekeeping, she placed the ring, along with other pieces of jewelry, in a plastic bag and stashed it in an old chest of drawers.

As winter turned into spring, a friend planned a garage sale. Ginger decided to donate the old chest of drawers. Too late, she remembered her mother's jewelry was inside. It had been sold.

Fortunately, Ginger's friend had the phone number of the woman who had bought the chest. Relieved, Ginger called but was shocked when the woman denied having any of the valuable pieces.

With an aching heart, Ginger eventually turned the situation over to God and prayed for deliverance from her anger.

Two years later, the woman who bought the jewelry called and said her own mother had died. Suffering with back pain, she had been unable to attend her own mother's funeral. She returned the cherished ring to Ginger, as well as some of the other pieces of her mother's jewelry. Within a short time, the woman's back pain began to disappear.

How often we cling to material things! We need to pray for contentment with what we have. It's a sure thing that we'll take nothing with us when we leave![29]

I am always content with what happens,
for what God chooses is
better than what I choose.

Kitchen-Sink Legacy

"Do to others as you would have them do to you."

LUKE 6:31

Corinna's grandmother never went to seminary, but she sure could preach. From her kitchen-sink pulpit, Grandma would sermonize while she scrubbed the supper dishes. Her congregation of assembled relatives labored alongside her, clearing the table, drying the dishes, and putting away the pots and pans.

Corinna wanted to be like the neighbor children who gulped down their meals and left their dishes on the table as they flew out the back door to play. But Grandma would have none of that. By the time Grandma finished her sermonizing, it would be dark outside, and Corinna would have to wait until the next day to play with her friends. She quickly learned to do her chores without excuse or complaint; otherwise Grandma would remind her to "do everything without grumbling or complaining."

It seemed Grandma had a saying for every situation. If someone was upset about the treatment they had received from a friend, a clerk, or a neighbor, Grandma answered with, "Do to others as you would have them do to you." Or if she overheard one of the kids hinting that they were considering mischief, she quickly countered with, "Be sure your sin will find you out."

Only much later did Corinna discover that Grandma's gems of wisdom came from God's Word. Grandma's example demonstrates that everyday chores can be used as an opportunity to share God's love.

We should behave to our friends as we would wish our friends to behave to us.

A time WHEN I WAS TREATED WITH UNUSUAL KINDNESS WAS . . .

The Quiet Touch of Stillness

In repentance and rest is your salvation,
in quietness and trust is your strength.
ISAIAH 30:15

I enjoy
QUIETNESS
BECAUSE . . .

A late-night snowfall blanketed the city one Saturday. When everyone awoke on Sunday morning, evergreens were layered with sparkling white icing. The roofs of houses looked as if someone had draped each one with a fluffy quilt.

But more striking than the beautiful whitewash was the pervasive stillness. The city noises were gone. No horns honking or dogs barking. No cars screeching or boom boxes blaring. No doors slamming or machines running. Just stillness—quietness.

The quiet didn't last long, however. Soon city snowplows were out, clearing and salting the streets. The sounds of shovels and snowblowers mixed with window scrapers and revving car engines as neighbors began to dig out from the storm. It was not the first snowstorm of the season, nor would it be the last.

But amazingly, the quiet start to the morning left its imprint on the entire day. The pace slowed for a moment, granting people an opportunity for reflection and allowing neighbors time to connect with others. And when normal activities resumed, some people were even able to hold on to the stillness for a while.

When Monday came, it brought with it all the noise of a busy week. But it also brought the remembrance of God's words to His people—that in quietness and trust they would find strength. Let God's quietness fill a corner of your heart today, and find the joy that can be found in stillness.

The great mind knows the
power of gentleness.

The Egg Test

*As the heavens are higher than the earth, so are
my ways higher than your ways and
my thoughts than your thoughts.*

ISAIAH 55:9

Have you ever tried to read a recipe while you're cracking an egg into a mixing bowl? If you have—and you're not very adept at it—you know it's not a pretty picture. If you don't keep your eyes on the egg, you'll end up with more egg on the counter than in the mixing bowl. Yuck! Any experienced cook will tell you that you'll have better success if you read the recipe first and then keep your eyes on the eggs.

The Bible agrees. Well, maybe it doesn't talk about eggs and mixing bowls, but it does talk about our choices in life. When the Israelites first camped on the edge of the Promised Land, God instructed them to do some reconnaissance. Twelve men were sent to look the land over and report back to Moses with their findings. All twelve had seen God miraculously deliver them from slavery. All twelve had heard God's promise of protection. All twelve had experienced God's provision for their journey.

But only two men remembered God and His faithfulness. Only two kept their focus on God—ten men were distracted by the sights and smells of Canaan. Ten men turned their eyes away from God and made a mess for the Israelites that took forty years to clean up.

Let the egg test be your reminder to keep your eyes focused on God.

*By asking for the impossible,
we obtain the best possible.*

I need TO
FOCUS CLOSER
ON GOD
WHEN I AM . . .

Perseverance

I will praise You, for You have answered me and have become my salvation.
PSALM 118:21 NKJV

With
PERSEVERANCE
AND GOD'S
HELP I CAN . . .

Rafael Solano, a diamond prospector in Venezuela, was one of many impoverished natives and fortune seekers who came to sift through the rocks of a dried-up riverbed reputed to have diamonds. No one, however, found any diamonds in the sand and pebbles for some time. One by one, those who came left the site—their dreams shattered, and their bodies drained.

Discouraged and exhausted, Solano had just about decided it was time for him to give up too. Then Solano stooped down and scooped up a handful of pebbles, if only so he could say he had personally inspected every pebble in his claim. He pulled out one that seemed a little different. It seemed heavy. He measured it and weighed it on a scale. Could it be?

Sure enough, Solano had found a diamond! New York jewelry dealer Harry Winston paid Solano $200,000 for that stone. When it was cut and polished, it became known as the Liberator, the largest and purest unmined diamond in the world.

The Scriptures teem with examples of men and women who, on the verge of disaster or failure, experienced God's creative work in their lives. Remind yourself . . .

God's Word is true.
God can do the impossible.
God can heal the incurable.
God can conquer your enemies.
God loves you.

You may have been plugging away at a project for weeks, even months or years, without seeing much progress. Today may be the day. Don't give up!

*Perseverance is the rope that ties
the soul to the doorpost of heaven.*

Voice from the Past

Faith by itself, if it is not accompanied by action, is dead. But someone will say, "You have faith; I have deeds." Show me your faith without deeds, and I will show you my faith by what I do.

JAMES 2:17-18

There IS A FRIEND IN MY LIFE THAT I NEED TO TELL . . .

Laura was mixing cake batter when the phone rang. "This is Carrie," the voice said. *Of course,* Laura thought. Carrie had been a member of her writers' group. In fact, she had written beautiful and thought-provoking fiction. Her work was good, and she could have been published if she had pursued it. Instead, Carrie chose to end an unhappy marriage and get on with her life, leaving her writing far behind.

Carrie bubbled with excitement. "I'm sailing with friends on a forty-two-foot sailboat from Nova Scotia to Scotland." Laura listened intently. Was this the same Carrie who had needed lots of support from her friends? The same Carrie who had wrapped herself safely in a little shell? To Laura's surprise, Carrie had changed. She was now taking control of her life and doing exciting things.

As Carrie was closing the conversation, she said, "I wanted to make certain my good friends knew I was going on this trip." Laura's breath caught in her throat. She had never thought of herself as Carrie's good friend. Sure, she'd taken her to the doctor once, visited her apartment, and even lunched at a pizza place with her and her children, but she'd never thought of herself as her good friend. She couldn't even recall her last name.

How often do we touch someone's life with a random act of kindness? God uses ordinary people to make an extraordinary difference in the world around them. Find a way to be kind to another person today.

❧

He who plants kindness gathers love.

Just Like Paul

*Encourage one another and build each
other up, just as in fact you are doing.*
1 THESSALONIANS 5:11

I would
DESCRIBE MY
FAVORITE
HOME
PLACE AS . . .

Prior to his conversion, the apostle Paul perse-cuted scores of Christians. But God met this ruth-less Pharisee in a special vision on the road to Damascus and changed his heart.

Yet wherever Paul went after his conversion, he caused controversy. The book of Acts tells us that many Christians were unwilling to accept his con-version as a real change of heart.

For several chapters, the book of Acts is silent about the life of Paul. But when he reappears in the narrative in Acts 11, no one questions his change of heart. No one misunderstands his intentions. Something is different about Paul.

While the Bible does not tell us what happened to Paul during that time, perhaps he went home to his family. Think of a time when you returned home after a long and maybe difficult absence. There's something reassuring about sitting at the same old kitchen table, cooking on the same old stove, listening to the same noises, and smelling the same aromas from your younger days—a simpler time. The four walls of the family home become a place to regenerate and renew. And when it comes time to move on again, you are refreshed and ready—just like Paul.

Whether you're sharing a favorite meal with a family member or a conversation with a friend, let your home be a haven . . . a place of refreshment. After all, you just might be strengthening another soul for ministry—someone like Paul.

❧

*Tell a man he is brave, and
you help him to become so.*

Sunbeam Blessings

"I am the light of the world. Whoever follows me will never walk in darkness, but will have the light of life."
JOHN 8:12

As Gloria sat alone at the dining table, a single sunbeam shone through the closed blinds. At the point where the light entered the window, it was just a tiny speck, but as it spread across the room, all the colors of the rainbow burst into an array of splendor. It highlighted the old shadowbox that hung on the wall and reflected on its glass front that protected her treasures from dust and grime.

She spotted the golden tree figurine covered with her birthstones and thought of how her mother often spoke of what a glorious day it was when she was born. She saw the animal figurines that resembled her pets from long ago. The angel standing over the small boy and girl on the bridge reminded her of her childhood years, as she and her brother played together.

The baby figurine took her back to the days when her children were small. The fellow pointing to a carving in a tree that said, "I Love You," made her smile. It had been a gift from her husband on one of their anniversaries. Many fond memories came alive as Gloria spied the tiny angel holding the Bible, and she thanked God for the many blessings in her life.

Even in the midst of difficult circumstances, try to remember the good things God has done for you, no matter how small or insignificant. It will get your eyes off your problem and on the Solver of problems instead.

*There are no days when
God's fountain does not flow.*

Five THINGS
I HAVE TO BE
THANKFUL FOR
TODAY ARE . . .

The God of Tomorrow

I am the Lord—I do not change.
MALACHI 3:6 TLB

What CHERISHED THINGS FROM THE PAST WOULD I LIKE TO SEE AGAIN?

When the microwave buzzed, Rebecca slid her chair away from her laptop computer and retrieved the hot water for her tea. She had been writing an article about new technologies and how they would impact our lives in the next century. The whole topic was unsettling. The more research she did on the Internet, the more disturbed she became about cloning, supercomputers, and spy satellites. Where would it all end?

Suddenly, she had an urge to hear the comforting whistle of a teakettle and the crackling of a real fire instead of the hiss of a gas log. The world was moving too fast, and at times like these, she wanted to crawl up onto her grandpa's lap and smell his sweet cherry pipe.

"Grandpa," she remembered asking one time, "did they have spaceships when you were little?"

He chuckled and said, "No, Honey, when I was a little boy, we rode in a horse-drawn wagon to town. And airplanes had just really gotten off the ground."

I wonder what Grandpa would think about life today? She knew. He'd tell her not to worry. "Honey," he'd say, "I've been in some pretty tight places in my day: train wrecks, labor strikes, and world wars. I reckon if God pulled us through all of that, He can see us the rest of the way home."

She "reckoned" He would. The God of her grandpa's era would be the same God in the twenty-first century. And *that* was a comforting thought.

God's investment in us is so great
He could not possibly abandon us.

Changing Seasons

The grass withers and the flowers fall,
but the word of our God stands forever.
ISAIAH 40:8

I am GLAD
TO BE THE AGE
I AM TODAY
BECAUSE . . .

Marie had always enjoyed washing dishes by hand. It gave her an opportunity to slow down, think, and observe the changing of the seasons as she gazed out her kitchen window.

As the cycle of seasons began, Marie watched flowers pop up through the soil when the weather got warmer. Their brilliantly colored blossoms always brought her happiness. In the summer, the green grass filled her heart with peace and tranquility. And as the green leaves gradually transformed to shades of gold, she sensed the autumn nip in the air, a sure sign that winter would follow.

Life is like the changing seasons. During the springtime of Marie's life, her days were filled with fun and joy as she played with frogs and tadpoles. Her teen and young adult years—the summer of her life—were marked by enthusiasm as she tried to find herself in the fast lane of life. Today, Marie is beginning to sense the contentment of autumn. She sees security in the eyes of her husband and joy in the lives of her grown children, and she realizes that winter soon will be upon her.

There's nothing wrong with looking back at the previous seasons of our lives. But God has a purpose for allowing us to be in the season we're in right now. So enjoy where you're at on the way to where you're going!

As dew to the blossom, the bud
to the bee, as the scent to the rose,
are those memories to me.

Monday Morning Mindset

Let us continually offer to God a sacrifice of praise.
HEBREWS 13:15

Lord,
THANK YOU
FOR THE
BLESSING
OF . . .

On Monday, the television newscaster looked grim as he read the statistics of the latest crime spree. The weatherman predicted a heavy snowstorm with possible ice damage and power outages. The car mechanic indicated that the repairs to the brake system would cost more than expected. The doctor's office called, requesting an immediate appointment to discuss the results of a biopsy.

But also on Monday, Grandma went to the oncologist and received a survivor pin commemorating five cancer-free years. Amy pulled through labor and delivery with no complications and gave birth to a healthy little girl. Sam's blood test revealed that he was merely overstressed and overtired, not diabetic. Frank passed a college exam with flying colors. Erin believed she had found someone to marry.

Concerns and problems are a part of life. Things go wrong. Plans fail. But we have a choice. We can either focus entirely on the problems, or we can focus on God. A problem-filled focus yields a fearful heart, and fear is a thief that robs us of the joy of today. However, a focus that acknowledges God's control over everything fills our hearts with peace, comfort, and joy despite our problems. We can listen to the newscaster and the weatherman, the mechanic and the physician, but we need to make some time to focus on our daily blessings, too, thanking God for those little reminders of His care.

Tell Him about the heartache,
And tell Him the longings too,
Tell Him the baffled purpose
When we scarce know what to do.
Then, leaving all our weakness
With the One divinely strong,
Forget that we bore the burden
And carry away the song.[30]

The Better Way

Since, then, you have been raised with Christ,
set your hearts on things above, where Christ
is seated at the right hand of God.

COLOSSIANS 3:1

Martha was a dedicated homemaker. She was an expert at entertaining her guests while preparing a scrumptious meal at the same time. One day when Jesus was passing through the village, Martha opened her home to Him. Her house was spotless, and the aroma coming from her kitchen was delightful. As a wonderful hostess, she made sure that Jesus felt welcome in her home.

Her sister, Mary, also was there. While Martha opened her home to Jesus, Mary opened her heart to Him and sat at His feet. She knew that true wisdom would be hers if she listened to His teachings and applied them to her everyday life.

Meanwhile, Martha began to grumble. She felt that Mary should be more involved in the work at hand. She went to Jesus to ask Him to send her sister to help her in the kitchen.

Jesus' response probably surprised her. He taught Martha some things about priorities, while sharing with her a better way to serve Him. Mary, He said, had chosen the better way, and it would not be taken away from her.

While working and serving are vital parts of living, they cannot be the most important parts. Seek God's guidance today through prayer and Bible study. The wisdom that you gain will benefit not only you, but others as well, for your life will serve as a shining example for Him.

Deep in your heart it is not guidance
that you want as much as a guide.

In THE LAST FEW DAYS, GOD HAS BEEN TEACHING ME . . .

Someone Who Cares

An anxious heart weighs a man down,
but a kind word cheers him up.
PROVERBS 12:25

Who DO I
REALLY CARE
ABOUT?

Maureen wearily rinsed out her coffee cup and stacked it in the nearly full dishwasher. Her life had been difficult for months. As her husband's illness rapidly progressed, her sense of security waned, and a fear of losing him filled her heart. After a few weeks in the hospital, her husband of forty-five years was forced to live in a nursing home. It seemed that Maureen couldn't stop crying. Her heart felt heavier after each visit.

At first, people asked if there was anything they could do to help. Others telephoned and visited her. But after a few weeks, the calls and visits dwindled as her friends got on with their lives. She was overcome with weariness, and joy seemed so remote.

One day before she left for her daily visit to the nursing home, she stopped by the mailbox. A small "thinking of you" card was tucked inside. It was signed, "Someone who cares." A ray of sunshine touched her heart as she read those simple words.

Someone really cares, she thought. She didn't know who it was, but she knew that someone was concerned about the situation that overshadowed her life. As the weeks and months passed, Maureen continued to receive greeting cards from this anonymous person. The signature was always the same. But no one ever confessed to being the sender. Only God knew who uplifted her spirit. And for the sender, that was enough.

Kindness is a language
the dumb can speak, the deaf can hear,
and the blind can see.

A Continual Feast

All the days of the oppressed are wretched,
but the cheerful heart has a continual feast.
PROVERBS 15:15

From
WHERE I SIT, I
CAN SEE SEVEN
BEAUTIFUL
THINGS.
THEY ARE . . .

Minnie, Janice's patient, was bent at the waist and shuffling slowly with the use of a walker. Her stiff and gnarled hands were white with the pressure. It took Minnie what seemed like hours to make her way across the small expanse of tile.

Finally, with much effort and painful exertion, Minnie turned and settled into the seat. Janice folded up the walker and leaned it against the wall, feeling her own aches and pains as she did so.

"Janice?" Minnie's voice was barely above a whisper as she beckoned Janice closer.

"Yes, Minnie?"

"Isn't it a beautiful day?"

Janice followed Minnie's line of vision, trying to see what beauty she saw. There was little to notice: a plant, a painting, a few friends. Janice looked into her eyes. They were bright and capable, although her body no longer followed suit. Minnie knew exactly what she was saying when she commented on the beauty of the day. Janice had to smile as she replied, "Yes, Minnie, it's a beautiful day."

Pain is real, and it's a struggle when life doesn't cooperate with our plans. But always, there is more. Always, there is something that God will place in our line of vision that is worth celebrating. It doesn't always take away the pain, but as He promises in Proverbs 15:15, "The cheerful heart has a continual feast." Once you start noticing the sublime, He makes it far too good to ever pass up again.

Cheerfulness: the habit of looking
at the good side of things.

A Kite's Tale

Each of us has one body with many members, and these members do not all have the same function.
ROMANS 12:4

Of ALL THE
PEOPLE I WORK
WITH I AM
INSPIRED
BY . . . WHY?

On a breezy March day, the town mayor happened through the park where a small boy was flying the largest, most beautiful kite he had ever seen. It soared so high and floated so gently, the mayor was sure it must be visible from the next town. The mayor decided to award a "key to the city" to the one responsible for setting this spectacle aloft.

"Who is responsible for flying this kite?" the mayor inquired.

"I am," said the boy. "I made the kite with my own hands. I painted all the beautiful pictures and constructed it with scraps I found in my father's workshop. I fly the kite," he declared.

"I am," said the wind. "It is my whim that keeps it aloft and sets the direction it will go. Unless I blow, the kite will not fly at all. I fly the kite," the wind cooed.

"Not so," exclaimed the kite's tail. "I make it sail and give it stability against the wind's whims. Without me, the kite would spin out of control and crash to earth. I fly the kite," declared the tail.

"Now who flies the kite?" the pastor asked the children.

"They all do!" said several kids in concert. Smart kids!

Take a moment to consider each of your coworkers. Ask yourself, *How would our progress be changed if that person's job didn't exist?* Next time you pass their work area, tell them you're glad they are part of the team.

❧

The heart hungers for a kind word.

The Gift of Words

There are different kinds of gifts, but the same Spirit. There are different kinds of service, but the same Lord.

1 CORINTHIANS 12:4-5

Melissa wanted more than anything to be able to sing and play the piano! Unfortunately, she simply had no musical talent, no matter how hard she tried or how much she practiced. She finally came to the conclusion that she had no sense of rhythm and no ability to carry a tune.

Marrying a preacher with a beautiful voice didn't help matters. Everyone knows that the pastor's wife is supposed to play the piano. She had never seen it written in any book, but she saw it written on every church member's face.

For years she prayed, "God, give me the ability to sing," but during the congregational hymns, she realized that nothing had happened. Her voice was just as bad as it was before she prayed. She took piano lessons until a well-meaning teacher kindly told her that she was wasting her money. Many times she wondered why God didn't answer her prayer in the way she would have liked.

One day, Melissa gave up on the idea of being an accomplished pianist or soloist. She sang in the shower after everyone had left for the day and hummed as she cooked before anyone arrived back home in the evening.

She taught Sunday school and later started writing. She discovered that God had given her the gift of words.

God does not give everyone the same talents. We're all unique and special in His eyes. Discovering her talent gave Melissa an entirely different outlook on life.

A bit of fragrance always clings to the hand that gives you roses.

What TALENTS DO I SEE IN MYSELF THAT I'VE OVERLOOKED?

Guilty Snacking

"Watch and pray so that you will not fall into temptation. The spirit is willing, but the body is weak."
MARK 14:38

If I AM NOT COMPLETELY HONEST, HOW MIGHT IT AFFECT MY RELATION- SHIPS?

Stacie was sitting in her office when she first heard the commotion.

"No way!"

"Check it out!"

"Who's got some quarters?"

Stacie got up from her desk and walked cautiously toward the sound of money and elation. She rounded the corner to discover three of her coworkers gathered around the vending machine. They were inserting change, picking out items, and receiving both the snack and their money back. The machine had a loose wire and was giving out free food.

Stacie grinned. No breakfast that morning and quarters in her pocket made for a happy young woman. She pushed her way through the crowd and gave it a try. Three quarters—some powdered donuts. Three quarters back—a big cinnamon roll. Three quarters back—a bag of chips. Carrying her quarters and her unexpected breakfast, she headed back to her desk with a smile on her face.

It wasn't until she sat down that the guilt (and the calories) settled heavily on her conscience. It wasn't right! No matter that everyone else seemed to be okay with it. No matter that the vending machine guy was always grumpy and never stocked the items she liked . . . no matter about any of that! This was wrong. It was stealing, and she couldn't do it.

Sometimes it's easier to join others who believe that if no one knows, it can't possibly hurt. Today, take a stand for the little acts of truth—the small steps of honesty and courage.

Courage is fear that has said its prayers.

Fear Not

Those of steadfast mind you keep in peace—
in peace because they trust in you.
ISAIAH 26:3 NRSV

Driving across the country by herself, a young woman recorded this experience:

I was on the second leg of a three-leg journey, and all I wanted to do was fall into bed for a good eight hours. But I couldn't stop, because I was still more than two hours from Tucumcari, New Mexico, and tired though I was, I was determined to get as close to the Texas border as I could.

What I hadn't reckoned on was bad weather. California and Arizona had been sunny and warm, and I wrongly assumed that New Mexico in late March would hold no unpleasant surprises.

The sun was sinking fast behind me, and soon disappeared altogether. On cross-country trips, I prefer not to drive at night—especially on unfamiliar roads—but I pushed on.

A quarter hour or so after sunset, I saw snow gliding past the glow of my headlights. Soon it was coming down fast and furiously at a slant, directly into my windshield, having a kaleidoscopic effect.

Panic took hold. There were few cars on the interstate, no lights along the route, no parking lots to pull into and wait it out.

Since I couldn't see where I was going as well as I would have liked, I had to put all my faith and trust in Someone who could.

I made it safely to my destination that night because I learned a long time ago Who it is who really keeps my car on the road.

Fear knocked at the door.
Faith answered.
No one was there.

When HAVE I BEEN IN A FEARFUL SITUATION? HOW DID I HANDLE IT?

The God Factor

*"Where your treasure is,
there your heart will be also."*
MATTHEW 6:21

God WILL
HELP ME WHEN
I TRUST HIM
ABOUT . . .

Surrounded by stacks of invoices and receipts, Theresa's fingers flew over the number pad of her keyboard, recalculating and checking the year's expenditures and income. It looked like they were going to make a good profit for the first time this year. *Thank God!* she thought wearily. They had finally licked their turnover problem by providing better health-care coverage and dental insurance.

Theresa picked up her coffee cup and walked down the hall to the small kitchen their company provided. One of her employees sat at the table reading her Bible and eating a microwave dinner.

"What are you doing here so late?" Theresa asked, pouring another cup of coffee.

"Oh, hi, Mrs. Chase," Angela said. "I thought I'd work tonight and get out that report you needed by tomorrow afternoon."

"You don't have to do that," Theresa said.

"I know, but I just wanted to double-check my figures."

"I appreciate all your hard work."

"Thanks," Angela said, smiling and closing her Bible. "And thanks for letting us start a Bible study group in the morning. We've been praying for you and the business too."

"It's working!" Theresa said. "Keep it up."

It takes a cooperative effort to achieve success. Some companies finally are realizing that there is a "God factor" at work when a business cares sincerely for its employees and sows appreciation as well as benefits into their lives. Invite God into your workplace, and He will honor your trust in Him.

❧

*A wise man will make more
opportunities than he finds.*

A Heart of Hospitality

*When Priscilla and Aquila heard him,
they invited him to their home and explained
to him the way of God more adequately.*

ACTS 18:26

Because of Jeff's profession, he and Rochelle relocated many times over the years. However, one of the relocations was memorable, not because of something that happened, but rather because of something that *didn't* happen.

Jeff was required to begin his position in a new city before their home was ready for occupancy. A woman from a local church heard about his predicament and offered him the use of her family's guest room until their home was ready.

When they finally moved into their new house, Rochelle wanted to show her gratitude to the woman for her kindness to Jeff. She called and asked her to stop by for tea, apologizing that she might have to sit on a few packing boxes but assuring her that she would be most welcome. There was a slight pause before the woman replied, "No, dear. I'll wait until you have things the way you want them. Then we can have a nice visit."

The woman was no doubt only trying to give Rochelle some extra time to settle in. But Rochelle never seemed to get things "the way she wanted them." Soon, nine months had gone by, and Rochelle was too embarrassed to re-extend her invitation of hospitality.

Hospitality asks us to open our hearts to others, whether our homes are picture-perfect or not. And when we refuse hospitality, we may be hurting the heart of a stranger. Let's keep our hearts open to give and receive hospitality.

*When there is room in the heart
there is room in the house.*

When HAVE I VISITED SOMEONE AND FELT WELCOME? WHAT MADE IT HOSPITABLE?

The God Who Never Sleeps

*Cast all your anxiety on him
because he cares for you.*
1 PETER 5:7

What HAS
GOD DONE
THAT PROVES
HIS POWER
TO ME?

In March of 1975, a tornado raked an eight-mile path across Atlanta, Georgia, snapping pine trees like toothpicks. Civil defense officials estimated the damage to be as high as thirty million dollars.

Even today, Gloria remembers that day as though it were yesterday. She was a younger woman then and was working part-time as a secretary at a small office. The office was closed that Monday so employees could attend a memorial service for a coworker.

That morning as Gloria got ready for the service, she noticed the skies turn an ominous black. The wind picked up, and trees bowed like rubber. She watched metal garbage cans being tossed down the street. Then the driving rain hit. After attending the service, she drove home. Visibility was poor as the rain slanted in sheets across the road.

Not until later did she learn that tornadoes had whipped through Atlanta that day destroying the building where she worked. When she finally went back to the office and surveyed the damage, she found everything in shambles. She trembled when she saw the collapsed concrete wall on top of her desk and shuddered to think what might have happened had she gone to work.

What a blessing to know that God is omnipresent! He is the One who neither slumbers nor sleeps. He promises to be with us and deliver us even in the midst of a whirlwind. Look to God when darkness blankets your world, and He will show you the way home!

*To worry about tomorrow
is to be unhappy today.*

Feel the Power!

Whatever is true, whatever is noble, whatever is right, whatever is pure, whatever is lovely, whatever is admirable—if anything is excellent or praiseworthy—think about such things.

PHILIPPIANS 4:8

Pope John XXIII was once quoted as saying, "It often happens that I wake at night and begin to think about a serious problem and decide I must tell the Pope about it. Then I wake up completely and remember that I am the Pope."

Far too often we imagine that the solution to our problems, the cure for our ailments, and the guarantee for our happiness lie with someone or something outside ourselves. But do we really have so little power?

Martha Washington thought otherwise, stating, "I have learned from experience that the greater part of our happiness or misery depends on our dispositions and not on our circumstances. We carry the seeds with us in our minds wherever we go."

Just think about it. How dramatically would your life be changed if you knew you had the seeds to your happiness waiting inside, longing to blossom whenever you would allow it? From the words of Mother Teresa, in her book *A Gift to God,* we can learn how to let those seeds spring to life:

We all long for Heaven where God is, but being happy with Him now means

- loving as He loves,
- helping as He helps,
- giving as He gives,
- serving as He serves,
- rescuing as He rescues,
- being with Him for all the twenty-four hours,
- touching Him in His distressing disguise.

Happiness is not a destination, but a journey.

What IS THE HAPPIEST THING ABOUT BEING ME?

The Kingdom Family

"Whoever does the will of my Father in heaven is my brother and sister and mother."
MATTHEW 12:50

Who is THE SPECIAL PERSON GOD ADDED TO MY LIFE?

Charlene walked down the aisle alone. This had been the moment she was supposed to share with her father—the precious time when he would give his blessing to her marriage and officially hand her over, as she made the transition from daughter to wife.

Yet her father was not there. Nor was her mother or sister. Her family had a previous commitment, a convention they had to attend, and that convention had been more important than her wedding. It had been a tough blow, and Charlene could feel the pain clouding this special moment.

There, waiting at the altar, was her pastor—her shepherd. His warm and tender smile received her into his presence. Charlene felt her longing subside as she looked into his kind face. The pastor and his wife had become more than family. They had counseled, laughed, and cried with Charlene as she worked through premarital jitters. They had prayed with her and held her hand. They were more father and mother to her than her biological parents had ever been.

Charlene smiled from the depths of her heart at her waiting bridegroom. This was a time to celebrate the new, and God had been faithful in surrounding her with parents, brothers, and sisters that were part of His kingdom.

Your family doesn't have to come from the same womb or share the same blood. Allow God to give you the gift of His family. We are meant to be that for each other.

The Lord gives His blessing when He finds the vessel empty.

Light and Fluffy

*"What shall I compare the kingdom of God to?
It is like yeast that a woman took and
mixed into a large amount of flour until
it worked all through the dough."*

LUKE 13:20-21

"What's that, Grandma?" the little girl asked, as she watched her grandmother carefully mix the ingredients for bread.

"Yeast," Grandma replied. "That's what makes the bread rise. We have to cover the dough with a cloth and put it in a warm place if we want our rolls to be light and fluffy."

Not fully understanding the way yeast works, Mary was impatient. She continued to lift the cloth in order to see the round balls of dough that sat in the baking dish. After a while, she realized that they were growing larger.

Finally, Grandma placed the rolls in the pre-heated oven. Mary watched through the glass window as the tops began to turn golden brown. The scent permeated the whole house. When the rolls were done, Mary was allowed to brush a small amount of butter on the top of each one.

Mary's grandmother thought about the look of amazement on her granddaughter's face when she saw how the bread had doubled in size. Her own faith, she realized, was a lot like that dough. The more she prayed and studied God's Word, the larger her faith grew. And just as the rolls needed to remain warm in order to rise, she needed to keep her heart warm in order to serve God and others.

With a "light and fluffy" attitude toward life, we can rise up in the midst of trouble and show others the warmth that only God can provide.

Your faith will cause you to rise to the top.

What ACTS LIKE YEAST IN MY LIFE AND MAKES ME GROW?

Closing the Door

*We want each of you to show this same diligence
to the very end, in order to make your hope sure.*
HEBREWS 6:11

I need TO
SAY GOODBYE
AND SHUT THE
DOOR ON . . .

Michelle looked around her office. She had worked so hard for all of this and had put so many hours into her vision, especially at the beginning, when her company had only been a dream and her energy was committed to making it a reality. Someone else had appreciated her creativity—a bigger, larger company that had bought her out in a forceful merger. Now all that was once hers belonged to an unseen face.

Michelle looked out of her office window at her employees. She knew they had been looking to her, waiting to see how she would handle herself over the past four weeks. She was tempted to throw all her energy into a new pursuit, but she also knew that she had a commitment to see this old one to its end. It was a matter of integrity. When she finally handed this company over, she would do so knowing that she had done her best to the very end.

Change takes place in all of our lives. One season ends, and another begins. With each ending, we have a choice. We can walk away without looking back and ignore the closure and attention that's needed; or we can take the time, painful as it may be, to finish well—to tie up loose ends, to say our good-byes, to work hard right to the end, knowing we have closed out the old one with integrity.

When one door is shut, another opens.

Help!

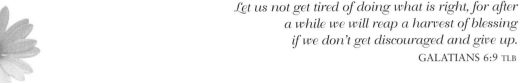

Let us not get tired of doing what is right, for after a while we will reap a harvest of blessing if we don't get discouraged and give up.
GALATIANS 6:9 TLB

What was I thinking? Kristy thought as she stood in the middle of the church's commercial kitchen and turned around slowly. As the hubbub from the fellowship hall continued, the dirty dishes were piling up on every possible surface.

"I've loaded the dishwasher," her friend Carol said. "You can wash pots and pans until the cycle is finished. I'm sorry, but I really have to run."

Kristy felt overwhelmed, but she didn't want to complain. "No problem . . . really."

By the time the dishes were washed, dried, and put away, she and another woman were the only ones left in the kitchen. Mrs. Carson, an elderly woman who had been in their church forever, had taken pity on her and stayed to help.

"I don't know what I would have done if you hadn't stayed," Kristy said, smiling. She hugged her plump helper.

"You should have been here before we had a dishwasher," Mrs. Carson said.

"I can't imagine."

"Of course, people were a little different back then. We all pitched in, and the work was done in no time. Now people are so busy. I suppose even you have to go to work in the morning."

"Yes, ma'am."

"Well, you might not get many thank-yous from other people, but God sees your heart. He's pleased with you. Now let's get you home."

When you feel like no one else cares about doing what's right or pitching in to help, remember, God cares, and He will extend His grace to you.

For grace is given not because we have done good works, but in order that we may be able to do them.

I know
GOD CARES
ABOUT . . .

One Lonely Seedling

*Let us not give up meeting together,
as some are in the habit of doing,
but let us encourage one another.*
HEBREWS 10:25

The GROUP
I'M IN HAS
HELPED ME TO
SURVIVE BY . . .

One fall, Margaret decided to dig out a flower bed by her front door. After the first killing frost, she yanked out the alyssum, tugged out the zinnias, and hauled the cosmos to the compost heap. Then she added fertilizer and mixed it into the dirt with her roto tiller.

The following April, as Margaret cleared out the debris that winter winds had blown into the flower bed, she discovered a solitary cosmos seedling struggling to grow in a corner. The leggy and weak-stemmed cosmos leaned toward the sun in a pathetic call for help. Margaret couldn't imagine how the cosmos seed managed to germinate after all her fall digging.

Margaret transplanted the single seedling into another bed with other baby cosmos. The flower grew strong and radiant within the cosmos congregation.

Like the one lonely seedling, we can't reach our full potential alone. Without being joined to a body of believers, spiritual growth can be one-sided or erratic. The transplanted cosmos worked with the other flowers to attract bees and butterflies. This made it possible for each flower to benefit. In the same way, believers are responsible for helping and encouraging each other for the benefit of all.

Joining with others strengthens our faith, expands our experiences, and refreshes our souls. This keeps us spiritually healthy. When we feel isolated or when we pull away from others, perhaps our lonely seedling needs a gentle transplanting.

*Blessed is the influence of one
true loving soul on another.*

Kitchen Friends

Share with God's people who are in need.
Practice hospitality.
ROMANS 12:13

How wonderful to see the goodness of God in my own kitchen! Jennifer thought as she browsed through her cookbook collection. He had provided abundantly for her and her family. Not only did they enjoy a variety of good foods, He had provided the kitchen and all its tools. He also had given her a talent she loved—cooking—a blessing to her and her entire family.

People loved to visit around her kitchen table, probably because her yellow kitchen was bright and cheerful. They seemed to feel warm and accepted there. Over the years, her table had been the scene of a lot of sharing, delight, heartbreak, good times, games, food, and plenty of fellowship. On holidays, everyone trooped in and out of the kitchen, helping with the cooking, visiting, carrying cups of coffee or other drinks to family members, stirring, laughing, and bumping into each other.

One day, Jennifer saw a holiday commercial on television in which the woman was thankful for instant food so she could get out of the kitchen and spend more time with her family. She wondered why the woman's family didn't spend more time in the kitchen with *her!*

Is your kitchen the kind of place where everyone feels comfortable and welcome? If not, how can you make it a spot that binds you closer to your family, friends, and God? It might be as easy as planning a pizza night or baking chocolate chip cookies together. Give it a try!

❧

Happy is the house that shelters a friend.

If I COULD CHANGE MY HOME, I WOULD MAKE IT . . .

The Real Stuff

APRIL 7

O LORD, you have searched me and you know me.
PSALM 139:1

What PLACE
DO I FEEL
WELCOME?
WHY?

Veronica placed the cake on the dining-room table. Wiping the sweat from her brow, she surveyed the scene before her. Streamers lined the ceiling, cups and plates were set out, and the warm glow of candles added the perfect touch. It was her Henry's seventieth birthday; she was determined that it would be an extra special occasion.

The guests began to arrive, and Veronica directed them to the living room. It didn't work. It never seemed to work. Every time she had a gathering, people always seemed to gravitate toward the kitchen. She sighed as she pushed through the crowd to finish her preparations. Everyone was laughing, talking, and seemed right at home. Veronica stopped for a moment as a friend warmly embraced her.

The kitchen was the heartbeat of her home. She smiled. The mess didn't matter; the fancy decorations in the other rooms didn't matter. It was the heart that people wanted—the real stuff—the comfort of home.

God is the same way in His love for us. He doesn't need the fancy stuff. He doesn't require hanging out with us at our formal best. He loves who we are—the messy, comfortable heartbeat of our very beings. That's who He wants to spend time with, who He's drawn to, who He created. You don't have to fake it with God. Just let Him love you.

You are not accepted by God
because you deserve to be, or because
you have worked hard for him;
but because Jesus died for you.

A Loaf of Bread

Love your neighbor as yourself.
LEVITICUS 19:18

It IS THE
ACTION
THAT COUNTS.
WHY?

Janice looked at the recipe book and then back to the mixing bowl. She kept up a constant stream of conversation with herself as she added each ingredient. "Don't mess this up, just take it slow. They'll love it!" She paused. "What if they don't love it? What if they think I'm a horrid cook, out to poison the neighborhood?"

Later that evening, Janice wrapped her slightly misshapen loaves of banana bread in plastic wrap. After a deep breath, she walked to her neighbor's home and rang the doorbell. An older man answered and greeted her in surprise. "Hi."

"Oh, hi! Yes . . . um . . . I'm your neighbor, Janice. I thought you might like this loaf of banana bread." Her cheeks reddened. "Not that I'm a great cook or anything."

His grin interrupted her. "Really?" He reached out a tentative hand and took a loaf. "That was so very kind of you. I love banana bread." Janice wanted to grab it back. He loved it? Oh, no! What if it was terrible?

He seemed to read her frantic thoughts. "I'm sure it's wonderful, Janice. Thank you. You made my evening . . . just with your thoughtfulness."

It's risky to give of ourselves! Sometimes we hardly know how to share friendship and love with our neighbors. What we do, though, isn't really important. It's the thought, the time, the interest we show that make a difference to those around us.

∽⚬∾

The way in which something is given
is worth more than the gift itself.

Clubfoot

There was given to me a thorn in the flesh.
2 CORINTHIANS 12:7 KJV

God HAS
BLESSED ME,
HEALED ME,
AND RENEWED
ME THIS YEAR
THROUGH . . .

Phillip Carey, an orphan and the main character in the novel *Of Human Bondage*, was born with what was once called a "clubfoot." Because of his deformity, his school classmates often made fun of him and excluded him from their boyhood games.

In one poignant scene, young Phillip is convinced that if he prays hard enough, God will heal his foot. He daydreams for hours about the reaction of his classmates when he returns to school with a new foot: he sees himself outrunning the swiftest boy in his class and takes great pleasure in the shocked amazement of his former tormentors. At last he goes to sleep knowing that when he awakes in the morning, his foot will be whole. But the next day brings no change. He still has a clubfoot.

Although just one of many disappointments for young Phillip, this proves to be a pivotal point in his learning to cope with the harsh realities of his life. Drawing upon an inner strength he did not know he had, he decided that his clubfoot would not determine his destiny. He began to see his handicap as nothing more than an obstacle to be overcome, and it did not hold him back.

Life is filled with grand opportunities cleverly camouflaged as devastating disappointments. Whatever it is in your life, don't despair. With God's help, you can be a woman who turns your scars into stars, your handicaps into strengths.

*Our trials, our sorrows,
and our griefs develop us.*

Faith Is a Verb

Faith is the assurance of things hoped for,
the conviction of things not seen.
HEBREWS 11:1 NASB

In *You Can't Afford the Luxury of a Negative Thought,* John Roger and Peter McWilliams offered a new description of faith. They chose the word *faithing* to describe their proactive approach to confidence in life's outcomes.

In their thinking, faithing works in the present, acknowledging that there is a purpose to everything and life is unfolding exactly as it should. It is actively trusting that God can handle our troubles and needs better than we can. All we must do is let them go so that He can do His work.

What
BLESSINGS HAS
GOD SENT MY
WAY LATELY?

"The Two Boxes"

I have in my hands two boxes
Which God gave me to hold.
He said, "Put all your sorrows in the black,
And all your joys in the gold."
I heeded His words, and in the two boxes
Both my joys and sorrows I store,
But though the gold became heavier each day
The black was as light as before.
With curiosity, I opened the black.
I wanted to find out why.
And I saw, in the base of the box, a hole
Which my sorrows had fallen out by.
I showed the hole to God, and mused aloud,
"I wonder where all my sorrows could be."
He smiled a gentle smile at me.
"My child, they're all here, with Me."
I asked, "God, why give me the boxes,
Why the gold, and the black with the hole?"
"My child, the gold is to count your blessings,
the black is for you to let go."[31]

Trust involves letting go and
knowing God will catch you.

Cradled

*Now will I arise, saith the LORD; I will set
him in safety from him that puffeth at him.*
PSALM 12:5 KJV

When I
WAS IN CRISIS,
GOD COM-
FORTED ME
THROUGH . . .

A number of years ago, two young women boarded a ferry to cross the English Channel from England to France. About halfway through their five-hour journey, as they were eating lunch on deck, the ferry hit rough waters. The ferry tossed about rather violently on the waves, to the point where even the seasoned crew felt ill.

When it became apparent that the pitching of the boat was not going to abate, one of the women decided to return to her seat in the middle of the ferry. She soon fell asleep and experienced no more seasickness. After the ferry had moved into calmer waters off the coast of France, the other woman joined her. "That was awful," she exclaimed. "I was nauseated for two hours!"

"I'm sorry to hear that," said the second woman.

"Weren't you sick?" the first woman asked in amazement.

"No," her friend admitted. "Here at our seats I must have been at the fulcrum of the boat's motion. I could see the front and back of the boat were moving up and down violently, but here, the motion was relatively calm. I simply imagined myself being rocked in the arms of God, and I fell asleep."

All around you today, life may have been unsettling and stormy. It may seem like your entire life is bouncing about on rough waters. But when you return to the "Center" of your life, the Lord, He will set you in safety. Let Him rock you gently to sleep.

*All I have seen teaches me to trust
the Creator for all I have not seen.*

Uniquely Fashioned

I will praise thee; for I am fearfully and wonderfully made: marvellous are thy works; and that my soul knoweth right well.

PSALM 139:14 KJV

When you stop to think about all the intricate details involved in the normal functioning of your body—which is just one creation among countless species and organisms on the planet—you must conclude, "The Designer of *this* piece of work had a marvelous plan."

Listen to your heartbeat. Flex your fingers and toes. As you do these things, keep in mind the following facts:

- No one else among all humanity has your exact fingerprints, handprints, or footprints.
- No one else has your voiceprint.
- No one else has your genetic code—the exact positioning of the many genes that define your physical characteristics.

Furthermore, no one else has your exact history in time and space. No one else has gone where you've gone, done what you've done, said what you've said, or created what you've created. You are truly a one-of-a-kind masterpiece.

The Lord knows precisely *how* you were made and *why* you were made. When something in your life goes amiss, He knows how to fix it. When you err or stray from His commandments, He knows how to woo you back and work even the worst tragedies and mistakes for your good when you repent.

You have been uniquely fashioned for a specific purpose on the earth. He has a "design" for your life. It is His own imprint, His own mark.

In order to be irreplaceable, one must always be different.

In WHAT WAYS AM I UNIQUE?

Age Is an Attitude

The righteous flourish like the palm tree.
They still bring forth fruit in old age.
PSALMS 92:12,14 RSV

When
I AM OLD .
I HOPE
TO BE . . .

Helen Keller was once asked how she would approach old age. She responded:

"Age seems to be only another physical handicap, and it excites no dread in me. Once I had a dear friend of eighty, who impressed upon me the fact that he enjoyed life more than he had done at twenty-five.

"It is as natural for me, certainly, to believe that the richest harvest of happiness comes with age as that true sight and hearing are within, not without. Confidently I climb the broad stairway that love and faith have built to heights where I shall "attain to a boundless reach of sky.""[32]

The poem "How Old Are You?" reinforces this idea that *outlook* is what determines our age:

Age is a quality of mind:
If you have left your dream behind,
If hope is cold,
If you no longer look ahead,
If your ambition fires are dead—
Then you are old.
But if from life you take the best,
And if in life you keep the jest,
If love you hold;
No matter how the years go by,
No matter how the birthdays fly,
You are not old.[33]

Years before we reach what we would call "old age" we determine whether that time will be a gracious and pleasant time or a time when we rehearse life's hurts.

It's not how old you are but how you are old.

The Sunset Decision

If serving the Lord seems undesirable to you, then choose for yourselves this day whom you will serve. But as for me and my household, we will serve the Lord.

JOSHUA 24:15

Jenny Lind, known as "The Swedish Nightingale," won worldwide success as a talented opera singer. She sang for heads of state and thrilled hundreds of thousands of people in an era when all performances were live.

Not only did her fame grow, but her fortune increased as well. Yet at the height of her career, at a time when her voice was at its peak, she left the stage and never returned.

She must have missed the fame, the money, and the applause of thousands—or so her fans surmised—but Jenny Lind was content to live in quiet seclusion with her husband.

Once an English friend went to visit her. He found her on the beach with a Bible on her knee. As he approached, he saw that her attention was fixed upon a magnificent sunset.

They talked of old days and former acquaintances, and eventually the conversation turned to her new life. "How is it that you came to abandon the stage at the apex of your career?" he asked.

Jenny offered a quiet answer that reflected her peace of heart: "When every day, it made me think less of this (laying a finger on the Bible) and nothing at all of that (pointing to the sunset), what else could I do?"

Nothing in life is as precious as your relationship with your Heavenly Father, and then your relationships with family members and friends. Ultimate fulfillment comes not in career or money, but in relationship with God and others.

The MOST PRECIOUS THINGS IN MY LIFE ARE . . .

If we fully comprehend the brevity of life, our greatest desire would be to please God and to serve one another.

Running on Empty

There remains, then, a Sabbath-rest for the people of God; for anyone who enters God's rest also rests from his own work, just as God did from his.
HEBREWS 4:9-10

My
FAVORITE
PLACE TO
REST IS . . .

Some years ago, a research physician made an extensive study of the amount of oxygen a person needs throughout the day. He was able to demonstrate that average workers breathe thirty ounces of oxygen during a day's work, but they use thirty-one. At the close of the day they are one ounce short, and their bodies are tired.

They go to sleep and breathe more oxygen than they use to sleep, so in the morning they have regained five-sixths of the ounce they were short. The night's rest does not fully balance the day's work!

By the seventh day, they are six-sixths or one whole ounce in debt again. They must rest an entire day to replenish their bodies' oxygen requirements.

Further, he demonstrated that replenishing an entire ounce of oxygen requires thirty to thirty-six hours (one twenty-four-hour day plus the preceding and following nights) when part of the resting is done while one is awake and moving about.

Over time, failure to replenish the oxygen supply results in the actual death of cells and, eventually, the premature death of the person.

A person is restored as long as he or she takes the seventh day as a day of rest.[34]

The God who created us not only *invites* us to rest, but He created our bodies in such a fashion that they *demand* rest.

In turning your attention to God, you can find true rest and replenishment in every area of your life—spirit, soul, *and* body.

I feel as if God had, by giving the Sabbath, given fifty-two springs in every year.

Discretionary Time

In all your getting, get understanding.
PROVERBS 4:7 NKJV

Twenty-year-old college student Amy Wu wrote about her aunt who "tends to her house as if it were her child." The house is spotlessly clean and usually smells of home-cooked meals. Roses from the garden are artfully arranged in beautiful vases. Her aunt could afford a housekeeper, but she truly enjoys doing her own housework.

Amy went on, "I'm a failure at housework. I've chosen to be inept and unlearned at what my aunt has spent so much time perfecting. Up to now, I've thought there were more important things to do." But those "more important things" didn't turn out to be all that important.

One day she decided to make a meal for her family. While the dinner was cooking, she wrote a letter to her cousin. Then she made a chocolate cake to celebrate her sister's birthday. It was a success: "That night I grinned as my father and sister dug into the pasta, then the cake, licking their lips in appreciation. It had been a long time since I'd felt so proud. A week later my cousin called and thanked me for my letter, the first handwritten correspondence she'd received in two years."

She concluded, "Sure, my generation has all the technological advances at our fingertips. We're computer-savvy, and we have more time. But what are we really saving it for? In the end, we may lose more than we've gained by forgetting the important things in life."[35]

The great rule of moral conduct is, next to God, to respect time.

If MY APPLIANCES SAVED ME AN HOUR A DAY, I COULD SPEND IT ON . . .

Resting in the Lord

He who dwells in the shelter of the Most High
will rest in the shadow of the Almighty.
PSALM 91:1

A song
I ALWAYS
LOVE TO HEAR
IS . . . WHY?

There is a story about an English steamer that was wrecked on a rocky coast many years ago. Twelve women set out into the dark stormy waters in a lifeboat, and the boisterous sea immediately carried them away from the wreckage. Having no oars, they were at the mercy of the wind and the waves. They spent a fearful night being tossed about by the raging tempest.

They probably would have lost all hope if it had not been for the spiritual stamina of one of the ladies, who was well known for her work in sacred oratorios. Calmly she prayed aloud for divine protection. Then, urging her companions to put their trust in the Lord, she encouraged them by singing hymns of comfort.

Throughout the dark hours her voice rang out across the water. Early the next morning a small craft came searching for survivors. The man at the helm would have missed the women in the fog if he had not heard one woman singing the selection from *Elijah,* "Oh, rest in the Lord, wait patiently for Him!" Steering in the direction of her strong voice, he soon spotted the drifting lifeboat. While many others were lost that night, these trusting few were rescued.

Have you ever had a long sleepless night when the trials and "storms" of the day refused to leave you? Instead of laying there awash in worry, frustration, fear, or anger, try singing hymns of faith—either aloud or silently—in your mind.

God washes the eyes by tears until
they can behold the invisible land
where tears shall come no more.

Ultimate Worth

You are Christ's, and Christ is God's.
1 CORINTHIANS 3:23 NKJV

The bidding was over, and the auctioneer's gavel fell. The winning bid for a rocking chair that had been valued between $3,000 and $5,000 was $453,500.

This had been the case through the duration of the auction. A used automobile valued between $18,000 and $22,000 was sold for $79,500. A set of green tumblers valued at $500 sold for $38,000. A necklace valued at $500 to $700 went for $211,500. For four days articles of common, ordinary value were sold for wildly inflated prices. Why? The items auctioned were from the estate of Jacqueline Kennedy Onassis.

As in the sale of the items of the Kennedy estate, some things are valuable solely because of the one to whom they belong.

We may inflate a person's worth because of their financial status, their influence, or their potential to benefit us; or we may say a person has no value because they have few assets or cannot help us. But the Scriptures tell us that when we were still sinners, Jesus Christ died for us. (See Romans 5:8.) When we had no value and were even opposed to God, He paid the price to redeem our lives.

Whenever you feel depressed and worthless, meditate on this: Your value is determined by God. He loved and valued you so much, He sent His Son to die so you could become His child. Never doubt your importance and worth!

All I could never be, all men ignored in me—this, I was worth to God.

What KIND OF VALUE DO I PLACE ON MY FRIENDS?

Rituals

A heart at peace gives life to the body.
PROVERBS 14:30

What
RITUAL IS
IMPORTANT TO
ME? WILL IT
ALWAYS BE SO?

The word "ritual" is derived from the word, "rite," which means "a ceremonial or formal, solemn act, observance, or procedure in accordance with prescribed rule or custom."[36] A ritual refers to a system of rites—in other words, doing the same thing in the same way, every time. Rituals are common customs unique to an era or group of people.

The word rite originally had a religious connotation. The best-known rites of the church have been baptism, communion, joining the church, marriage, and burial. These rites give a comforting continuity when the meanings remain alive and cherished.

On a more mundane level, in present-day society a ritual can be anything performed on a regular basis. It can now refer to something as simple as brushing our teeth. Whether we realize it or not, we all have rituals. The things we do to prepare for work in the morning and the things we do when we get home each night are rituals that give order, meaning, and security to our lives.

Just like religious rituals, our daily rituals can bring us peace and comfort. A devotional time before bed touches every area of our lives. Praying purifies the heart, reading the Word of God renews the mind, receiving more of the Heavenly Father's unconditional love evokes feelings of serenity, communing with the Lord gives us a sense of belonging and guides us in our work—and all these things put the body in a relaxed, peaceful state.

*When I am with God my fear is gone
in the great quiet of God. My troubles
are like pebbles on the road,
my joys are like the everlasting hills.*

Invited to Breakfast

You, O Lord . . . know the hearts of all.
ACTS 1:24 NKJV

An EXAMPLE
OF HOW
GOOD GOD
HAS BEEN
TO ME IS THE
TIME . . .

For the apostle Peter, the crowing rooster on the early morning of Jesus' crucifixion was a "wake-up call"—it woke him up to who he really was. In Peter's worst moment he had denied knowing his Friend and Teacher, Jesus. He wept bitterly over his betrayal and must have felt terrible guilt and shame afterward.

Then one morning after His resurrection, Jesus appeared to the disciples, who were fishing at the Sea of Tiberias. He called out from the shore and asked if they had caught any fish. The disciples didn't recognize Him and called back no. Jesus told them to throw the net on the other side of the boat, and the catch was so great they were unable to haul it in. Now they knew the Man directing them was Jesus, and they headed to shore.

When the disciples got there, Jesus invited them to eat with Him. "Come and have breakfast," He said. In the dawning hours of the day, the resurrected Jesus cooked breakfast for them.

How do you think Peter felt when, after the greatest failure of his life, Jesus wanted to spend time with him, eat with him, and even help him fish? Jesus sought out the disciple who had let Him down when He needed him most. Moreover, He called Peter to lead His followers.

Whatever mistakes or compromises we made yesterday, Jesus still loves us today and says, "Come and have breakfast with Me."

*Whether we stumble or whether we fall,
we must only think of rising again
and going on in our course.*

The Empty Tomb

*"Be honest in your judgment and do not decide
at a glance (superficially and by appearances);
but judge fairly and righteously."*
JOHN 7:24 AMP

My DIFFER-
ENCE FROM
OTHERS IS
GOOD
BECAUSE . . .

Philip was born with Down's syndrome. He was a happy child, but as he grew older he became increasingly aware that he was different from other children.

He went to Sunday school with boys and girls his own age, and the class had wonderful experiences together—learning, laughing, playing. But Philip remained an outsider.

As an Easter lesson, the Sunday school teacher gave each student a large egg-shaped plastic container. The children were asked to explore the church grounds, find something that symbolized new life to them, put it in their "egg," and bring it back to share with the class.

The children had a grand time running about the churchyard collecting symbols. Then they gathered back in the classroom and watched with great anticipation as the teacher opened each egg. In one egg, there was a flower, in another a butterfly. The students responded with great glee and enthusiasm as the teacher revealed the contents of each egg.

When the teacher opened Philip's egg, there was nothing inside. As could be expected, the eight-year-olds responded, "That's stupid! You didn't do it right."

"I did so do it right," Philip responded. "It's empty—the tomb is empty!"

The classroom fell silent. From that day on things were different. Philip became a full-fledged part of the class. The children took him into their friendship. He had been freed from the tomb of his difference, and he entered into a new life among his peers.[37]

~~

*You must look into people,
as well as at them.*

Power Steering

Whatever is born of God overcomes
the world; and this is the victory that
has overcome the world—our faith.

1 JOHN 5:4 NASB

When SOMEONE IS RUDE TO ME, I COULD RESPOND PEACEFULLY. WHY SHOULD I?

Few things in life make us feel as powerful as sitting behind the steering wheel of a car. Realizing the vehicle weighs two tons and is capable of traveling up to one hundred miles per hour, we have a tendency to feel almost invincible—which is a good feeling after a long, hard day at work.

Unfortunately, this heady sensation often results in dangerous or rude behavior, such as changing lanes without signaling, driving too fast, tailgating, failing to yield to merging traffic, running red lights or stop signs, flashing head-lights, and blaring horns. When we give in to the urge to do just one of these things, reasoning, "It won't hurt to do it this once," or "I'm in a hurry," or "Everyone else does it," we become part of a problem instead of part of a solution.

How should you act when you're in the driver's seat at the end of your workday, headed for home? Pop some uplifting music, such as praise songs, into the tape deck, or listen to the soothing sounds of a classical station. Say a quick prayer for safety before you start the engine, and decide you'll be a friendly, courteous driver and not a road hazard. Use this time for personal rejoicing over the work you've just completed.

What do you do when other drivers seem to be going out of their way to make your drive time a "drive you crazy" time? Say a prayer for them, smile, and wave.

Beware in your prayer, above everything,
of limiting God, not only by unbelief, but
by fancying that you know what He can do.

Take Time for Beauty

One thing I have desired of the LORD, that
will I seek: to behold the beauty of the LORD.
PSALM 27:4 NKJV

What HAVE I
EXPERIENCED
IN NATURE
THAT PUT
ME IN AWE
OF GOD?

Beauty feeds our souls like food nourishes our bodies. Beauty points us to the transcendent, takes us beyond our finiteness, and opens our hearts to that which is greater and larger than ourselves. There is something about great beauty that brings us into the awesome presence of the infinite and the eternal.

In reflecting on his priorities, a prominent British scientist said he would give more time to the enjoyment of things that are beautiful. He said:

If I had my life to live over again, I would have made a rule to read some poetry and listen to some music at least once a week; for perhaps the part of my brain now atrophied would have thus been kept active through use. The loss of these tastes is a loss of happiness, and may possibly be injurious to the intellect, and more probably to the moral character, by enfeebling the emotional part of our nature.[38]

We sometimes need to be reminded to slow down enough to find beauty in those things we hurry by each day. Let's take time for beauty. Make a date with yourself to stroll through an art gallery, visit a beautiful church, or linger in a park or garden.

If there simply is not time, then remember the beautiful places captured in memories—moments of sheer joy or a mental "snapshot" of a majestic, snow-capped mountain or moonlit night.

Let God use the beauty He created to
awaken in you the desire for more of Him.
At cool of day, with God I walk in my
garden's grateful shade; I hear His voice
among the trees and I am not afraid.

Underwater

He knoweth the way that I take: when he hath tried me, I shall come forth as gold.

JOB 23:10 KJV

I feel THAT I AM GENUINE WHEN I . . .

As the shadows of the day grow longer, our tempers can grow short. Drawing on the refreshing power of the Holy Spirit, however, will get us to the end of a stressful day. We can gain renewed patience, a fresh sense of humor, and a new surge of creativity and insight by enlisting the aid of the Spirit's ministry within us. Frequently it's during those late afternoon hours when we most need His extra help.

Jewelers claim one of the surest tests for diamonds is the underwater test. "An imitation diamond is never so brilliant as a genuine stone. If your eye is not experienced to detect the difference, a simple test is to place the stone underwater. The imitation diamond is practically extinguished, while a genuine diamond sparkles even underwater and is distinctly visible. If a genuine stone is placed beside an imitation one underwater, the contrast will be apparent to the least experienced eye."

That is how it should be with Christians when their heads are "underwater" at the end of the day. The power of the Holy Spirit should so sparkle within them, refreshing and renewing them in spite of the day's harassments, that it should be easy for the average person to tell there is something genuinely different about their lives.

Pray that the Holy Spirit will help you in the ways you need Him most—to make you shine like a diamond underwater!

❧

In the morning, prayer is the key that opens to us the treasures of God's mercies and blessings; in the evening, it is the key that shuts us up under His protection and safeguard.

Is Anyone Out There?

"Let your light shine before men, that they may see your good deeds and praise your Father in heaven."
MATTHEW 5:16

What COULD I SHARE THAT WOULD CHEER SOMEONE ELSE?

When a uniform factory in the Midwest closed its doors for what was presumably the last time, one of its customers did something kind for a person he had never met. As the factory workers were facing certain unemployment in their small town, this gentleman decided to buy and reopen the plant. Needless to say, the workers were amazed, pleased, and disbelieving.

The man, a native Midwesterner who owned several uniform shops on the West Coast, had come into a large fortune. He believed that if your cup was full and running over, you should share your blessings with others. When he tried to place an order and found out that the uniform factory had gone out of business, he decided to put his philosophy into action.

The man bought the factory and began to put people back to work. He provided his employees with their first health plan, jazzed up the uniform styles to make them more attractive to buyers, began replacing outdated machinery, and made other improvements to the plant.[39]

Do you have to be rich to bring a ray of sunshine into someone's life? Not at all! Sometimes money is involved in making a meaningful change, but it's really the person who signs the check and his or her desire to do something good that is behind it.

No matter how much or how little we have, we can each do something to make someone else's path a little smoother.

Give to the world the best you have, and the best will come back to you.

Circadian Meetings

To everything there is a season, a time for every purpose under heaven.

ECCLESIASTES 3:1 NKJV

A business consultant once advised executives to follow this pattern for scheduling their meetings and appointments:

- Have breakfast meetings to set agendas, give assignments, and introduce new projects.
- Have lunch meetings to negotiate deals, give advice to key staff members, and discuss midcourse corrections.
- Have afternoon meetings to interview prospective employees, clients, or vendors, to return phone calls; and to resolve personnel issues.

From this consultant's perspective, morning hours are best spent in task activities, midday hours in problem-solving, and afternoon hours in people-intensive activities. The reason has little to do with management and much to do with biology. Our "circadian rhythms" seem to put us at a high-energy time in the morning and a low-energy time in the afternoon. Meeting with people requires less energy than attention to task and detail.

This afternoon, perhaps you can meet a friend or invite colleagues into your office for a bit of refreshment and conversation. Take time out for a brief end-of-the-day conversation with a secretary or another person who works under your supervision. Allow time for light conversation and share about personal matters—such as the antics of a toddler or accomplishments of a teen in the family.

Jesus no doubt spent full days in ministry, preaching, teaching, and healing those who flocked to Him. But at the close of His ministry-intensive hours, Jesus spent time with His friends. We are wise to follow His example!

Hast thou a friend, as heart may wish at will? Then use him so, to have his friendship still. Wouldst have a friend, wouldst know what friend is best? Have God thy friend, who passeth all the rest.

A favorite MEMORY OF A BYGONE FRIEND IS . . .

Playtime!

Blessed be the Lord your God,
who delighted in you.
1 KINGS 10:9 NKJV

If I WERE
ASKED TO TELL
GOD A JOKE,
I WOULD TELL
HIM THE ONE
ABOUT . . .

For most children, the time immediately following school is set aside for the following things:

- Unstructured fun—no more assignments to be completed in a specific class period.
- Noise and activity—no more restrictions to sit still and be quiet.
- Friendships—no more working on your own to read a book or complete an assignment.
- Games—workbooks are left behind, and homework is yet to come.

Whatever happened to those good ol' days? you may wonder. Perhaps it is time to recapture them.

Build in a little playtime at the end of your workday. Let it be unstructured. Allow yourself to be a little noisy. Move about, and flex those tired muscles. Spend a little time with friends. Play a game—perhaps handball with a colleague, a set of tennis with a friend, or a game of hopscotch with your child.

The Lord made you with a capacity for fun, an ability to smile and laugh, a desire to kick up your heels and frolic a bit, and a need for freedom of motion. He created the world for you to enjoy—and to enjoy it with Him!

The Scriptures say that the Lord "delights" in us. Could it be that the Lord delights in what delights us? Could it be that the Lord desires to have someone with whom to have complete fellowship, including someone with whom to laugh, play, and relax?

Could it be? Why not find out today!

❧

Human fellowship can go to great lengths,
but not all the way. Fellowship
with God can go to all lengths.

The Tea Cart

Be kind to one another, tenderhearted.
EPHESIANS 4:32 NKJV

What NICETY COULD I SHARE WITH MY FAMILY? HOW MIGHT THIS AFFECT THEIR ATTITUDES?

A number of years ago, a corporation experimented with the recommendation of one of its vice-presidents. At three o'clock each afternoon for a month, a tea cart pushed by a maid in uniform mysteriously appeared on the executive floor. The cart was laden with fine china and linen napkins, as well as silver urns and trays of simple but elegant sweets. Executives and their administrative assistants were invited to come out of their offices and from behind their desks to select a flavor of tea and a sweet treat from the cart.

Moments of pleasantry and conversation followed naturally. In many cases, people who had worked on the executive floor for years met their colleagues for the first time or became better acquainted with them.

After a month, the president of the company conducted an informal poll among those who had enjoyed a "month of tea." He discovered that, without exception, each person reported a new air of civility on the floor. Many employees commented on how much they had enjoyed the tea break and on how they felt this service had increased morale.

Encouraged by such positive results, the president ordered a "tea cart" service for each of the floors in the corporate building. The same benefits were noted by all of the employees.

A kind word, a kind deed, a kind attitude—they all impact the way we think of ourselves and others, which impacts the way we work.

❧

Make a rule, and pray to God to help you keep it, never, if possible, to lie down at night without being able to say: "I have made one human being at least a bit wiser, or a little happier, or at least a little better this day."

Opposites Balanced

The day is Yours, the night also is Yours;
You have prepared the light and the sun.
You have set all the borders of the earth;
You have made summer and winter.
PSALMS 74:16-17 NKJV

When
I NEED TO
REST, I LIKE
TO . . .

Much of our lives seem to be suspended between opposites. We grow up learning to label things as good or bad, hurtful or helpful, naughty or nice. People are kind or mean. The thermostat can be adjusted to avoid extremes of heat and cold. We look forward to the changing of seasons from summer to winter. Time is divided by day and night.

Not only are these opposites helpful to us in defining or "bordering" our lives, but they can also help us release stress. Very often people engaged in physical, muscle-intensive work all day choose a mental activity with which to relax and unwind. Those who have idea-intensive jobs often enjoy relaxing with hobbies that make use of their hands, such as woodcarving or needlework. Those in sterile, well-ordered environments look forward to going home to weed their gardens.

Structured tasks and routines are good relaxation for those involved in the creative arts. The musician runs home to the computer. The surgeon delights in growing orchids in a hothouse. The factory worker enjoys crossword puzzles. The executive unwinds in the kitchen, preparing gourmet meals.

When you feel stressed out at day's end, try engaging in an activity that is opposite in nature to the work you have been doing. If you have been using your mind, turn to an activity that is physical. If you have been exerting physical energy, turn to an activity that is mental.

Nothing is at last sacred but
the integrity of your own mind.

A Little Ceremony, Please

"Ye shall find rest unto your souls."
MATTHEW 11:29 KJV

How ARE
PRAYER TIME
AND TEA TIME
ALIKE TO ME?

Afternoon tea at London's Ritz Hotel is described as the last delicious morsel of Edwardian London. Helen Simpson offers this description in *The London Ritz Book of Afternoon Tea:*

"In the elegantly columned Palm Court, the light is kind, the cakes are frivolous and the tempo is calm, confident and leisurely. Takers of tea perch on rose-coloured Louis XVI chairs at marble tables, sipping their steaming cups of tea. . . . There are no clocks, and although it is just possible to glimpse the flash of Piccadilly's taxis and buses if you look hard in the direction of the doors, a strange sense of taking a holiday from time heightens the pleasure of taking tea here. People look more beautiful than they do in real life due to the flattering lighting. Here is one of the few places outside church where a woman may wear a hat and feel entirely at ease."[40]

Why all that fuss over a cup of tea and a snack? Because the "ceremony" of drinking afternoon tea causes the participants to cease all other activities for a short period of time, take in a little sustenance, and give attention to others who are sharing the repast.

Teatime also provides a natural opportunity for the spirit to be refreshed. Taking tea alone gives one the chance to reflect on the ups and downs of the day in quiet prayer, receiving fuel to move confidently through the rest of the day.

Praise is more than singing,
it's the saint reflecting the life of Christ.

Wildflower Worth

"Look at the lilies and how they grow. They don't work or make their clothing, yet Solomon in all his glory was not dressed as beautifully as they are. And if God cares so wonderfully for flowers that are here today and gone tomorrow, won't he more surely care for you?"
LUKE 12:27-28 NLT

God PROVED

HIS LOVE FOR

ME WHEN . . .

Each spring, wildflowers bloom in profusion at a place in Idaho called "Craters of the Moon." Nourished by snowmelt and occasional rains, the flowers spring up in the lava rock left by an eons-old volcano. It is a stunning sight to see the small, delicate wildflower blossoms bursting into life amid the huge, rugged boulders.

Sightseers can follow footpaths all through the lava rocks to discover the surprising spots that dusty maiden, dwarf monkey flower, and Indian paintbrush find to grow. The life span for the fragile flowers can be as brief as one day if the hot desert winds blow into the area. Even without the winds, three weeks is about their longest show.

When Jesus taught His followers, He often sat outside. Perhaps He sat on a Judean hillside among the spring wildflowers when He pointed at the lilies, encouraging the worriers not to be blinded to the fact that God takes care of all His creation, even a short-lived wildflower. If He takes care of them, He certainly will care for us.

How do we avoid worry? By increasing our faith in our God who loves us. By starting each day focusing on Him instead of our fears. And by remembering His loving care even for the brief life of a wildflower.

A day of worry is more exhausting than a day of work.

The Celebrity Garden

*I am a rose of Sharon . . . Like a lily among
thorns is my darling among the maidens.*
SONG OF SONGS 2:1-2

In THE
GARDEN OF
MY LIFE, WHO
ARE THE
CELEBRITIES?

Sherry had finally cleaned a spot in her back yard for a rose garden—her dream for many years. As she thumbed through a rose catalog, she sighed at the magnitude of her choices. *Just like a Christmas wish list,* she thought. *Which ones should I pick? A white John F. Kennedy, a large, pink Peggy Lee, a red Mr. Lincoln, the delicate Queen Elizabeth rose?*

Sherry closed her eyes as if in deep thought. Suddenly, she had an idea, *I'll plant my own celebrity garden.*

The next day Sherry hurried to her local nursery and bought a dozen roses—all colors and sizes. She worked hard that week, carefully planting each rose. Finally, her task was done, and she decided to throw a party and invite all her friends to help her celebrate her celebrity rose garden.

Imagine their surprise when her friends watched Sherry unveil the celebrity names she had placed on each rose. One by one, they read their own names beside the flowers. The celebrities in Sherry's garden were none other than her friends. But in the middle of the fragrant bouquet, one rose still remained a mystery.

She unveiled the label which read, "Rose of Sharon" and said, "This One is the Love of my life, and everything else centers around Him."

Relationships, like a healthy garden, need ample doses of love and affirmation. When Christ is at the center of our affection, all other loves will fall into place.

*He who would have beautiful roses
in his garden must have
beautiful roses in his heart.*

Spontaneous Love Bouquets

"Freely you have received, freely give."
MATTHEW 10:8

What
GIFT HAVE
I RECEIVED
THAT WAS A
SURPRISE?
WHAT DID IT
MEAN TO ME?

Melanie read the suggestions carefully. "Place contrasting colors together, like peach with blue. Or try red, white, and blue for a bright, patriotic bed. If you prefer, naturalize your bulbs, incorporating them into your yard's natural habitat. This works particularly well if you live in a wooded, grassy area."

She grabbed her gardener's tools and set to work, planting some in circles and others in rows. Melanie reserved a handful of varied-sized bulbs, and like a mother hiding Easter eggs for her expectant child, she tossed bulbs randomly on the grass. Wherever they landed, she carved a hole and dropped them in the ground.

Weeks passed, and Melanie forgot about the bulbs—including their secret hiding places. One early spring day, she walked out in her back yard and saw green shoots poking through the earth. In the next few weeks, her yard looked like a magical wonderland. As she strolled through the green terrain, she realized the most fun part was seeing the bulbs pop up among the natural setting—beside trees, in the middle of a grassy slope, or tucked away in a corner. Nature had worked its magic and rewarded Melanie's long-forgotten efforts with a harvest of beautiful flowers.

Christlike deeds are like the bulbs in Melanie's garden. Some we plant in deliberate, orderly fashion. Others, because of the God-nature planted within us, spill out from our lives naturally like spontaneous love gifts to those around us.

If you have love in your heart,
you always have something to give.

Larkspur Lives

Sing to the Lord a new song; sing to the Lord, all the earth. Sing to the Lord, praise his name; proclaim his salvation day after day. Declare his glory among the nations, his marvelous deeds among all peoples.

PSALMS 96:1-3

Pauline misread the instructions for planting larkspur seeds and placed the seeds too close together. When the larkspurs emerged from the soil, they looked like a tiny hedge of carrot tops. They seemed so whimsical, she didn't have the heart to thin them as much as perhaps she should have.

Despite her haphazard gardening procedures, Pauline found that the larkspur sprouted and grew in abundance. When a slight breeze ruffled through them, she was sure she heard tiny giggles of joy because the larkspurs knew God had created their beauty.

Their tall flower stalks formed a chorus of pink, blue, white, purple, and occasional splashes of lilac singers. The larkspur choir sang a new song of praise that delighted Pauline's soul. Flowers have the delightful capacity to sing songs for the eyes instead of the ears. The larkspurs stood tall and straight like vertical musical staffs filled with trills of colored notes all the way up their stalks.

As Pauline cut the mature ones for drying, even more larkspurs shot up and bloomed. The flowers were still singing praises in her garden past the first few light frosts of fall.

Our Christian walk can be a larkspur life. We can daily sing praises to our Lord. We can strive to make our lives of faith an observable witness of God's marvelous deeds.

Can others hear you singing?

*O for a thousand tongues to sing
my great Redeemer's praise!*

How CAN I PRAISE MY GOD IN A FRESH NEW WAY?

Flower Power

We dare not make ourselves of the number, or compare ourselves with some that commend themselves: but they measuring themselves by themselves, and comparing themselves among themselves, are not wise.
2 CORINTHIANS 10:12 KJV

What KIND
OF FLOWER
DOES GOD
INTEND ME
TO BE?

Butchart Gardens is one of the most famous tourist attractions in Victoria, British Columbia. The elaborate display dates back to 1904 when Jenny Butchart decided to transform part of her husband's limestone quarry into a sunken garden. Today it is open all year and includes a botanical array of breathtaking beauty.

When one walks through these delightful grounds, it is impossible to choose the most outstanding exhibition. The plants are obviously healthy and well attended. Each provides colorful blossoms that are distinct, yet make a significant contribution in the overall scheme and design.

Likewise, part of our spiritual growth is to realize our importance in God's garden, especially when we exercise the talents and abilities He has given. Many feel inferior about their own gifts, and they compare themselves unfavorably with others. And yet God designs different people just as He created various kinds of flowers. The lily and the rose each have their own features. In fact, every blossom has its own unique characteristics. Tulips and lilacs and hyacinths are not alike, and yet each kind of flower adds a particular fragrance and beauty to any arrangement.

The same is true in life. Take a few moments to make an inventory of your gifts. Then ask the Holy Spirit to guide you. Through His power, you can make a difference in the lives of others as well as your own.

The real tragedy of life is not in being limited to one talent, but in the failure to use the one talent.

Flowerbox Faith

On my bed I remember you; I think of you through the watches of the night. Because you are my help, I sing in the shadow of your wings. My soul clings to you; your right hand upholds me.

PSALMS 63:6-8

One Labor Day weekend, Shannon's husband constructed a large flowerbox for her. With great care, she picked out and purchased two hundred top-quality bulbs. Next, she filled the flowerbox with the perfect mixture of soil, fertilizer, and peat moss. Then, she spent hours planting the bulbs in a delightful design.

All through the long Idaho winter, she thought about her tulips, daffodils, and hyacinths. If they followed God's plan and waited for His perfect timing, they would change from dull, brown clumps into colorful celebrations of spring.

Maintaining our faith in God during times of forced inactivity is similar to a dormant bulb planted in a flowerbox. At certain times in our lives, we may be compelled to stop all activity and take time out to heal. Instead of lying in our beds fretting about our restraining circumstances, we simply need to wait and rest.

Dormancy for a bulb is nature's solution to getting through times of difficult weather conditions. God's gift of rest is His way of helping us through difficult health conditions. All bulbs store food to carry them through their dormant periods. We can use our times of dormancy to nourish our souls by planting our hearts in the fertile soil of His Scriptures.

Like bulbs waiting for spring, we can rest in God's promises as we wait for our recovery. We can look forward to the certain celebration of life through Christ. He alone will bring the colors of spring to our souls.

Resting

IN GOD'S

PROMISE

MEANS

I WILL . . .

Simply wait upon him. So doing, we shall be directed, supplied, protected, corrected, and rewarded.

Bumper Crop

Do not be interested only in your own life, but be interested in the lives of others. In your lives you must think and act like Christ Jesus.
PHILIPPIANS 2:4-5 NCV

What SELF-PAMPERING DO I DO THAT KEEPS ME FROM PRODUCING THE FRUIT OF MEEKNESS?

Dorothy wasn't allowed to plant a garden outside the townhouse they rented, so she decided to do the next best thing. She bought large pots and created a container garden on her patio. One evening while she relaxed on the patio, her husband said, "Look! Our neighbor has tomatoes already. Why don't we?"

Much to her amazement, her neighbor had an abundance of fat green tomatoes covering her vines. All that Dorothy had growing were the tiny yellow flowers that promised fruit.

Dorothy had babied her plant by gently positioning it up the rungs of its tomato cage as it grew. She had judiciously showered it with water and had moved the pots around for the best sunshine. Yet, all she had was a profusion of vines.

Dorothy searched through her gardening books and discovered that she needed to pinch back staked tomato plants. Pinching helps the plant focus its energy on producing its fruit instead of merely growing taller.

Many of us are like Dorothy's tomato plant. We love showing the abundant leaves of our spiritual insights. We take pride in how we are climbing the rungs of increased Bible knowledge. But do we only *promise* fruit, or do we apply what we've learned to our actions? Do we focus our energy on producing quality fruit?

When we pinch back our self-centeredness and concentrate on Christ, we might even grow a bumper crop of fruit to God's glory.

Self is the only prison that can ever bind the soul.

When Faith Flutters

You who are spiritual should restore him gently.
GALATIANS 6:1

Early one morning, Jill sat at her desk, enjoying the warm rays of spring sunshine as they streamed through her bedroom window. Just outside the window, Jill noticed a small, brownish butterfly go by—or so she thought. A few seconds later, she turned to look at the window and saw that same butterfly had not landed on a plant; yet it seemed strangely suspended in midair. Its wings fluttered helplessly, but the flying insect could not move.

Puzzled, Jill walked outside to get a closer look. Glistening in the sun, like a ladder of dew-dropped pearls, hung an almost invisible net. During the night, another one of nature's creatures had spun a magical web to trap its victims.

Jill observed the struggle briefly until she watched the butterfly's wings grow motionless. She reached over and very gently plucked the winged insect from the spider's deadly threads. At first, the butterfly seemed stunned and fell to the ground. Jill gingerly picked it up and lifted it toward the sky, releasing its wings again. This time, it soared into the air and over the fence.

Anyone can tumble into tangled webs of deception—believing a lie, following the wrong leader, or confusing priorities. Disillusionment sets in. With faith fluttering, we can easily lose the strength to fight. At that point, a gentle, steady hand may be all we need to help free our fragile wings and send us soaring again on our heavenly way.

❦

*A lie travels around the world
while truth is putting her boots on.*

Some OF THE
PEOPLE WHO
HAVE HELPED
ME KEEP
FLYING ARE . . .

Flowers of Blessings

How can we thank God enough for you in return for all the joy we have in the presence of our God because of you?
1 THESSALONIANS 3:9

What
SPECIAL
PERSON HAVE I
KNOWN WHO
WAS A GIVER?

Bill and Casey's grades were so close that the faculty asked them both to speak on graduation night. In his speech, Bill spent twenty minutes enumerating his successes and honors throughout high school.

Casey, on the other hand, thanked each of her teachers. Then she named friends and family members who had encouraged her through many discouraging times. "These people are the real stars," she said. "They believed in me when I had no faith. They wished me success when I could not dream. But most of all, I thank my God who has given me grace to come this far."

She continued, "With friends, loved ones, and God's help, you, too, can live your dream. Next year I will enter college and prepare to teach. Although I often wanted to quit, these heroes never did. I can never repay them for their generosity and kindness."

As a close friend gently pushed Casey in her wheelchair down the ramp, the entire student body gave Casey a standing ovation.

Oswald Chambers says, "Whenever you get a blessing from God, give it back to Him as a love-gift . . . if you hoard it for yourself, it will turn into spiritual dry rot . . . a blessing . . . must be given back to Him so that He can make it a blessing to others."

Like a grateful gardener, Casey had taken her "flowers" of blessings and presented them back to the ones who helped her grow them.

❧

*Kindness is the sunshine
in which virtue grows.*

A Garden Fair

Their life shall be like a watered garden,
And they shall never languish again.
JEREMIAH 31:12 NASB

A creative
WAY FOR ME
TO SHARE MY
FAITH IS . . .

When Pat's daughter needed financial support to do mission work in Hong Kong, she had an idea. Why not host a "Country Garden Fair," charge admission, and give the proceeds to the mission trip? Four hundred guests showed up to enjoy the breathtaking beauty of poppies, larkspur, delphiniums, hollyhocks, and other flowers in her four-acre English country garden. A year later at a second fair, the number of guests tripled. Pat honored her initial commitment and gave the proceeds to missions.

Later Pat took advantage of the high interest in her garden to hold an evangelistic outreach event. She desired that unbelievers would meet God and that existing believers would have a closer walk with Him. Guests admired the brightly colored flowers while listening to hymns and classical music, reading Scripture verses posted along the trails, and soaking up the peace and serenity of God's creation. The Garden Fair, which began as a way to meet a need, flourished as a creative way of planting spiritual seeds in numerous lives.

Because life began in the first garden with Adam and Eve working the soil, we may feel a pull to return to our roots. In a mysterious way, we feel at home when we dig and plant. Because of Pat's love for gardens, for God, and for people, many others can now also look forward to someday strolling the grounds of their heavenly home.

How far that little candle throws its beams!
So shines a good deed.

Carrot Hearts

"The good man brings good things out of the good stored up in his heart, and the evil man brings evil things out of the evil stored up in his heart. For out of the overflow of his heart his mouth speaks."
LUKE 6:45

What
ROCKS ARE
HIDDEN IN
MY HEART?

When Peggy moved from Missouri to Idaho, she knew she needed information about gardening in the mountains.

"Your safest bet is the root crops," a native Idahoan told her. "Potatoes, beets, onions, carrots—those kinds of veggies."

Taking his advice, Peggy planted her regular eight-inch carrot seeds totally unaware of the problems that lurked underground. She didn't know stones constantly pushed their way up through mountain soil. She thought her neighbors were joking when they said, "It's a great place to garden. We even grow rocks!"

When Peggy harvested her carrots, she made a disappointing discovery. Her poor carrots had pushed and twisted their way around the rocks trying with all their little carrot hearts to grow. Most of them came out of the ground looking like bright orange corkscrews.

As she tossed her curiously shaped carrots into a bucket, Pauline thought of people whose public appearance came across as just right, but who exposed their twisted hearts whenever they spoke.

She wondered, *Are my words good things that I've stored up, or are they harmful? Do I encourage others and speak words of truth that I've planted in my heart through daily times in God's Word? Or, are my words destructive, coming from a critical heart?*

She quietly asked God to help her confront the harmful rocks hidden in her heart. She was acutely aware of her need for God's help. On her knees in the garden was the perfect place to start.

Nothing is impossible to a willing heart.

His Way

In quietness and confidence shall be your strength.
ISAIAH 30:15 NKJV

A Danish author tells the story of an old peasant who made an unusual request of his son as he lay dying. He asked his son to go into the best room of the house every day and sit there alone for half an hour. The son agreed to the strange request and promised his father he would do what he had been asked.

After his father's death, the son was faithful to his promise. He did this unusual thing—spending a half hour alone each day. At first the time of quiet and solitude was uncomfortable. He became restless and anxious for the time to end. But over the weeks, that half hour of solitude grew into a cherished and even transforming habit. The son looked forward to this brief quiet period each day and even began to thrive on it. He began to experience deep and calming changes within himself.[41]

Are you willing to be alone for fifteen or thirty minutes each day, preferably when your mind is not overtired? Are you willing to take an adventure of expectant faith, not looking for a predefined experience or not seeking an emotional high, but asking Jesus to come to you in His own way?

With your body relaxed and comfortable, and looking only to Jesus, your heart will be turned to Him in adoration. People who devote time to be alone with the Lord find a renewed reservoir of personal strength and quiet confidence.

A happy life consists of tranquility of mind.

When I AM FINALLY ALONE, THE SOLITUDE MAKES ME . . .

Firstfruits

You shall observe the Feast of the Harvest of the first fruits of your labors from what you sow in the field.
EXODUS 23:16 NASB

Gardening opens doors for learning and produces a platform for teaching those around us about God's great provision. Appreciating the elements enough to tackle a garden opens our eyes to God's creativity. Planning helps us to seek and accept God's will for our lives. Tilling the soil and laboring to plant and care for the garden teaches us responsibility and good stewardship. Weeding is a reminder of the spiritual battle we face each day. Waiting for the harvest brings about patience.

Last but not least, reaping the harvest encourages us to be thankful, and sharing the harvest brings blessing to others and honors God.

Throughout history, God's people have been taught to give the firstfruits of their harvest as a thanksgiving offering to God. In some cultures, a bountiful harvest is cause for great celebration. In the United States, the Thanksgiving tradition is based on sharing the harvest with others and giving thanks for God's rich blessings.

Sometimes the best way to give our firstfruits to God means giving from our own abundance to those who are in need. Whether food or money, time or love, we can give what has been given to us. If done cheerfully and generously—with no strings attached—giving the firstfruits of our labors brings rich reward.

God showers His blessing upon us, and the cycle of giving thanks and sharing the bounty begins again.

In everything the Lord gives, we can learn principles for our walk with Him if we will allow the lessons to become a part of the gift to us.

The Lord gives His blessing when He finds the vessel empty.

Tools of the Trade

We are his workmanship.
EPHESIANS 2:10 RSV

We see it as we walk along an ocean shore, where steep cliffs meet with the rise and fall of the tides. The splashing of sand- and rock-laden waves have cut away at the towering sea cliffs. Day after day, night after night, the continual lapping of the ocean water silently undercuts the stone walls. Then in one sudden blow the entire structure can shift and fall thunderously into the sea. On a daily basis, the wear and tear of water on sea cliffs is imperceptible, yet we know that every wave hitting the rock is washing away some of its hard surface.[42]

When we are subjected to the endless wear and tear of life, we develop faults and cracks in our lives. In God's hands, however, those stresses and changes become His tools for shaping our lives for His purpose. As our lives are yielded to and shaped by Him, He creates within us the ability to resonate His presence.

The varied and often difficult experiences of life, given to God, are how He transforms each individual into something beautiful. The Holy Spirit can work wonders on the rough edges of our stubborn wills and hard hearts, conforming them to His own will.

Commit your life to the Lord again this afternoon. Trust Him to take all that happens to you—both good and bad—and make you stronger and wiser, using you in His great plan.

Whate'er we leave to God,
God does and blesses us.

A bad THING THAT HAPPENED TO ME ONCE HAS MADE ME BECOME . . .

"We Interrupt Your Life . . ."

I will sing to the LORD all my life; I will sing praise to my God as long as I live.
PSALM 104:33

How CAN
MY HANDS ACT
AS THE HANDS
OF GOD?

Living longer is supposed to be a good thing. None of us wants to die "before our time." We want to see children and grandchildren and sometimes great-grandchildren grow up. We want to travel, enjoy the homes we worked so hard to build, and do all those things we dreamed of before and after retirement.

Life doesn't always turn out the way we planned. Yes, we might be living longer, but so are our parents. And oftentimes, parents have major health concerns that require constant care.

Take positive steps if you find yourself in the role of caregiver for elderly parents. It helps to have a friend you can visit with from time to time—someone who isn't too close to the situation. You need the perspective he or she can give. It also helps to find a support group of people who have learned how to care for their parents with wisdom and joy.

Start each day by saying, "I'll do my best today," and avoid criticizing yourself for not doing everything perfectly. Take care of yourself! You can't help anyone if you get sick due to lack of rest, poor nutrition, or stress.

Above all, make your caregiving an act of love and not obligation. Ask the Lord for His grace and His peace to surround you, and whisper prayers to Him throughout the day.

Prayer serves as an edge and border to preserve the web of life from unraveling.

Power Naps

With him is an arm of flesh; but with us is the Lord our God to help us, and to fight our battles. And the people rested themselves upon the words of Hezekiah king of Judah.

2 CHRONICLES 32:8 KJV

Medical students are usually adept at taking power naps. They fall asleep immediately upon lying down, sleep for fifteen to twenty minutes, and then awake refreshed. Researchers have discovered these short naps are actually more beneficial than longer midday naps. The body relaxes, but does not fall into a "deep sleep," which can cause grogginess and disorientation.

Only one thing is required for people to sleep this quickly and benefit fully from a power nap—the ability to "turn off the mind." We quiet our minds by not thinking about all that remains to be done, worrying about all that might happen, or fretting over events in the past.

Power nappers are experts at inducing a form of inner peace that comes from knowing all will be well with the world while they check out for a few minutes. What they believe with their minds actually helps their bodies relax.

When King Hezekiah told the people the Lord was with them and would fight their battles, they *rested* upon his words. The Lord is with us also, to help us and to fight our battles. These simple lyrics from a Bible-school chorus say it well:

> You worry and you wonder how you're gonna
>   get it done,
> From the rising of the moon 'til the setting of
>   the sun.
> Plenty to do when your rest is through,
> Let Him have the world for a turn or two.
> Take time to rest today.

There will be plenty to do when you wake up . . . so sleep on for a few minutes. Rest and be thankful.

The MOST RELAXED PLACE I CAN REMEMBER IS . . .

Thirst-Quenchers

MAY 17

Whosoever will, let him take the water of life freely.
REVELATION 22:17 KJV

The LAST "DRINK" OF TRUTH I HAD FROM THE WORD OF GOD WAS . . .

Water is essential to the survival of plants, animals, and people. The life processes of an organism depend on its cells having moisture. A tree, for example, may be 80 percent sap, which is primarily water. Sap contains minerals, carbohydrates, vitamins, and proteins, which circulate through the tree's vascular system to feed all parts of the tree.

The amount of the water supply in an area determines whether it is a desert or a forest. It determines whether a tree is shriveled and stunted or towering and majestic. Water comes to trees through dew, clouds, mists, fog, summer rains, and winter snows. Trees also take in water through their roots, which tap into springs, streams, or rivers.

A tree does not hoard moisture for itself, but after the water travels through the framework of the tree, it is given off into the surrounding air. The moisture, along with the oxygen expelled into the air, give the forest a fresh fragrance.

The spiritual lesson we learn from nature is that it is nearly impossible to be a blessing to others when we are grossly undernourished ourselves. Like the tree, we must be well-watered with God's Word and His Spirit to bring a sweet fragrance to those around us.

If you are feeling empty and dry, go to the watering hole of God's Word and take a long, refreshing drink. Feel His truth permeate every cell of your being and rejuvenate love, peace, and joy in your heart.

What I kept, I lost. What I spent, I had.
What I gave, I have.

Decision-Free Hours

Sing to Him, sing psalms to Him; Talk of His wondrous works. Glory in His holy name.
PSALMS 105:2-3 NKJV

I should
TALK TO GOD
ABOUT . . .

Kate declared the hour between three and four o'clock in the afternoon a decision-free hour in her office! She announced this to her staff in a light-hearted way, but she was secretly intent upon making it a reality.

As the supervisor of nearly thirty people, all of whom had access to her because of her open-door policy and easy style of management, Kate was asked to make decisions incessantly. This left little time for creative interaction or easy conversation with her staff members and colleagues.

Over time, Kate found that people were quick to stop by her office between three and four o'clock just to say "hi," to share a bit of news, or to compliment a fellow employee. Her decision-free hour became the most positive hour in the day, and the information she received actually helped her become a better manager—and make wiser decisions.

Could it be that the Lord might also enjoy some decision-free, problem-free, no-answer-required-from-Me hours with us, His children and coworkers in the world? Could it be that He'd enjoy hearing prayers in which we simply tell Him what is happening, what we find funny or interesting about our lives, and what delights us or gives us joy? Could it be that He'd enjoy hearing a good joke from our lips, rather than a string of incessant petitions? It just might be.

He prays well who is so absorbed with God that he does not know he is praying.

Invisible Work

*Faith is the assurance of things hoped for,
the conviction of things not seen.*
HEBREWS 11:1 NRSV

Is it EVER
GOOD FOR ME
TO SIT BACK
AND DO
NOTHING?
WHEN? WHY?

Trees have specific seasons for dormancy—a time when they appear to be inactive and not growing. This season of rest comes immediately prior to a season of rapid and accelerated growth. During dormancy, the cells and tissues within the tree are repaired and built up. This activity is invisible to the eye. The tree quietly prepares for the vigor of spring.

Dormancy is one of the most important periods in the life cycle of the tree. It is how a tree becomes fit for the later demands of adding new wood to its structure and bearing its fruit.

The benefits of dormancy apply to people as well. There is a mistaken notion that to be effective we must always be active. But people also have seasons in their lives when God is preparing them for what lies ahead.

Not knowing the future ourselves, we often have to come to a deep trust in God during times when nothing seems to be happening in our lives. Inactivity must not be equated with nonproductivity—God is at work behind the scenes!

It takes patience and humility to get through a time of dormancy. Most of us desire to be productive at all times so we can "get ahead" in our lives. We need to recognize there are times when, unbeknownst to us, God has to work in our hearts to prepare us for our destiny.

*It is vain to gather virtues without humility;
for the spirit of God delights to dwell
in the hearts of the humble.*

Write Away

The Lord answered me, and said,
Write the vision, and make it plain upon
tables, that he may run that readeth it.
HABAKKUK 2:2 KJV

As teenagers, our diaries were sacred. Woe to the curious sibling or friend who dared to unlock the secrets of our lives! Through the centuries, journals have been a precious possession to many—a place to chronicle days, record feelings, dream, complain, plot a course, and escape. Many journals have become valuable historical records, while others have served as the basis for novels or scholarly papers.

Most of us will never see our journals in print—we hope!—but we can benefit greatly from the writing process. Journaling is taking a journey through the past, the present, or the future.

Some people journal early in the morning, before the day begins, and record dreams from the night before or thoughts about the day ahead. Others journal at night, just before bed, to put the final punctuation on the day. Still others use journaling as a good excuse to take a break during the day.

Journaling on paper might not be suited to you. Sitting quietly and thinking about what's happened that day, and then mentally turning the frustrating parts over to God, might be your way of bringing closure to what is beyond your control. However you choose to journal, make and keep a daily appointment with the Lord for reflection. Such a time can help you sort through your thoughts and find a suitable stride for finishing out your day.

Of all those arts in which the wise excel,
nature's chief masterpiece is writing well.

Today, I WOULD LOVE TO WATCH THE SUNSET AND THINK ABOUT . . .

Parsley

Ye are washed, but ye are sanctified, but
ye are justified in the name of the Lord Jesus,
and by the Spirit of our God.
1 CORINTHIANS 6:11 KJV

I look
FORWARD
TO THE DAY
WHEN . . .

Most of us are very familiar with parsley, those sprigs of greenery that give color to our dinner plates in restaurants. Parsley is sometimes used as a lush bedding for salad bars or as a garnish on pasta dishes and bowls of soup.

For the most part, parsley seems decorative—a pretty splash of green to brighten the culinary scene. Few of us ever eat the parsley made available to us or even think to try it. And yet that is why parsley was originally provided. It was intended to be eaten in small quantities—a few leaves consumed as the final bite from the plate. For what purpose?

Parsley is a food known to gourmets as a "palate cleanser." Eating it removes the lingering taste of foods just eaten to allow a person to experience more fully the new tastes of the next course.

Like clover, parsley is a "trinity" plant. Each time a stem divides into stalks or leaves, it divides into three parts.

What a wonderful spiritual analogy we have in parsley! For surely it is our Father, Son, and Holy Spirit who cleanse us from the dust, dirt, and evil grime of the world and prepare us for the beautiful new world which Jesus called the Kingdom of Heaven. God is the One who has the capacity to remove all memories of sorrow and pain, and replace them with overflowing joy and hope for the future!

The Christian life that is joyless is a discredit
to God and a disgrace to itself.

A Servant's Heart

Serve one another in love.
GALATIANS 5:13

I can
CHANGE
THE WORLD
IN WHAT
SMALL WAYS?

Work is over, and you're headed home, but first there are several errands to run. When the last stop has been made and you're pulling into your driveway, you marvel once again at the all-too-common coldness of your fellow humans.

Doesn't anyone smile anymore? Can't people help me find what I'm looking for without treating me like a nuisance? Doesn't anyone apologize for making a person wait or for giving bad service?

The boss of a moving company in the Northeast has a wonderful philosophy. Knowing what a traumatic experience it is to pack up and start a new life in a new place, he makes a point of letting his clients know he understands and cares about what they're going through. In the process, he has found it is just as easy to be kind as it is to be abrupt.

The best example we have of how to serve is the Lord Jesus. In Matthew 20:28, He told His disciples, "The Son of Man did not come to be served, but to serve." Jesus' dedication to service was evident in all He did, from teaching in the synagogues and preaching the good news, to healing the sick and performing miracles.

The law of sowing and reaping tells us that what we sow we will reap. (See Galatians 6:7.) As we become more and more servants of love and kindness to others, we will find ourselves being served with love and kindness in return.

The most acceptable service of
God is doing good to man.

Stubborn as an Old Goat

*Even so now yield your members servants
to righteousness unto holiness.*
ROMANS 6:19 KJV

The LAST
TIME I HELD
MY TONGUE
AND TRULY LIS-
TENED TO MY
FRIEND, I
LEARNED . . .

Martin Luther had a favorite illustration he used in his sermons:

If two goats meet each other in a narrow path above a piece of water, what do they do? They cannot turn back, and they cannot pass each other; and there is not an inch of spare room. If they were to butt each other, both would fall into the water below and drown. What will they do, do you suppose?

As it happens, one goat will inevitably lie down while the other goat passes over it. Once the walking goat is safely on its way, the other will rise and continue on its chosen path. This way, both get where they wish to go safely.

There is a great deal of concern in today's world about allowing others to "walk all over us." But lying down to give way to another in order that both might achieve their goal is not the same as being a doormat. Nothing Jesus ever did could be considered weak and helpless. In strength and power, He laid down His life for us.

When you come to impasses with people, consider what might happen if you simply yielded your pride for a moment and allowed them to:

- speak their opinions,
- present their arguments,
- offer their ideas,
- suggest courses of action, or
- perhaps even make decisions.

Prostrating ourselves for the benefit of others rarely costs us anything, but it may yield great rewards, both now and for eternity!

*What we have done for ourselves alone dies
with us. What we have done for others
and the world remains and is immortal.*

Taste Berries

Oh, that men would give thanks to
the LORD for His goodness, and for His
wonderful works to the children of men!
PSALM 107:8 NKJV

Today,
I AM TRULY
THANKFUL
FOR . . .

In Africa there is a fruit called the "taste berry," so named because it makes everything eaten after it taste sweet and pleasant. Sour fruit, even if eaten several hours after the "taste berry," seems sweet and delicious.

For Christians, gratitude is the "taste berry" that makes everything else taste sweet. When our hearts are filled with gratitude, nothing that comes our way seems unpleasant to us.

A habit of giving thanks in all circumstances helps us to look beyond our immediate situation and see our lives from a higher perspective.

Sometimes the gifts given to us may not appear to be good gifts or gifts we desire. But when we learn to thank God in all things, we discover that the gifts we've received are exactly what we need.

Gratitude can also help a person who is mourning or lighten the load of a person carrying a heavy burden. It can dispel loneliness and give strength to a person in ill health.

George Herbert wrote this beautiful thank-you prayer:

Thou hast given so much to me,
Give one thing more—a grateful heart.
Not thankful when it pleases me,
As if Thy blessings had spare days,
But such a heart, whose pulse may be Thy praise.

Keep the "taste berry" of gratitude in your hearts, and all of life will be sweeter.

May silent thanks at least to
God be given with a full heart;
Our thoughts are heard in heaven.

Kindness Bouquet

*A kind man benefits himself, but a
cruel man brings trouble on himself.*
PROVERBS 11:17

What SMALL
ACT HAS
SOMEONE
DONE FOR
MY SAKE?
HOW DID IT
AFFECT ME?

Not surprisingly, Kristina, a middle-aged woman who regularly practices kindness in her life, has a lot of friends. One day Peg confessed to her that she was depressed. Peg had two small children who required much care, and she worked part-time as a secretary to help with finances. "The hardest thing I do every day is get out of bed in the morning," Peg said. "I'm so down that I don't know what to do."

Kristina, in her usual manner, remembered that her friend loved flowers. So she went into her back yard and picked an assortment of wild purple, yellow, and red flowers that gave a wonderful aroma. Next she picked a handful of wild greenery and arranged the flowers in a vase.

When Kristina delivered the flowers to Peg, her friend's brown eyes lit up. She asked, "Those are for me?"

"Yes, I picked them from my back yard."

Several days later, Kristina spotted Peg at the grocery store and asked, "How are you feeling?"

"Terrific!" Peg exclaimed with a wide grin. "You made me feel so special when you picked those flowers just for me. You know, I never appreciated the beautiful dandelion bouquets my children gave me, but now I do. I look at them and see that in my busy world there are so many tiny beautiful things I'd never noticed before. It's a miracle really. I'm not feeling depressed anymore."

A little act of kindness can touch someone's life forever.

∞

*Little deeds of kindness,
little words of love, Help to make
earth happy like the heaven above.*

Consider the Heavens

*When I consider your heavens, the work of your
fingers, the moon and the stars, which you have
set in place, what is man that you are mindful
of him, the son of man that you care for him?*

PSALM 8:3-4

Astronomers keep finding light in our dark universe.

Helen Sawyer was born in 1905, in Lowell, Massachusetts, and twenty-five years later married Canadian astronomer Frank S. Hogg. Noted for her research on variable stars, Helen found more than two hundred and fifty such stars that display different degrees of brightness.

Receiving her doctorate in astronomy from Radcliffe College in 1931, Helen studied globular star clusters in the Milky Way galaxy. By studying the variable stars, she was able to determine the time required for some of these stars to change from bright light to dim light and back to bright light again. This information helped other scientists to calculate how far certain stars are from the earth.

For centuries, scientists have discovered more and more information about the light at night in our huge universe. Today scientists know that the heavens contain a mind-boggling number of stars, moons, planets, and galaxies. Most are far beyond what the naked eye can see, and much of the light in our night sky can't even be seen with today's powerful and gigantic telescopes.

Tonight, enjoy your night-light. Gaze out your windows and count the stars. Study the moon with a telescope. Search for the Big Dipper, the Little Dipper, the North Star, and other famous night-light spots. As you enjoy light at night, you'll inevitably come to appreciate the tremendous amount of light God has provided in the universe.

*When I
LOOK UP AT
THE STARS
I FEEL . . .*

*Darkness is my point of view, my right
to myself. Light is God's point of view.*

155

Anybody Home?

The Lord blesses the home of the righteous.
PROVERBS 3:33

The HARDEST
LETTING GO
I HAVE EVER
DONE WAS
WHEN . . .

Jennifer was resting after returning home from a weekend retreat with her husband when she heard the door open.

"Hello!" a familiar young lady's voice said. "Anybody home?"

Both Jennifer and John hurried to the door to greet their beautiful daughter. At twenty years of age, Becky was trying to discover her place in the world. Gradually, she attempted to let go of her parents' hands and enter a world of new beginnings, a place where she would find true happiness and joy as she used the talents and abilities with which God had blessed her.

Letting go of their children had been very difficult for Jennifer and John. Since Becky was the baby of the family and the only girl, it was much more difficult. Her mother had spent many sleepless nights worrying about her. At night when Jennifer would hear the door unlock, signaling Becky's safe return, she would whisper a prayer of thanks to God for placing His protective hand over her.

As the nights passed, she learned to depend on God more often. She realized that although she couldn't be with Becky every moment of every day, God could. Over the previous year, she placed Becky in the hands of God, allowing Him to guide her steps.

"I'm glad you're home," Becky said to them. "I missed you both so much."

Aren't we glad that God is always home? He always offers the security that we need to live each day to its fullest.

*The knowledge that we are never
alone calms the troubled sea of our
lives and speaks peace to our souls.*

Are You Rich?

*The sleep of a laborer is sweet, whether
he eats little or much, but the abundance
of a rich man permits him no sleep.*
ECCLESIASTES 5:12

Amy, a young mother, longed to be rich, thinking that wealth would ease the financial strain on her self-employed husband. They lived in a moderately priced middle-class home, but she wanted a more expensive one.

One day Amy visited her sister in her new home and was impressed. A chandelier hung from the dining room ceiling. The kitchen featured every built-in appliance and gadget possible. The den boasted a large-screen television, loads of CDs, and an enviable stereo system. Amy thought, *Joe and I could enjoy a home like this, too, if I went to work.*

Later, after the tour of the house was over, she asked her sister what time she had to get up for work every morning. "Five-thirty," Janice replied.

Back in her own home, Amy looked at her husband with tears of gratitude in her large brown eyes. "Do you realize how rich we are?" she asked him.

"What do you mean?" Joe frowned.

"I don't have to get up early in the morning and leave our precious son at a sitter's house. I can enjoy him all day. I'm rich! I just never realized it before."

Tonight, take a look at your surroundings. See how rich you are—not with expensive, material things, but with the things that count. No matter what you have, take note of your blessings tonight and enjoy them.

*There are two ways of being rich.
One is to have all you want; the other
is to be satisfied with what you have.*

I want
TO PRAISE
GOD FOR . . .

The Tarnished Cup

*Be kind to each other, tenderhearted,
forgiving one another, just as God has
forgiven you because you belong to Christ.*
EPHESIANS 4:32 TLB

What STEPS
CAN I TAKE TO
"POLISH UP"
MY RELATION-
SHIPS?

After hours of searching through dusty cartons in the basement and brushing aside spider webs and dust bunnies, Kelly found the box that contained the baby cup that had been her grandmother's. It was wrapped in yellowed newspaper from many years earlier, as evidenced by the dates on the paper. Kelly removed the wrapping and discovered that the cup was now blackened by tarnish. Frustrated and disappointed, she stuffed the cup back into the carton.

That night she was unable to sleep. After an hour of tossing and turning, it finally occurred to her that she was uneasy because her neglect and lack of concern had allowed the cup to deteriorate. She ran downstairs to the basement to retrieve it and brought it back up to the kitchen.

Finding some silver polish, she gently cleaned the cup until the beautiful silver was again revealed. With much work and love, the cup was restored to its original beauty.

Often our relationships with family and friends become tarnished, and they deteriorate under layers of hurt feelings, anger, and misunderstanding. Many times the deterioration begins with a comment made in the heat of the moment or under the strain of another problem entirely. If the air isn't cleared immediately, the relationship becomes tarnished.

When we put work and love into our relationships, they can be restored. Then we rediscover the beauty that lies underneath the tarnish and realize that it has been there all along.[43]

*We achieve inner health only through
forgiveness—the forgiveness not only
of others but also of ourselves.*

Without Words

Show proper respect to everyone.
1 PETER 2:17

I can SERVE GOD WHEN I SERVE MY FELLOW MAN BY . . .

The Franklin Delano Roosevelt memorial in Washington, D.C., gives testimony to the fact that President Roosevelt and his wife, Eleanor, served America during some of its darkest years. It is a fitting design, for as visitors approach it, nothing really stands out. All one sees is a flat granite wall, perhaps twenty feet in height, with a simple quote from FDR; but this is just the beginning.

The memorial stretches directly away from the entrance. After rounding the wall, visitors move from area to area—every one marked by unique stillness. Each succeeding area is creatively set apart from the previous one, making it a tribute in its own right. Visitors find themselves looking at human-sized sculptures of men and women standing in breadlines, reading quotes decrying the savagery of war, staring eye to eye with Eleanor Roosevelt, and eventually looking up and across to see FDR in his wheelchair with his Scottish terrier beside him.

The strength of the memorial comes from its ability to draw the visitor into the presence of one man's passionate belief in serving his country. The impact of the memorial is that it makes each visitor more aware of the awesome responsibility of leadership—not just the leadership of presidents, but leadership of all people.

Whenever you have doubts about your purpose, remember the words of Martin Luther King Jr., "Everyone can be great because everyone can serve."

A candle loses nothing by lighting another candle.

Food in My House

Bring the whole tithe into the storehouse, that there may be food in my house.
MALACHI 3:10

When I BEGIN TO GET DEPRESSED, WHAT CAN I FIND TO DO FOR OTHERS?

"What? You just lost your job?" Deborah took a deep breath, then sat down quickly. She watched the laugh lines at the corners of her husband's eyes turn somber.

Although her husband had been a faithful employee of the same company for more than twenty-six years, he was let go when the company's earnings dropped. The woman watched as her husband mentally battled the onslaught of depression. "Hey," she said. "I'll take you out to eat tonight."

"Why?" he asked. "I just lost my job."

"Because I'm trying to keep you from getting depressed," she said. A grin spread across his face, and she knew she'd hit home.

When they got home, they finished the evening with a time of prayer, asking specifically for God's guidance. At church, they asked people to pray. Her husband began sending out résumés and making phone calls.

Months dragged on, and depression crept into the couple's lives after they received little response from prospective employers. But when Deborah heard about Hurricane Mitch's devastation in Honduras, she immediately began gathering clothes and canned goods for the victims. Her husband stopped her, asking, "What are you doing? That's our food."

"Those people need clothes and food more than we do," she said. "I also think we should tithe on your unused vacation pay and give that to them." After writing the check, the Lord released a flood of joy in both of them. The next day, two companies called to schedule interviews.

As we give, we live.

Unfailing Love

The LORD delights in those who fear him,
who put their hope in his unfailing love.
PSALM 147:11

Writer Marion Bond West wrote about "The Healing Tree" at a time when things weren't going right and she doubted her roles as wife and mother. At the time, her self-reliant older daughter was pregnant, she and her teenage daughter couldn't seem to get along, and the twin boys preferred their father.

One afternoon, she asked her husband if he wanted to go for a walk. "No," he said in a matter-of-fact way.

Disappointed, West drove to the woods and began to walk by herself. The only sounds were her footsteps and rushing water in a stream. In the distance, she saw a lone black walnut tree. She felt like that tree—alone. At the base of the tree, she sat down.

Thinking of her husband, West picked up a branch. She prayed to release those things about him that troubled her. She tossed the stick into the water. Picking up a smaller stick, she thought, *This fragile stick is Jennifer. Please let me stop controlling my daughter's life.* She threw the stick as far as she could.

One by one, she released her children to the Lord.

The last stick was hers. *Lord,* she prayed, *There's so much in me that is selfish and demanding. Do things Your way; love my family with Your unconditional love.* She dropped her stick into the stream. Immediately, she began to feel a sense of freedom, a respite from her bondage.

There's freedom in releasing our loved ones and ourselves to the Lord.[44]

To take all that we are and have and hand it
over to God may not be easy; but it can
be done, and when it is done, the world
has in it one less candidate for misery.

I know THAT
I WILL FIND
FREEDOM
WHEN I LET
GO OF . . .

Finishing Strong

When Jesus had cried with a loud voice, he said, Father, into thy hands I commend my spirit: and having said thus, he gave up the ghost.
LUKE 23:46 KJV

What WORK
DO I NOW
NEED TO
FINISH AND
GIVE TO GOD?

The Gospel accounts of Matthew, Mark, and Luke tell us that Jesus ended His earthly life and ministry by crying with a loud voice, obviously from a great surge of energy. Luke tells us further that in His cry, Jesus commended His spirit to the Lord, giving His all to the Father.

What a wonderful example of how we might end our work each day!

First, we need to "finish strong." In the afternoon, we often must refocus and double our efforts. Those who work in offices often find their most productive hour is the last hour of the day, when everyone else has gone home and the phone has stopped ringing. Those who work at home also tend to experience an end-of-the-day urgency to get things done before shifting to more relaxed hours.

We are wise to pray as we enter the home stretch of a day, "Father, give me Your strength and energy to bring to a conclusion what I have started. Help me now to go the extra mile."

Second, we need to commend our work to the Lord. As we finish our work, we need to say, "Thank You, Lord, for the energy, health, and creativity to do what I have done today. Now, I turn over to You all rights to what I have done. I trust You to winnow out what is worthless and to cause that which is worthy to last and benefit others. I give it all to You."

Religion is no more possible without prayer than poetry without language or music without atmosphere.

Nothing Is Impossible

"I tell you the truth, if you have faith as small as a mustard seed, you can say to this mountain, 'Move from here to there' and it will move. Nothing will be impossible for you."

MATTHEW 17:20

When Jama Hedgecoth was five, she found a hungry cat. Even at that age, Jama loved animals and couldn't stand to see one in need. The daughter of traveling evangelists, Jama believed strongly in God. Years later, her faith became reality. Today, Jama is now married with four children and lives on 122 acres of farm county in Georgia, where she began Noah's Ark, a safe haven and rehabilitation center for more than a thousand animals.

When Jama first saw the property, she knew without a doubt that God would give it to her. And he did. Her truck-driver husband was amazed.

And Jama continued to believe God, although Noah's Ark passed through troubling waters. Three times, the center was nearly evicted, but God brought one miracle after another. Once when Noah's Ark was near financial ruin, an Atlanta businessman offered to pay off the center's mortgage and build a foster children's home, where twelve children are housed.

A spirit of unconditional love runs through Jama's family. Through her faith in God, Jama has taken in animals that no one wanted, including wildcats, lions, monkeys, and emus. And she has opened up her heart to foster children as well.

How big is your faith? Sometimes God wants us to step out in our faith—not to prove to Him that we have faith, but to prove to ourselves how much we believe in the power of our God. Are you willing to step out in faith?[45]

To have faith is to believe the task ahead of us is never as great as the Power behind us.

How MUCH FAITH DO I REALLY HAVE THAT GOD WILL HELP ME ACHIEVE MY DREAMS?

Braveheart

Beloved, thou doest a faithful work in whatsoever thou doest toward them that are brethren and strangers withal.
3 JOHN 1:5 ASV

What
PERSON
HAS BEEN A
HERO TO ME?

Karen tells the story of a dear friend and fellow church member who passed away after a long life of love and service.

At the funeral, her children stood up one by one to tell stories about their mother, and soon there was a recurring theme: that her single most outstanding trait was her willingness to serve others, no matter what the need. She was one of those people who was always ready to lend a hand—to run an errand, do odd jobs, or give someone a ride home.

More often than not, when we hear the word courage, we think of heroic acts in times of crisis. But in our everyday lives, we shouldn't overlook the courageousness of simply being there. Lives are changed when we faithfully care for our families, tend to the elderly, or lend an ear to a troubled friend. Persistence in making this world a better place to live—for ourselves and others—is definitely a form of courage.

Albert Schweitzer, the great Christian missionary, doctor, and theologian, was once asked in an interview to name the greatest living person. He immediately replied, "The greatest person in the world is some unknown individual who at this very moment has gone in love to help another."

As you go about your work today, remember that you could be someone else's hero.

The greatest work any of us can do for another, whether old or young, is to teach the soul to draw its water from the wells of God.

A Flash Prayer

Dear friends, since God so loved us, we also ought to love one another. No one has ever seen God; but if we love one another, God lives in us and his love is made complete in us.

1 JOHN 4:11-12

A woman, hoping to change her own outlook on life, decided to hand out smiles—not forced smiles, but caring smiles that radiated the love of Jesus. For some, she whispered a "flash prayer" that their day would be blessed by the Heavenly Father.

Her smiles brought blessings from God in the form of a grandmother who rushed to her side to share a funny story, a man who asked her opinion on which handbag to buy for his wife, and a boy who allowed her to take his place in the express lane.

A smile even began a friendship with a young grocery store bagger who had Down's syndrome. One winter day with snow clouds slung low across the sky, the young man carried the woman's groceries to her car. Digging in her purse for a tip, she was embarrassed when she found she had nothing to give him.

"I'm sorry," she said, not wanting to disappoint the young man.

A smile as bright as the summer sun spread across his face. "That's okay," he said. Then he wrapped his arms around her. "I love you," he said.

Shivering in the cold, she whispered a "flash prayer" for this very special child of God. "Lord, bless this precious child," she whispered.

As Christians, we need to be reaching out to all of God's children. It seems that "the least of these" can teach many of us a lesson in humility, but the greatest lesson in humility is found in Jesus Christ.[46]

A smile is a curve that helps to set things straight.

An IMPORTANT LESSON I LEARNED THROUGH AN HUMBLING MISTAKE WAS . . .

Uniquely Positioned

When I consider your heavens, the work of your fingers, the moon and the stars, which you have set in place, what is man that you are mindful of him?
PSALMS 8:3-4

Why DO I
BELIEVE THAT
MANKIND WAS
GOD'S GREAT-
EST CREATION?

A number of years ago, IMAX filmmakers produced a movie titled *Cosmos*. In it, they explored the "edges" of creation—both outer space as viewed through the most powerful telescope, and inner space as viewed through the most powerful microscope. Viewers saw that at the far reaches of space, clumps of matter (huge stars) seem to be suspended in fixed motion and separated by vast areas of seemingly empty blackness.

They also saw that the same can be said for the depths of inner space—clumps of matter are suspended in fixed orbits, separated by vast areas of seemingly empty blackness. In fact, the world of the distant stars is almost identical in appearance and form to the world of the tiniest neutrinos! Furthermore, neither of these "edges" of creation has been explored fully.

In sharp contrast, the created earth as we experience it daily is uniquely suspended between these two opposite poles. Our world is filled with varied colors, dynamic forms, differing patterns, changing seasons, and adaptable functions.

It is as if God has placed human beings at the very center of His vast creation, with the maximum amount of complexity, meaning, and choice. We are "hung in the balances" literally, as well as figuratively—the pivot point between the great and the small, the vastness of outer space and the vastness of inner space.

We are not only fearfully and wonderfully made, but we are fearfully and wonderfully positioned in God's creation.

When God conceived the world, that was poetry. He formed it, and that was sculpture. He colored it, and that was painting. He peopled it with living beings, and that was the grand, divine, eternal drama.

Stormy Weather

God did not give us a spirit of timidity, but a spirit of power, of love and of self-discipline.

2 TIMOTHY 1:7

I will NOT
BE FEARFUL
WHEN I
REMEMBER...

Elizabeth stared out the window at low-hanging rain clouds. Kissing the top of her newborn's head, she wrapped the blanket around him, wishing her husband was home.

That afternoon, the rain started slowly. By nighttime, it had turned into a tap-tapping sound, and Elizabeth realized it was now sleet.

The child opened his slate-blue eyes and cooed. As her heart filled with love for this new human being, she felt an inexplicable warmth pass between them. She wondered if perhaps this was the way God felt about His children.

Later, the sleet turned to freezing rain. Peeking outside, she could see the ice-coated pine trees bowing to their knees. Nervously, she said out loud, "Jim, where are you?"

Just as she started toward the telephone, the lights went out. She found a candle and lit it. As time passed, the house became chilled. She wrapped another blanket around the baby and put a cap on his head, then pulled on her coat.

What if the lights don't come back on soon? What if they don't come on for days? Her mind raced through all the possibilities. *Where is my husband? In all this bad weather, has he been in an accident?* "Oh, Lord," she whispered, "I'm so afraid."

In the darkness and deepening silence, she heard an inner voice remind her that God is our Refuge and Strength, an ever-present Help in trouble. Within the hour, her husband came home, and not long after, the lights blinked on.

Relinquishment of burdens and fears begins where adoration and worship of God become the occupation of the soul.

Active Trust

"Do not let your hearts be troubled, trust in God; trust also in me."
JOHN 14:1

I am
LEARNING TO
TRUST GOD
FOR . . .

In her book *Beyond Our Selves,* Catherine Marshall writes about her husband's active trust in God. A popular Presbyterian minister, her husband, Peter Marshall, also served as chaplain of the United States Senate during the late 1940s.

Catherine once said, "I thought that faith was believing this or that specific thing in my mind. Now I know that faith is nothing more or less than actively trusting God." To demonstrate this, she provided an illustration her husband used:

Suppose a child has a broken toy. He brings the toy to his father, saying that he himself has tried to fix it and has failed. He asks his father to do it for him. The father gladly agrees, takes the toy and begins to work. Now obviously the father can do his work most quickly and easily if the child makes no attempt to interfere, simply sits quietly watching, or even goes about other business, with never a doubt that the toy is being successfully mended.

But what do most of God's children do in such a situation? Often we stand by offering a lot of meaningless advice and some rather silly criticism. We even get impatient and try to help, and so get our hands in the Father's way, generally hindering the work.

Try putting your trust in a Father who tends His flock like a shepherd, gathering His children in His arms and carrying them close to His heart.[47]

A mighty fortress is our God,
A bulwark never failing; Our helper
He amid the flood of mortal ills prevailing.

First Cup

In the morning my prayer comes before You.

PSALM 88:13 NKJV

God HAS
TOUCHED ME
THROUGH . . .

Many people wouldn't dream of starting their day without a cup of coffee. They count on that "first cup of the day" to wake them up and get them going.

There are others who have discovered an even more potent day-starter: first-thing-in-the-morning prayer.

For some, this is a prayer voiced to God before getting out of bed. For others, it is a planned time of prayer between getting dressed and leaving for work. For still others, it is a commitment to get to work half an hour early to spend quiet, focused time in prayer before the workday begins.

Henry Ward Beecher, one of the most notable preachers of the last century, had this to say about starting the day with prayer:

In the morning, prayer is the key that opens to us the treasure of God's mercies and blessings. The first act of the soul in early morning should be a draught at the heavenly fountain. It will sweeten the taste for the day.[48]

A popular song in Christian groups read, "Fill my cup, Lord; I lift it up, Lord. Come and quench this thirsting of my soul. Bread of heaven, feed me till I want no more; Fill my cup, fill it up and make me whole."[49]

Morning prayer is a time to have your cup filled to overflowing with peace. Then, as you have contact with other people, you can pour that same peace into them. And the good news is—unlimited free refills are readily available!

Without prayer, no work is well begun.

Today's Sure Thing

The steps of a good man are ordered by the Lord.
PSALM 37:23 NKJV

A promise
GOD MADE
TO ME AND
KEPT WAS . . .

In his book for children, *The Chance World*, Henry Drummond describes a place in which nothing is predictable. The sun may rise, or it may not. The sun might suddenly appear at any hour, or the moon might rise instead of the sun. When children are born in Drummond's fantasy world, they might have one head or a dozen heads, and their head or heads may not be positioned between their shoulders.

If one jumps into the air in the "chance world," it is impossible to predict whether the person will come down again. That the person came down yesterday is no guarantee he or she will come down the next time. All the natural laws change from hour to hour.

Today, a child's body might be so light it is impossible for him or her to descend from a chair to the floor. Tomorrow, the same child might descend with great force, landing near the center of the earth.

In the final analysis, *The Chance World* describes a frightening world. While most people enjoy a certain amount of spontaneity in their lives, they enjoy life more when it is lived against a backdrop of predictability, surety, and trustworthiness.

The Scriptures promise us that the Lord changes not. He is the same yesterday, today, and forever. (See Hebrews 13:8.) Furthermore, His natural laws do not change unless He authorizes their change for the good of His people. His commandments do not change. His promises to us are sure promises.

All but God is changing day by day.

Share the Secret

I have learned the secret of being content.
PHILIPPIANS 4:12

A woman named Frances once knew a young person at church named Debbie. Debbie always seemed effervescent and happy, although Frances knew she had faced struggles in her life. Her long-awaited marriage had quickly ended in divorce, and she had struggled to get a grip on her single life. She hadn't chosen it, but she decided she would live it with utmost enjoyment and satisfaction.

Frances enjoyed knowing Debbie because her whole face seemed to smile, and she always greeted Frances with a hug. One day she asked Debbie, "How is it that you are always so happy—you have so much energy, and you never seem to get down?"

With her eyes smiling, Debbie said, "I know the secret!"

"What secret is that? What are you talking about?" Frances asked.

Debbie replied, "I'll tell you all about it, but you have to promise to share the 'secret' with others."

Frances agreed, "Okay, now what is it?"

"The secret is this: I have learned there is little I can do in my life that will make me truly happy. I must depend on God for that. When a need arises in my life, I have to trust God to supply according to His riches. I have learned most of the time I don't need half of what I think I do. He has never let me down. Since I learned that secret—I have been happy."

*Teach us to put our trust in Thee
and to await Thy helping hand.*

Some OF THE THINGS THAT MAKE ME HAPPY ARE . . .

Ruminating on God's Word

This Book of the Law shall not depart from your mouth, but you shall meditate in it day and night, that you may observe to do according to all that is written in it.

JOSHUA 1:8 NKJV

Some SPECIAL PROM-ISES FROM GOD THAT I LIKE TO MEDIATE ON ARE . . . WHY?

Have you ever watched the news before going to bed and then dreamed about one of the news stories on the broadcast? The last thing we think about just before we doze off settles deep within our subconscious mind. Like clothes in a washing machine on the spin cycle, thoughts spin around all night in our minds. Then they often return to our consciousness as the first thought we have in the morning.

King David said in Psalm 4:4 NKJV, "Meditate within your heart on your bed and be still." Before you fall asleep, think about God's Word and what God is doing in your life. Ask yourself, *What is the condition of my spirit? Am I fulfilling God's plan for my life?* That will not only deepen your relationship with God, it also will expand your knowledge of Him.

Meditate—or ruminate—on God's Word as you lie on your bed at night. To ruminate, as defined by Webster's dictionary, means "to go over in the mind repeatedly and often casually or slowly." By spending time going over and over a Scripture, you can draw from it the depth of its meaning. The Bible reminds us to be transformed by the renewing of the mind.

Before retiring for the night, read a passage or two of Scripture. As you drift off to sleep, meditate on it. When you wake, you will have "ruminated" all night on God's Word, waking refreshed and renewed. Then in the morning, you can praise God as King David did: "My voice You shall hear in the morning, O LORD; In the morning I will direct it to You, and I will look up" (Psalm 5:3 NKJV).

Think often on God, by day, by night, in your business, and even in your diversions. He is always near you and with you; leave Him not alone. You would think it rude to leave a friend alone who came to visit you; why, then, must God be neglected?

A Kind Word

Thou hast lifted me up, and hast not made my foes to rejoice over me.

PSALM 30:1 KJV

The Reverend Purnell Bailey tells of a convict from Darlington, England, who had just been released from prison. He had spent three long years in prison for embezzlement, and though he wanted to return to his hometown, he was concerned about the social ostracism and possible ridicule he might have to endure from some of the townsfolk. Still, he was lonesome for his home and decided to risk the worst.

He had barely set foot on the main street of town when he encountered the mayor himself.

"Hello!" greeted the mayor in a cheery voice. "I'm glad to see you! How are you?" The man appeared ill at ease, so the mayor moved on.

Years later, the former mayor and the ex-convict accidentally met in another town. The latter said, "I want you to know what you did for me when I came out of prison."

"What did I do?" asked the mayor.

"You spoke a kind word to me and changed my life," replied the grateful man.[50]

We cannot always know how important the seed of a kind word may be to the one who receives it. More often than we know, words of encouragement or recognition provide a turning point in a person's outlook on life.

Just as Jesus spoke with love and acceptance to the hated tax collector Zaccheus, the mayor set the tone for others' contacts with the ex-convict by openly and warmly addressing him as a neighbor. People watch those they respect for cues regarding their own relationships with certain people.

Genuine, kind words cost the giver nothing but can mean the world to the one receiving them.

Today, don't be put off when someone to whom you offer a kind word seems uncomfortable or embarrassed. Recognize that they may be unpracticed at receiving your love and compassion, even though they need it greatly.

Who CAN I OFFER A KIND WORD TO TODAY THAT I THINK REALLY COULD USE SOME ENCOURAGMENT?

Be kind; everyone you meet is fighting a hard battle.

True Value

"The last will be first, and the first will be last."
MATTHEW 20:16

I find IT
HARDEST TO
DO WHAT
IS RIGHT
WHEN . . .

In the J. M. Barrie play *The Admirable Crichton*, the Earl of Loam, his family, and several friends are shipwrecked on a desert island. These nobles were adept at chattering senselessly, playing bridge, and scorning poorer people. However, they could not build an outdoor fire, clean fish, or cook food—the skills they needed to survive.

Stranded on a desert island, what the Earl's family and friends did know was entirely useless for their survival. Had it not been for their resourceful butler Crichton, they would have starved to death. He was the only one who possessed the basic skills to sustain life.

In a great turnabout, Crichton became the group's chief executive officer. He taught the Earl and his family and friends the skills they needed and organized their efforts to ensure their survival until their rescue.

It is always good to remind ourselves of our "relative" place in society. If we are on top, we need to remember we can soon be at the bottom. If we perceive ourselves as at the bottom, we need to know that in God's order we are among "the first."

We may not achieve the fame and recognition from people that we would like to have in this life, but God doesn't call us to be well known or admired. He calls us to be faithful to Him in whatever situation we find ourselves. When we are, we can see more clearly when He promotes us and gives us favor with others.

❧

When men cease to be faithful to their God,
he who expects to find them so to each
other will be much disappointed.

Seeds of Care

> *"A new command I give you: Love one another. As I have loved you, so you must love one another."*
>
> JOHN 13:34

A person
WHO REACHED
OUT TO ME
WITH HANDS
THAT I
CANNOT
FORGET
WAS . . .

The snapshots in her mind were sharp and clear as Jennifer remembered her mother marrying the man from Alabama. Jennifer had been a teenager from the city, and she couldn't stand this man from the "sticks." To her, he was nothing but a country bumpkin.

But early one spring morning, that changed. Jennifer was sitting on the backyard swing, watching as he turned the soil with a shovel on a sunny spot behind the house. Each day, he did something different: he'd break up dirt clods, toss rocks out, and add compost, finally raking the soil smooth. Curious, Jennifer walked across the garden, feeling the coolness of the newly worked earth between her toes.

"Here," said her stepfather, pouring some seeds into her open hand.

Then he gently demonstrated how to plant the seeds, cover them with dirt, and pat them down.

Later that summer, she enjoyed looking under the leaves of the squash plants and plucking the golden vegetables. She also liked the taste of a young cucumber, but most of all, she loved the green tomatoes her stepfather taught her to fry.

Jennifer smiled at the memory. What her stepfather had done that day was to crumble the wall between them, much like he'd broken up the soil.

Take the time to nurture and care for your "seeds." Break up the hard ground of resentment, and allow God to cause your love to grow in someone's heart.[50]

Love, that all gentle hearts so quickly know.

On the Road Again

God did not give us a spirit of timidity, but
a spirit of power, of love and of self-discipline.
2 TIMOTHY 1:7

After A NICE
WALK ON A
SUNNY DAY
I FEEL . . .

Getting yourself out of bed in the morning is one thing. Feeling prepared to face whatever comes your way that day is another. Where do you turn for a confidence-booster? Believe it or not, one of the best confidence-builders you can find may be inside those fuzzy slippers you like to wear: your own two feet.

Researchers have discovered that regular exercise—thirty minutes, three or four times a week—boosts the confidence level of both men and women. This is due in part to the way exercise strengthens, tones, and improves the body's appearance. It also has to do with brain chemistry.

When a person exercises, changes take place inside the brain. Endorphins, released as one exercises, are proteins that work in the pleasure centers of the brain and make a person feel more exhilarated. When the heart rate increases during exercise, neurotrophins are also released, causing a person to feel more alert and focused.

Are you feeling anxious about your day? Take a walk, jog, cycle, or do some calisthenics first thing in the morning.

Those who exercise regularly also feel that if they can discipline themselves to exercise, they can discipline themselves to do just about anything!

The human body is one of the most awesome examples of God's creative power—an example we live with daily. He has created us not only to draw confidence from reading His Word and experiencing His presence through prayer, but also from the use of our body.

Walking and talking with
God is great soul exercise!

Where Does the Time Go?

"While it is daytime, we must continue doing the work of the One who sent me. The Night is coming. And no one can work."
JOHN 9:4 NCV

Most of us can look around and find reminders of good intentions. We readily see areas where we never followed through to reach a goal. The seldom-used exercise equipment needs dusting. A piano, intended to fulfill our dreams of happy family sing-a-longs, sits silent. The books piled on the nightstand remain to be read. And the laptop computer we intended to take on vacation to write a novel is still in its original packaging.

More importantly, there are the children in our family who wait for our attention. Every child has gifts and abilities waiting to be developed—but that takes time. To tap into potential takes intentional, concerted effort. It doesn't just happen. Time for meaningful interaction and activity doesn't always "appear" to us as we juggle a full day of appointments and other commitments.

The time God gives to us is ours to spend—we determine how to use it. We can fill it with life-building activities, or we can let it sift through our fingers hour by hour, day by day, week by week, until before we know it, an entire year is gone and very little accomplished.

As long as you are alive, your time—24 hours, 1,440 minutes, 86,400 seconds a day—will be spent. It is up to you to decide how you are going to spend it. Accept the challenge to make every moment count!

We always have time enough, if we use it.

What HAVE I BEEN INTENDING TO DO, BUT HAVEN'T?

See the Light

Thou art my lamp, O Lord; and the Lord illumines my darkness.
2 SAMUEL 22:29 NASB

I choose TO
BE CHEERFUL
TODAY BY . . .

Helen Keller may have lost her ability to see, hear, and speak at a very early age, but she did not lose her gift of inspiring others. Keller spoke eloquently about darkness—the kind that invades the hearts and minds of the sighted:

Truly I have looked into the very heart of darkness, and refused to yield to its paralyzing influence, but in spirit I am one of those who walk the morning. What if all dark, discouraging moods of the human mind come across my way as thick as the dry leaves of autumn? Other feet have traveled that road before me, and I know the desert leads to God as surely as the green, refreshing fields and fruitful orchards.

I, too, have been profoundly humiliated, and brought to realize my littleness amid the immensity of creation. The more I learn, the less I think I know, and the more I understand of my sense-experience, the more I perceive its shortcomings and its inadequacy as a basis of life. Sometimes the points of view of the optimist and the pessimist are placed before me so skillfully balanced that only by sheer force of spirit can I keep my hold upon a practical, livable philosophy of life. But I use my will, choose life and reject its opposite—nothingness.[51]

When the day ahead of you seems shadowed or darkness threatens to overcome you, choose life! Take Helen Keller's words to heart and reject "nothingness" by turning to the Lord.

'Tisn't life that matters!
'Tis the courage you bring to it!

The Value of Disaster

We . . . glory in tribulations, knowing that tribulation produces perseverance.

ROMANS 5:3 NKJV

God HAS GIVEN ME RENEWED HOPE TO START AGAIN ON . . .

For ten years Thomas Edison attempted to invent a storage battery. His efforts greatly strained his finances and, in December 1914, nearly brought him to ruin when a spontaneous combustion broke out in his film room. Within minutes all the packing compounds, celluloid for records and film, and other flammable goods were ablaze. Though fire departments came from eight surrounding towns, the intense heat and low water pressure made attempts to douse the flames futile. Everything was destroyed.

The inventor's twenty-four-year-old son, Charles, searched frantically for his father, afraid that his spirit would be broken. Charles finally found him, calmly watching the fire, his face glowing in the reflection, white hair blowing in the wind.

"My heart ached for him," said Charles. "He was sixty-seven—no longer a young man—and everything was going up in flames.

"When he saw me, he shouted, 'Charles, where's your mother?' When I told him I didn't know, he said, 'Find her. Bring her here. She will never see anything like this as long as she lives.'"

The next morning, Edison looked at the ruins and said, "There is great value in disaster. All our mistakes are burned up. Thank God we can start anew." Three weeks after the fire, Edison managed to deliver the first phonograph.[52]

With each new day, we have the opportunity to start again, to start fresh—no matter what our circumstances. Let the Lord show you how to salvage hope from debris. You never know what joys lie ahead.

Hope is like the sun,
which, as we journey towards it,
casts a shadow of our burden behind us.

Making Connections

My help comes from the Lord,
Who made heaven and earth.
PSALM 121:2 NKJV

I have
FOUND
TRUSTING
GOD MEANS . . .

In *Silent Strength for My Life,* Lloyd John Ogilvie tells the story of a young boy he met while traveling. Boarding began, and the young child was sent ahead of the adult passengers to find his seat. When Ogilvie got on the aircraft, he discovered the boy had been assigned the seat next to his.

The boy was polite when Ogilvie engaged him in conversation and then quietly spent time coloring in an airline coloring book. During the flight, the plane flew into a very bad storm, which caused the jetliner to bounce around like a "kite in the wind." The air turbulence and subsequent pitching and lurching of the aircraft frightened some of the passengers, but the young boy seemed to take it all in stride.

A female passenger seated across the aisle from the boy became alarmed by the wild rolling of the aircraft. She asked the boy, "Little boy, aren't you scared?"

"No, Ma'am," he replied, looking up just briefly from his coloring book. "My dad's the pilot."

There are times when we feel like we are in the middle of a turbulent storm. We may have the sensation of being suspended in midair with nothing to hold on to, nothing to stand on, and no sure way to get to safety.

In the midst of the storm, however, we can remember that our Heavenly Father is our Pilot. Despite the circumstances, our lives are in the hands of the One who created Heaven and earth.[53]

The Pilot knows the unknown seas,
and he will bring us through.

The Power to Let It Go

If you forgive men when they sin against you,
your heavenly Father will also forgive you.

MATTHEW 6:14

I can MOVE
FORWARD IF I
LET GO OF. . .

Unforgiveness is a destructive and insidious force, having more effect on the one who is unforgiving than on the unforgiven. A great example of this was an experience of one of the outstanding intellects of all history, Leonardo da Vinci.

Just before he commenced work on his depiction of the Last Supper, he had a violent quarrel with a fellow painter. Leonardo was so enraged and bitter, he determined to use the face of his enemy as the face of Judas, thus taking his revenge by handing the man down to succeeding generations in infamy and scorn.

The face of Judas was, therefore, one of the first that he finished, and everyone readily recognized it as the face of the painter with whom he had quarreled.

However, when he attempted to paint the face of Jesus Christ, Leonardo could make no progress. Something seemed to baffle him—holding him back and frustrating his efforts. At length, he came to the conclusion that what was hindering and frustrating him was that he had painted his enemy into the face of Judas.

When he painted over the face of his enemy in the portrait of Judas, he commenced anew on the face of Jesus. This depiction became a success which has been acclaimed through the ages.

You cannot be painting the features of Jesus Christ into your own life, and at the same time be painting another face with the colors of enmity and hatred.

If you are harboring unforgiveness and bitterness, forgive your offender and put them and the situation in God's hands. Ask Him to cleanse you of those negative feelings and to release you from their bondage. As you forgive, you will be forgiven and set free to live your life with inner peace.

He that demands mercy, and
shows none, ruins the bridge over
which he himself is to pass.

Taking a Stand

*Be strong and of a good courage, fear not,
nor be afraid of them: for the Lord thy God,
he it is that doth go with thee; he will not
fail thee, nor forsake thee.*
DEUTERONOMY 31:6 KJV

What
CHANGE FOR
THE BETTER
WOULD I LIKE
TO SEE MADE?

Nine-year-old Kevin was upset at learning one of his favorite Popsicle flavors was being discontinued. But what's a kid going to do? Fighting City Hall when you're under voting age can seem like a fruitless endeavor.

"But you're a consumer," the boy's mother reminded him. "Yes, you can make a difference. You can start a protest. You can stand up and be counted." So Kevin took his mother's advice.

With the help of his cousins, he launched a petition drive, eventually gathering 130 signatures. The children also constructed picket signs with catchy sayings. Finally, on a rainy January day, Kevin and nearly a dozen family members marched at the Popsicle company's headquarters.

The company's CEO saw the marchers from the window of his office and invited them inside. He listened to the children's pleas and then explained the company's position. Extensive marketing research had been done, and thousands of dollars had already been spent to present a new flavor. In the end, however, Kevin and his group won the day. The CEO decided to forget the new flavor and grant the petitioners' plea to return the old flavor to the marketplace.

Never give in to the notion that you are too insignificant to lead the move toward a positive change in your world. As a band leader once pointed out in an inspirational speech to a group of students: the smallest person in the band, the head twirler, is the one who is leading us down the street!

*Obstacles will look large or small to you
according to whether you are large or small.*

Shake It Up

Prepare your minds for action.
1 PETER 1:13 NASB

If I COULD
CHANGE PART
OF MY
ROUTINE, I
WOULD . . .

What can I do to shake things up a bit? a woman asked herself one morning as she arose at her usual time. She had done all she needed to do to get her children off to school and her husband to work. Now she was home alone, looking for the motivation to face her day.

She said to herself, *I know what I'll do. I'll turn things upside-down. Instead of sticking to my usual schedule, I'll reverse the order.*

That meant her first item of business was preparing dinner. She thought she might feel strange preparing meat and vegetables at 9 A.M., but she was surprised to find she felt a sense of relief at having this "chore" done early. Somehow, it made the rest of the housework and errands less stressful.

She found a little extra time to write a letter and catch up on some reading, and by the time her children came in from school, she felt happier than she had in weeks. She was already thinking of other ways to add variety to her daily routine. Who says you have to do the same things in the same way at the same time every day?

The Bible clearly tells us that our God is a God of infinite variety! While His commandments are not negotiable, His methods often change. That's part of His nature as our Creator. The Lord is continually creating new methods to reach us with His love and to show us His care.

※

Variety's the very spice of life,
that gives it all its flavour.

As to the Lord

JUNE 24

With good will render service,
as to the Lord, and not to men.
EPHESIANS 6:7 NASB

What JOB
DO I DO THAT
SEEMS WORTH-
LESS? HOW
MIGHT I SERVE
GOD BY
DOING IT?

When we think of the most noble professions, we nearly always think of those that offer a service, such as doctors, lawyers, or teachers. Perhaps at the pinnacle of the service professions are those who are involved in full-time ministry—the helping of others in their spiritual lives in the name of the Lord.

Ministry, however, is not limited to those who earn their living by it. Ministry is the call and challenge of God to all Christians. Ministry is giving to others and living our lives as unto the Lord.

Ministry happens in the home, in the school, on the street, at the grocery store, in the boardroom, at the committee meeting, and in the gym. It happens wherever and whenever a person, motivated by the love of Jesus Christ, performs an act of loving service for another person.

Gandhi once wrote:

If when we plunge our hand into a bowl of water,
Or stir up the fire with the bellows
Or tabulate interminable columns of figures on
　　our bookkeeping table,
Or, burnt by the sun, we are plunged in the
　　mud of the rice field,
Or standing by the smelter's furnace
We do not fulfill the same religious life as if in
　　prayer in a monastery, the world will never
　　be saved.[54]

There is no ignoble work except that which is void of ministry! There is no lack of meaning in any job performed with God's love and "as unto the Lord."

Be satisfied with nothing but your best.

Leader of the Pack

See, the former things have taken place,
and new things I declare; before they
spring into being I announce them to you.

ISAIAH 42:9

Being the owner of a small business is not easy. Just when you start to build a clientele, along comes a crafty competitor who copies your style or improves on your methods. Next thing you know, revenues are falling, and you find yourself looking over your shoulder, trying to avoid being hit by another wave of wanna-bes.

A man on the West Coast found himself in this situation. His first venture was commercial fishing. When larger companies took over the water, he began renting out small sailboats and kayaks to people who wanted to explore the bay. Soon others with stronger financial backing moved in on that business.

Once again, he needed a new idea. How about submarine tours? After doing some research, the entrepreneur realized the cost of buying and maintaining a sub was beyond his reach. But a semi-submersible underwater viewing boat was not! The boat looks like a sub, but it doesn't dive. Passengers can go below deck and view the fascinating world under the sea.[55]

When your income seems to be going out with the tide, you may need to be a little creative. Talk with other people, do some research, consider even the "crazy" ideas, and glean what you can from them. You never know which wave might be the one that carries you safely and profitably to the shore.

Small opportunities are often the
beginning of great enterprises.

The BEST
IDEA I EVER
HAD WAS . . .

Bearing Fruit

*Meditate upon these things; give thyself wholly
to them; that thy profiting may appear to all.*
1 TIMOTHY 4:15 KJV

My
FAVORITE
BIBLE VERSE IS
. . . BECAUSE . . .

Two brothers were out walking on their father's vast acreage when they came upon a peach tree, its branches heavy with fruit. Each brother ate several juicy, tree-ripened peaches. When they started toward the house, one brother gathered enough peaches for a delicious peach cobbler and several jars of jam. But the second brother cut a limb from the tree to start a new peach tree. When he got home, he carefully tended the tree-cutting until he could plant it outdoors. The branch took root and eventually produced healthy crops of peaches for him to enjoy year after year.

The Bible is like the fruit-bearing tree. Hearing the Word of God is like the first brother. He gathered fruit from hearing the Word and had enough to take home with him to eat later. But that doesn't compare with having your own peach tree in the backyard. Memorizing the Word is like having the fruit tree in your backyard. It is there to nourish you all the time.

One of the greatest values of Scripture memory is that it keeps us from sin. In Psalm 119:11 NKJV the psalmist wrote: "Your word I have hidden in my heart, That I might not sin against You." [56]

Scripture memorization is often considered a dull, burdensome task. But we could get highly motivated if we were given one hundred dollars for every Bible verse we memorized! The rewards of Scripture memory may not always be monetary but are a better treasure for life.

*The Bible is God's chart for you to
steer by, to keep you from the bottom
of the sea, and to show you where
the harbour is, and how to reach it
without running on rocks and bars.*

Whose Will?

"Not as I will, but as Thou wilt."
MATTHEW 26:39 NASB

The
HARDEST
THING GOD
EVER ASKED OF
ME WAS . . .

A Christian woman once confided to a friend that she found it nearly impossible to pray, "Thy will be done." She was afraid of what the Lord might call her to do. Very specifically, she feared being called to a snake-infested swamp to take the Gospel to head-hunting natives. As the mother of a young child, she simply could not bear the thought that God might call her to leave her child and sacrifice her life on the mission field.

Her friend said to her, "Suppose your little girl came to you tomorrow morning and said, 'Mommy, I have made up my mind to let you have your own way with me from now on. I'm always going to obey you, and I trust you completely to do everything you think is best for me.' How would you feel?"

The woman replied, "Why, I'd feel wonderful. I'd shower her with hugs and kisses and do everything in my power to give her all the things that were good for her and that would help her find her talents and use them to their fullest."

The friend said, "Well, that's how the Lord feels as your Heavenly Father. His will is going to be far better than anything you have imagined, not far worse."

Make your prayer today, "Thy will be done, Lord." And then see what good things God has for you to experience!

⚬⚬⚬

God is perfect love and perfect wisdom.
We do not pray in order to change His will,
but to bring our wills into harmony with His.

Precious Ones

*Since thou wast precious in my sight, thou
hast been honourable, and I have loved thee.*
ISAIAH 43:4 KJV

When HAVE
I SHARED
GOD'S LOVE
WITH A
STRANGER?

June volunteered at a church agency that served
the poor and homeless of her city. One day June
met George, who had come in to get some help.
Winter was coming, and he needed a jacket and
some shoes. When he indicated he wanted a Bible,
June went to get one for him while he waited his
turn in the clothing room. When she returned with
a Bible, she sat down to talk with him for a while.

George looked like he was in his late fifties. His
thin hair was beginning to gray. Deep lines marked
his face. His hands were stiff, and he had lost part
of one finger. It was 1:30 in the afternoon, and he
smelled slightly of alcohol.

She wrote his name in the front of his Bible
along with the date. Then she showed him the
study helps in the back that would help him find
key passages.

As they talked, the thought occurred to her:
George is one of God's very precious creatures. She
wondered if George knew. She wondered how long
it had been since someone had told him. What if he
had never been told he was precious to God—and
to all God's other children as well?

God spoke to June through George that day,
saying, "My children need to know they are precious to Me. Please tell them that." Since then she
has made that message a part of every encounter
she has at the church agency.

❧

*Kindness is like a rose, which though
easily crushed and fragile, yet speaks
a language of silent power.*

The Big Picture

"I go to prepare a place for you. And if I go and prepare a place for you, I will come again and receive you to Myself; that where I am, there you may be also."
JOHN 14:2-3 NKJV

During World War II, parachutes were constructed by the thousands in factories across the United States. From the workers' point of view, the job was tedious. It required stitching endless lengths of colorless fabric, crouched over a sewing machine eight to ten hours a day. The result of a day's work was a formless, massive heap of cloth that had no visible resemblance to a parachute.

To keep the workers motivated and concerned with quality, the management in one factory held a meeting with its workers each morning. The workers were told approximately how many parachutes had been strapped onto the backs of pilots, copilots, and other "flying" personnel the previous day. They knew just how many men had jumped to safety from disabled planes. The managers encouraged their workers to see the "big picture" of their job.

As a second means of motivation, the workers were asked to form a mental picture of a husband, brother, or son who might be the one saved by the parachute they were sewing.

The level of quality in that factory was one of the highest on record!57

Don't let the tedium of each day's chores and responsibilities wear you down so you see only the "stitching" in front of you. Focus on why you do what you do and who will benefit from your work. You may not have all the answers to the question, "Why am I here?" but you can rest assured that the Lord does!

My JOB IS IMPORTANT BECAUSE . . .

I would not give one moment of heaven for all the joys and riches of the world, even if it lasted for thousands and thousands of years.

Which Day Planner?

The things that I purpose, do I
purpose according to the flesh?
2 CORINTHIANS 1:17 KJV

The PATH
AHEAD OF
ME LOOKS . . .

One of the challenges of our busy lives today is to be organized, so we can "get it all done." But sometimes we need to be challenged not to "get it all done," to slow down and reflect on what it is we are trying to accomplish. We must be sure we are headed in the right direction with our families, our work, our church, our community, and our personal lives.

If we are not careful and prayerful, we may find ourselves agreeing with the modern-day philosopher who noted, "So what if you win the rat race—you are still a rat!"

God has a different "daily planner." The psalmist wrote about it in Psalm 105:

- Give thanks to the Lord.
- Call on His name.
- Make known among the nations what He has done.
- Sing to Him, sing praise to Him.
- Tell of all His wonderful acts.
- Glory in His holy name.
- Let the hearts of those who seek the Lord rejoice.
- Look to the Lord and His strength.
- Seek His face always.

Remember the wonders He has done, His miracles, and the judgments He has pronounced.

Each day we have the privilege of consulting with the King of Kings and Lord of Lords to determine what path we will take, what tasks are most important, and who needs us the most.

People who are always in a hurry seemingly
get very little satisfaction out of life.

Every Little Bit Helps

He who began a good work in you
will carry it on to completion.
PHILIPPIANS 1:6

In TIME I
WANT TO
CHANGE . . .

Can the dead be raised in today's world? It all depends on what has died. Sometimes bringing something to life is simply a matter of hard work and time . . . perhaps even centuries. The staff at Redwood National Park in California will tell you that attempting to do this is definitely worth the effort.

In 1978, the park "grew" by sixty square miles of clear-cut forest. Congress gave the park's managers a challenge: restore the land to its natural state. A warning was also given: the final results of your work won't be visible for hundreds of years.

Work began. Since 1978, roads have been removed, stream and estuary habitats have been repaired, land that was stripped of vegetation has been replanted, and hundreds of haul roads and ski trails have been erased. In the process, the park has become something of a "living laboratory," a means of helping environmental researchers learn more about restoration ecology. What they have learned so far at Redwood has been beneficial to managing the health of other national and state parks.[58]

The next time you think your efforts may be too little too late, remember that the world's tallest tree—located at Redwood—did not grow to be 368 feet high overnight. It takes time to become magnificent.

Trust God today to be at work in your transformation—a project that may take all your lifetime and be complete only in eternity, but will end in your eventual wholeness.

⟳

To be what we are, and to
become what we are capable of
becoming, is the only end of life.

Perspective

*I have become all things to all men so that
by all possible means I might save some.*
1 CORINTHIANS 9:22

When I
LOOK AT MY
LIFE I SEE . . .
HOW DO
OTHERS
SEE ME?

Wouldn't it be wonderful if we could look at each day from a slightly different perspective and, with God's guidance, learn to serve Him better as a result?

A Bible translator named Fraiser learned the importance of different perspectives in a very interesting way. Known simply as "Fraiser of Lisuland" in northern Burma, he translated the Scriptures into the Lisu language. He then went on to do translation work somewhere else for a time, leaving a young fellow with the task of teaching the people to read.

When he returned six months later, he found three students and the teacher seated around a table, the Scriptures open in front of the teacher. Fraiser was amazed to see that as each of the students read for him, he left the Bible where it was—in front of him. The man on the left read it sideways, the man on the right read it sideways but from the other side, and the man across from the teacher read it upside down. Since they had always occupied the same chairs, they each had learned to read from that particular perspective, and they each thought that was how their language was written!

The principles of truth in God's Word never change, but our understanding of them does! Ask God to give you new insights about Him today. With your new perspective, you may see the solution to a problem that has plagued you for years.

*An investment in knowledge
always pays the best interest.*

The Morning Hour

Be still, and know that I am God; I will be exalted
among the nations, I will be exalted in the earth!
PSALM 46:10 NKJV

So many of us find the morning to be a time of "rushing." Family members scurry in different directions with different needs and different timetables.

In sharp contrast stands the age-old advice that we each need a "quiet time" in the morning to center ourselves and to renew our relationship with our Heavenly Father. Carving out that time for yourself may be your supreme challenge of the day, but it is an effort worth its weight in gold, as so aptly stated by Bruce Fogarty:

"The Morning Hour"

Alone with God, in quiet peace,
From earthly cares I find release;
New strength I borrow for each day
As there with God, I stop to pray.
Alone with God, my sins confess'd
He speaks in mercy, I am blest.
I know the kiss of pardon free,
I talk to God, He talks to me.
Alone with God, my vision clears
I see my guilt, the wasted years
I plead for grace to walk His way
And live for Him, from day to day.
Alone with God no sin between
His lovely face so plainly seen;
My guilt all gone, my heart at rest
With Christ, my Lord, my soul is blest.
Lord, keep my life alone for Thee;
From sin and self, Lord, set me free.
And when no more this earth I trod
They'll say, "He walked alone with God."[59]

Fools rush in where angels fear to tread.

I can HAVE
MORE TIME
FOR MYSELF
IF I STOP . . .

What Are You Doing Today?

Praise the LORD, all you Gentiles!
Laud Him, all you peoples!
For His merciful kindness is great toward us,
And the truth of the LORD endures forever.
PSALMS 117:1-2 NKJV

What ARE
THE BEAUTIFUL
THINGS ABOUT
MY WORK?

In the Middle Ages a man was sent to a building site in France to see how the workers felt about their labor. He approached the first worker and asked, "What are you doing?"

The worker snapped at him, "Are you blind? I'm cutting these impossible boulders with primitive tools and putting them together the way the boss tells me. I'm sweating under this hot sun. My back is breaking. I'm bored. I make next to nothing!"

The man quickly backed away and found a second worker, to whom he asked the same question: "What are you doing?"

The second worker replied, "I'm shaping these boulders into useable forms. Then they are put together according to the architect's plans. I earn five francs a week, and that supports my wife and family. It's a job. Could be worse."

A little encouraged but not overwhelmed by this response, the man went to yet a third worker. "What are you doing?" he asked.

"Why, can't you see?" the worker said as he lifted his arm to the sky. "I'm building a cathedral!"[60]

The more positive we feel about our work, the greater the satisfaction we have at day's end and the less damaging stress we internalize. Those who see value in their jobs enjoy a greater sense of purpose.

Any job can be done with grace, dignity, style, and purpose . . . you only have to choose to see it that way!

Reputation is precious,
but character is priceless.

Soul Shower

Create in me a clean heart, O God.
PSALM 51:10 NKJV

Don't forget to ask God to create a clean heart
   in you today!
Generous in love—God, give grace!
Huge in mercy—wipe out my bad record.
Scrub away my guilt,
soak out my sins in your laundry.
I know how bad I've been;
my sins are staring me down.
You're the One I've violated, and you've seen
   it all,
seen the full extent of my evil.
You have all the facts before you;
whatever you decide about me is fair.
I've been out of step with you for a long time.
What you're after is truth from the inside out.
Enter me, then; conceive a new, true life.
Soak me in your laundry and I'll come out clean,
scrub me and I'll have a snow-white life.
Tune me in to foot-tapping songs,
set these once-broken bones to dancing.
Don't look too close for blemishes,
give me a clean bill of health.
God, make a fresh start in me,
shape a Genesis week from the chaos of my life.
Don't throw me out with the trash,
or fail to breathe holiness in me.
Bring me back from gray exile,
put a fresh wind in my sails!
Give me a job teaching rebels your ways
   so the lost can find their way home.
Commute my death sentence, God,
my salvation God, and I'll sing anthems to your
   life-giving ways.
Unbutton my lips, dear God;
I'll let loose with your praise.

—Psalm 51, The Message[61]

How HAS GOD CHANGED MY ATTITUDE TOWARD THE WORLD?

Clean hands, clean heart
Help me, Lord, to do my part.

Reciprocity

Pray for each other so that you may be healed.
JAMES 5:16

TO MAKE
SOMEONE
ELSE'S LIFE
EASIER, I
COULD . . .

Sometimes when we focus on helping others, we end up solving our own problems. That certainly was true for David, an eight-year-old from Wisconsin who had a speech impediment. His problem made him hesitant to read aloud or speak up in class.

David's mother also had a problem—multiple sclerosis. One winter day she and David were out walking, and her cane slipped on an icy patch, causing her to fall. She was unhurt, but the incident left David wishing he could do something to help her.

Some time later, David's teacher assigned her students to come up with an invention for a national contest. He decided he would invent a cane that wouldn't slide on ice by putting a nail on the bottom of it. After his mother expressed concern about the nail damaging floor coverings, he developed a retractable system. Much like a ballpoint pen, the nail could be popped out of sight by releasing a button at the top of the cane.

David's invention earned him first prize in the contest. As the winner, he was required to make public appearances and communicate with those who expressed an interest in his project. The more he talked about the cane, the less noticeable his speech impediment became![62]

An outward expression toward others always does something inwardly that enables, empowers, and enhances the character of Christ Jesus in us. That's God's principle of reciprocity!

Little deeds of kindness,
Little words of love,
Help make earth happy
Like the heaven above.

Forgiveness

"Forgive us our debts, as we also have forgiven our debtors."

MATTHEW 6:12

A person
WHO FORGAVE
ME WHEN I
DID NOT
DESERVE
IT WAS . . .

One morning Denise Stovall's daughter, Deanna, taught her a special lesson about forgiveness. "Mama! How do you spell Louis?" Deanna asked as she rushed into the kitchen.

"Louis? Who's Louis?" asked Denise.

"You know," said the five-year-old. "He's the boy who gave me my black eye."

For several days Denise had asked herself how a child could be so mean to another child. "Why on earth do you want to know how to spell his name—especially after what he did to you?" she asked.

Deanna's reply reminded Denise of why Jesus said, "Let the little children come unto me, for of such is the kingdom of Heaven."

"W-e-l-l, at church yesterday, Miss Mae told us we should make paper chains for All Saints Day. She said to make a ring every time somebody does a nice thing like Jesus did, and then put that person's name on the ring. Louis told me on the bus today that he was sorry he hit me in my eye, and that was nice. I want to put his name on this ring and make it part of the chain, so we can pray for him so he won't do it again."

As Denise stood in the middle of the kitchen with her hands on her hips, the words of a recent sermon came back to convict her: "Forgiveness, no matter how long it takes or how difficult it is to attain, is the only path to healing and freedom."[63]

Forgiveness is the attribute of the strong. The weak can never forgive.

Restoration

Those who hope in the Lord will renew their strength. They will soar on wings like eagles; they will run and not grow weary, they will walk and not be faint.
ISAIAH 40:31

In THE EVENING, I FIND REST AND RESTORATION THROUGH . . .

In a remote Swiss village stood a beautiful church. It was known as the Mountain Valley Cathedral, and it had the most incredible pipe organ in the entire region. People would come from miles away—even from far-off lands—to hear the lovely tones of this organ.

One day a problem arose. An eerie silence enveloped the valley. The area no longer echoed with the glorious fine-tuned music of the pipe organ.

Musicians and experts from around the world tried to repair the instrument to no avail.

One day an old man appeared at the church door. He spoke with the sexton, and after a time the sexton reluctantly agreed to let the old man try his hand at repairing the organ. For two days the old man worked in almost total silence.

Then on the third day, at precisely high noon, the valley once again was filled with glorious music. Farmers dropped their plows, merchants closed their stores, everyone in town stopped what they were doing and headed for the cathedral.

After the old man finished playing, a brave soul asked him how he could have restored the magnificent instrument when the world's experts could not. The old man merely said, "It was I who built this organ fifty years ago. I created it—and now I have restored it."

God created you, and He knows exactly how to restore you at the end of a draining day—so you can play beautiful music tomorrow!

He who plants a tree plants a hope.

The Value of One

"There is joy in the presence of the angels of God over one sinner who repents."
LUKE 15:10 NASB

I can MAKE A SMALL DIFFER- ENCE IN THE WORLD BY . . .

A businessman and his wife once took a much-needed getaway at an oceanside hotel. During their stay a powerful storm arose, lashing the beach and sending massive breakers against the shore. Before daybreak the wind subsided.

The man went outside to survey the damage done by the storm. He walked along the beach and noticed it was covered with starfish that had been thrown ashore by the massive waves. They laid helpless on the sandy beach. Unable to get to the water, the starfish faced inevitable death as the sun's rays dried them out.

Farther down the beach, the man saw a figure walking along the shore. Every once in a while, the figure would stoop and pick something up. As he approached, he realized it was a young boy picking up the starfish one at a time and flinging them back into the ocean to safety.

As the man neared the young boy, he said, "Why are you doing that? One person will never make a difference—there are too many starfish to get back into the water before the sun comes up."

"Yes, that's true" the boy said bending down to pick up another starfish. "But I can sure make a difference to that one."

God never intended for an individual to solve all of life's problems. But He did intend for each one of us to use whatever resources and gifts He gave us to make a difference where we are.[64]

Those who bring sunshine to the lives of others cannot keep it from themselves.

Who Says You Can't?

*I can do all things through Christ
who strengthens me.*
PHILIPPIANS 4:13 NKJV

What JOB
SEEMS TOO
HARD FOR ME?
WHY DO I
THINK I
CAN DO IT?

You can do anything. That's what Kent Cullers' parents told him as he was growing up. That's what many parents tell their children. But Cullers was born blind. Even so, if a child hears the phrase *You can do anything* often enough, it eventually sinks in. It bears fruit. And it certainly did in Cullers' case.

As a young boy, he insisted on climbing trees and riding a bicycle. His father arranged a job transfer to California so the boy could attend a regular school, and Cullers became a straight-A student. He was valedictorian of his high school class and a National Merit Scholar. He went on to earn a Ph.D. in physics.

Cullers' first love has always been space, so it seems fitting that he found himself employed at NASA. As a researcher, one of his jobs is to design equipment to help scientists search for signs of intelligent communication in outer space.[65]

How does this blind man see what others can't? He uses his "mind's eye." He also uses his other senses—perhaps a little better than most people. Above all, he continues to tell himself what his parents taught him early in life: *You can do anything.*

The apostle Paul would have added a key phrase to Cullers' parental advice: *through Christ who gives me strength.* It is the Lord working in us to enable us, working through us to empower us, and working on our behalf to enrich us.

❧

*If you think you can or can't do
something . . . you're probably right.*

Procrastination Leads Nowhere

> *I will hasten and not delay*
> *to obey your commands.*
> PSALM 119:60

Morning is a great time to make a list of things to do and plan the day. It's also the best time to tackle those tasks that are the most difficult or least enjoyable. If we procrastinate as the day wears on, rationalization sets in, and sometimes even the tasks we had considered to be the most important are left undone.

Here's a little poem just for those who struggle with procrastination:

"How and When"

We are often greatly bothered
By two fussy little men,
Who sometimes block our pathway
Their names are How and When.
If we have a task or duty
Which we can put off a while,
And we do not go and do it
You should see those two rogues smile!
But there is a way to beat them,
And I will tell you how:
If you have a task or duty,
Do it well, and do it now.

—Author Unknown

Often we ask the Lord, "What do You want me to do?" but then fail to ask Him one of the key follow-up questions: "When do You want me to do this?" When we have a sense of God's timing, and in some cases His urgency about a matter, our conviction grows to get the job done right away.

God is concerned with how you use every moment of your time. Recognize that He desires to be part of your time-management and task-completion process today!

∾

Never leave till tomorrow that
which you can do today.

Today I NEED TO COMPLETE . . .

A Cork's Influence

*Let us behave decently, as in the daytime . . .
clothe yourselves with the Lord Jesus Christ.*
ROMANS 13:13-14

I can TOUCH
A FRIEND'S LIFE
TODAY BY
DOING . . .

On a factory tour, a group viewed an elongated bar of steel, which weighed five hundred pounds, suspended vertically by a chain. Near it, an average-sized cork was suspended by a silk thread.

"You will see something shortly which is seemingly impossible," said an attendant to the group of sightseers. "This cork is going to set this steel bar in motion!"

She took the cork in her hand, pulled it only slightly to the side of its original position, and released it. The cork swung gently against the steel bar, which remained motionless.

For ten minutes the cork, with pendulum-like regularity, struck the iron bar. Finally, the bar vibrated slightly. By the time the tour group passed through the room an hour later, the great bar was swinging like the pendulum of a clock!

Many of us feel we are not exerting a feather's weight of influence upon others or making a dent in the bastions of evil in the world. Not so! Other people can be powerfully impacted when they see us walking in God's goodness.

Not everyone is called to spread the love of Jesus through the pulpit, on the evangelistic trail, or in a full-time counseling ministry. Most of us are called to live our lives as "corks," through word and example—quietly, gently tapping away through the work of our daily lives. Tap by loving tap, in God's time, even the quietest Christian can make a huge difference in the lives of others.

*Wear a smile and have friends;
wear a scowl and have wrinkles.*

Staying Charged Up

Let the people renew their strength.
ISAIAH 41:1 KJV

My FAVORITE
PLACE TO REST
IN THE AFTER-
NOON IS . . .

Before automatic headlight controls were installed in automobiles, it was easy to park a car and leave the headlights on. Perhaps we were in a hurry, or it was light enough outside that we forgot we had turned the lights on. If we were gone for very long, we returned to find the car battery dead. To get the car running again, the battery had to be recharged.

Just like a car battery, our own supply of energy is not infinite. We must replenish it frequently with sleep, rest, food, and relaxation. Our busy nonstop days can be draining. Operating at top speed, we utilize all available emotional, physical, mental, and spiritual resources. Before we know it, our energy is consumed, and we feel "dead on our feet."

Being fatigued can cause our perception to be distorted and our responses to others to be negative. Furthermore, if we fail to do something about it, over time it can result in physical or emotional illness.

Charles Spurgeon, a well-known nineteenth-century preacher once said, "Without constant restoration we are not ready for the perpetual assaults. If we allow the good in our lives to get weak—or our 'light' to grow dim—the evil will surely gather strength and struggle desperately for the mastery over us."

You are wise to take a short break now and then during the day. Living this way will help you to maintain your energy supply and enable you to be more productive and content.

If you are swept off your feet,
it's time to get on your knees.

The Olive Press

He went away again a second time and prayed,
saying, "My Father, if this cannot pass away
unless I drink it, Thy will be done."
MATTHEW 26:42 NASB

What GOOD
THING CAN
BE PRESSED
OUT OF ME?

In Jerusalem one can stand in the Garden of Gethsemane on the Mount of Olives and look across the Kedron Valley to the Eastern Gate where Scriptures say Jesus will return one day. There in the garden, one of the olive trees is thought to be more than two thousand years old. Perhaps it is the same one Jesus knelt beneath when He agonized in prayer prior to the Crucifixion.

The Israelites were familiar with the procedure of making oil from the olives through a process of pressing that took about three days. Olive oil became a staple used for food and cooking. To this day, virgin olive oil is much favored by gourmet cooks. In biblical times, olive oil was burned in lamps as a source of light. It was used in preservation, anointing, and healing. There is much spiritual significance associated with olive oil.

Perhaps it is no wonder that Christ knelt beneath an olive tree as He chose the path of the Cross. When we follow Him, we reflect His love; we are a good seasoning for the world; and we are lights in the darkness. When we place our trust in Him, we are preserved until He comes again.

Today the Garden of Gethsemane is a favorite spot for visitors from around the globe. For each person, regardless of race or religion or background, the olive trees stand as constant reminders of God's grace and redeeming love.

❧

The grace of God is infinite and eternal.
As it had no beginning, so it can have
no end, and being an attribute of God,
it is as boundless as infinitude.

Day by Day

"Give us this day our daily bread."
MATTHEW 6:11 KJV

A mother once stopped by her recently married daughter's home unexpectedly and was promptly greeted with a flood of tears. Alarmed, the mother asked, "What happened, dear?"

Her daughter replied, "It's not what happened, but what keeps happening!"

Even more concerned, the mother asked, "What is it that keeps happening?"

The daughter replied, "Every day there are dishes to be washed. Every day there are meals to be prepared and a lunch to be packed. Every day there is laundry to be done and beds to be made and a house to be cleaned."

"And?" the mother asked.

"Don't you see?" the daughter said through her tears. "Life is just so daily."

On those days when the "daily-ness" of life seems to have you bogged down in boredom or drudgery, remind yourself the Lord said He would provide for the needs of His people on a daily basis. Manna was gathered in the wilderness every morning. Jesus taught His disciples to pray for their "daily bread." God wants to provide what we need, not only physically and materially, but also emotionally and spiritually, one day at a time.

Trust the Lord to give to you

- material goods, money, food, and supplies that you will need today.
- ideas and creative energy that you need for today's work.
- stamina, health, and strength that you need today to fulfill your many roles and responsibilities.
- spiritual nourishment and fortitude to face and conquer the temptations and trials of today.

An
EMOTIONAL
NEED IN MY
LIFE IS . . .

God gives us the ingredients for our daily bread, but He expects us to do the baking.

A Quiet Moment

Thus saith the Lord God, the Holy One of Israel;
In returning and rest shall ye be saved; in quietness
and in confidence shall be your strength.
ISAIAH 30:15 KJV

When I
CONTEMPLATE
THE WORD
"SILENCE,"
WHAT KIND OF
PLACE COMES
TO MIND?

Between the great issues of life there is quiet. Silence characterizes the highest in art and the deepest in nature. It's the silence between the notes that give them rhythm, interest, and emphasis.

The surest spiritual search is made in silence. Moses learned in Midian and Paul in Arabia what would have eluded them in the noisy streets of men.

Silence reaches beyond words. The highest point in drama is silence. The strongest of emotions don't always cry aloud. The most effective reproof is not a tongue-lashing. The sincerest sympathy is not wordy or noisy. The best preparation for an emergency is the calm of quietness.

Time spent in quiet prayer is the best preparation for intelligent action. The best proof of quality is often silence; the great engine is almost noiseless. The best indicator of confidence is almost always silence; people who are confident of their position do not argue or raise their voices or even try to explain everything.

Quiet times are most cherished in the middle of busy days. Sometimes the quiet does not offer itself; it must be sought out. At other times, the surroundings don't allow for true silence. It is in those moments when the Holy Spirit can supernaturally turn down the volume and allow moments of quiet communion with God from within.

A coffee break is a perfect time to seek a quiet spot for a few minutes of real refreshment in the presence of a "still small voice" (1 Kings 19:12 KJV).

Silence is a great peacemaker.

Wrong Route

Wait for the LORD; be strong and
take heart and wait for the LORD.
PSALM 27:14

Lizzy and Karen were in downtown Seattle, sitting in the hotel lobby and waiting for a bus. They had broken free of a conference and were ready to explore the city that surrounded them. They'd been waiting for the bus for twenty minutes and found themselves impatient and eager.

Good
REASONS TO
WAIT FOR
GOD'S TIMING
ARE . . .

Moments later, a bus pulled up. "It's not the one they said we should take," Lizzy said, smiling as she began walking toward the doors, "but it's headed in the same direction! Let's go!" They climbed on board—two Midwestern girls, heading for the sights. As the bus made its way through the dark and scary underbelly of the city, the girls huddled together in a small corner of the bus. The driver seemed amused by their predicament, and their fellow passengers seemed anything but willing to help them find their desired destination. They grasped each other's hands and tried to look less like tourists and more like residents. That only served to emphasize their discomfort. Lizzy and Karen ended up staying on the bus for the whole route.

Is there a bus you're tempted to climb aboard because you're tired of waiting? There is much to be gained by waiting in the lobby for the right bus. God will not abandon you in your search. He is there, ready and waiting with His answer, reminding you of His sovereign will and His ability to take you where you need to go.

All comes at the proper time to him
who knows how to wait.

Downshifting

*He who dwells in the shelter of the Most High
will rest in the shadow of the Almighty.*
PSALM 91:1

The CHORE
THAT SEEMS TO
HELP HEAL
AND CALM
ME IS . . .

We are a people on a mission: work nonstop, master the learning curve, and achieve as much as possible as fast as we can. For all our enthusiasm and energy, however, we start out strong in the morning and then fall prey to gloomy weather, dark moods, or weariness toward teatime. We feel driven to finish what's in front of us, but we don't have the stamina to go on. That's when we have to resort to Plan B.

Plan B says that if you don't want to leave your office yet, but you are burned out on weightier matters, you have to do something lighter. Select a job-related task that doesn't require a lot of brainpower.

In *The Spirit of Discipline,* Bishop Francis Paget writes:

When it is dull, cold and weary weather with us, when the light is hidden, and the mists are thick, and the sleet begins to fall, still we may get on with the work which can be done as well in the dark days as in the bright; work which otherwise will have to be hurried through in the sunshine, taking up its happiest and most fruitful hours. Very often, I think, the plainer work is the best way of getting back into the light and warmth. Through humbly and simply doing what we can, we retrieve the power of doing what we would.

*Inside myself is a place where I live all
alone, and that's where you renew
your springs that never dry up.*

Give Me a Word

The Word was God.
JOHN 1:1 NKJV

The TEN
MOST LOVELY
WORDS I
CAN THINK
OF ARE . . .

Marjorie Holmes writes in *Lord, Let Me Love* about her daughter, who had a fascination with words at a young age. From her earliest attempts at talking, she liked to try out new words and sounds. Often she would chant and sing words or make up strange combinations of sounds to build her own vocabulary.

She was impatient, however, because all the things she was learning far exceeded her ability to express them. Because she needed more words, she began asking her mother for words, just as she might ask her for a cookie or a hug.

The little girl would ask, "Give me a bright word, Mother." Marjorie would answer with nouns and adjectives that described the word bright, such as "sunshine, golden, luminous, shiny, and sparkling."

Then she would ask for a soft word. Marjorie responded, "Velvety soft like a blackberry or a pony's nose? Or furry, like your kitten?" And when her daughter was angry, she would demand a glad word. The game continued until the little girl's attitude was transformed by the happy thoughts prompted by happy words.[66]

Through words, God spoke creation into being. He said, "Let there be light." And there was light. He said, "Let us make the earth and the fullness of it." And foliage, animals, birds, and fish were created.

God gave us His Word so we could live full and satisfying lives while we are here on earth. The Bible is teeming with wonderful, powerful, beautiful words for our daily lives.

༄

Try these: a kind thought—
a kind word—and a good deed.

JULY 20

He has made everything appropriate in its time.
ECCLESIASTES 3:11 NASB

Lord, WHEN I
DO MY CHORES
TODAY, I WANT
TO TALK TO
YOU ABOUT . . .

Several years ago, a television ad focused on a lovely young woman's smiling face. She was looking down and obviously very busy at the task before her, although what she was doing was not shown. At the same time she was busy with this task, she was praying. The ad's emphasis was on taking time to pray no matter what else we must do during the day.

As the camera moved away from this young woman's face and down to what she was doing, it became clear that this was a young mother diapering her baby.

What a lovely picture of how easy it is for us to talk with the Lord! Setting a chunk of time aside every morning might not work every day for you, but during each twenty-four-hour day you can creatively find a portion of time that is just for God.

> We mutter and sputter,
> We fume and we spurt,
> We mumble and grumble,
> Our feelings get hurt.
> We can't understand things,
> Our vision grows dim,
> When all that we need is:
> A moment with Him.[67]

—Author Unknown

Most of us are so busy during the day that we find it increasingly difficult to set aside a block of time to spend in prayer, not just a quick prayer of thanks, but a time of genuine communication with the Lord. There are times we can be alone with the Savior, but we need to creatively look for them.

I cannot be the man I should be
without times of quietness. Stillness
is an essential part of growing deeper.

More than Atoms

Let each one examine his own work,
and then he will have rejoicing in
himself alone, and not in another.
GALATIANS 6:4 NKJV

Two young brothers were engaged in their ongoing battle for sibling superiority. Adam, age nine, was explaining to four-year-old Rob the science of living matter, taking no small pleasure in his advantage of a third grade education.

Soon, a skirmish broke loose, with cries of "Am not!" and "Are too!" ringing through the house. Rob ran crying to find his mother.

"Mo-o-o-m . . . is everything made of atoms?"

"Yes, that's true."

"But," he said, "I'm made of atoms!"

"Sweetie, he's right. Everything in the world is made of atoms."

Rob sank to the floor, sobbing as if his heart had broken. His perplexed mom picked him up, hugged him, and asked, "What on earth is the matter?"

"It's no fair!" he howled. "I don't want to be made of Adams—I want to be made of Robs!"

We all want recognition for our "specialness." But we should never strive to gain our self-worth from our society, feedback from others, or our own comparisons to others. Our self-esteem should be based in the fact that God created us with the utmost care and has called His creation good.[68]

In His foresight, we are all made of "the right stuff." Our self-worth then comes from how we use it—serving our families and communities, exercising our creative gifts, and becoming one with God. No amount of stature in the eyes of people can equal the reward of following God's will.

❧

Self-esteem is a fragile flower
and can be crushed so easily.

The REASON
I THINK MY
SIBLING IS
SPECIAL
IS HIS . . .

Obedience and Peaceful Abiding

"Abide in Me, and I in you."
JOHN 15:4 NASB

While on safari, a missionary family stopped for lunch. The children were playing under a tree a distance away from their parents and the other adults on the team. Suddenly the father of one child jumped up and yelled to his son, "Drop down!" and the son did so instantly. Others in the group were shocked to learn that a poisonous snake was slithering down the tree ready to strike the child. It would have meant certain death if the snake had bitten him. Only the father of the child saw the snake.

Amazement was expressed over the instant response of the child to his father's command. The father explained that the abiding love he and his son enjoyed had developed from the trust they had in each other. The boy did not question when his dad gave the command; he trusted him and responded accordingly. The missionary father also expected his son to respond to his command.

The peaceful rest that both of them were able to enjoy later that day was evidence of the abiding rest that God has for each of us as we learn to trust Him. Are you abiding in Christ?

God wants to abide in us, and He wants us to abide in Him. He is ready to equip us with what we need to endure and hold on to that place for as long as He wants us there. Abiding starts with trust and ends with complete rest.

*All I have seen teaches me to trust
the Creator for all I have not seen.*

But When?

Wait on the LORD; be of good courage,
and He shall strengthen your heart.
PSALM 27:14 NKJV

I have
GROWN
SPIRITUALLY
THIS YEAR IN
THE AREA
OF . . .

We have often smiled knowingly at that kitchen-magnet quip, "Lord, give me patience, and give it to me now!" And why not? Our society expects immediate accomplishment in almost everything we do—from microwave meals in minutes to global communication in seconds.

It seems, whatever the problem, there should be a button, switch, or pill to deliver fast results. This makes it all the more difficult to accept that, like it or not, spiritual growth takes time.

In a garden, all seedlings have average schedules of development. But as human beings with unique histories and needs, we can't rely on averages to determine when we might take that next step in our walk with God.

It's tempting, when faced with a flaw of the spirit or other growth issue, to pray for and expect immediate change. Sometimes it happens. But how lost and confused we feel if our prayers don't bring the instant relief we seek!

During such times, it's good to remember that all facets of our nature—whether traits we love about ourselves or those we want to improve—are part of our God-created being. Even our less-than-desirable parts are there for a reason and contain His lessons for us.

When change seems to come slowly, don't give up hope. Consider that the timetable for your growth is in the Lord's hands. Continue your daily communion with God and trust your spirit to be healed in His time.

He that can have patience
can have what he wills.

Morning Thirst

My soul thirsts for God, for the living God.
PSALM 42:2 NASB

The BOOK OF
THE BIBLE
THAT MOST
SPEAKS TO MY
HEART IS . . .

The need for a refreshing drink when we first wake in the morning is often so strong that we find ourselves anticipating the taste before we ever get a glass in our hands. That thirst is a driving force that nothing else will satisfy.

There is another thirst that needs to be quenched. It is a thirst we often ignore until it is so great, everything else in our lives—our relationships, our growth as children of God, our joy, our peace—begins to wither.

Patti did not have running water inside her home when she was a child. Not since then has she known that same level of satisfaction a morning drink of water can give. This was especially true if the water in the house ran out during the night when it was too cold or too stormy for anyone to make a trip to the source outside.

There is a source of living water that is available to us any time of the day or night. It never runs out, it never gets contaminated, it never freezes over, and it is always as refreshing throughout the day as it was with the first sip in the morning.

Renowned missionary Hudson Taylor once said, "There is a living God, He has spoken in the Bible and He means what He says and He will do all that He has promised." He has promised to quench our thirst in such a way that we will never be thirsty again!

*When you drink from the stream,
remember the spring.*

The Face of God

No one has beheld God at any time;
if we love one another, God abides in us,
and His love is perfected in us.
1 JOHN 4:12 NASB

Dutch psychologist and theologian Henri Nouwen was known for his determination to break down barriers, whether between Catholic and Protestant or therapist and patient. He spent most of his life pursuing a high-pressure career as a sought-after speaker and author.

But years of travel and dozens of books took such a toll on his health and spirit that he eventually retreated to Toronto, Canada, to become priest-in-residence at Daybreak, a home for the severely disabled.

Nouwen lived a quiet life at Daybreak, residing in a small, simple room and ministering to the patients at the facility. He had a special relationship with a resident named Adam, a profoundly retarded young man unable to walk, talk, or care for himself. Nouwen devoted nearly two hours every day to caring for Adam—bathing, shaving, combing his hair, and feeding him.

To onlookers, it seemed a great burden on the priest to spend so many hours on such menial duties. But when asked why he spent his time in this way, Nouwen insisted that it was he who benefited from the relationship. He described how the process of learning to love Adam, with all of his incapacities, taught him what it must be like for God to love us, even with all our frailties.

Ultimately, Henri Nouwen concluded that "the goal of education and formation for the ministry is continually to recognize the Lord's voice, His face, and His touch in every person we meet."[69]

There is no remedy for love
than to love more.

What JOB
HAS GOD
CALLED ME
TO DO THAT
HAS ETERNAL
VALUE?

What Do You Think?

The eyes of the LORD preserve knowledge.
PROVERBS 22:12 KJV

I love GOD
BECAUSE HE
TRUSTED ME
ENOUGH
TO . . .

"Dad, have you heard of this book?" Cindy asked, showing him a copy of a highly controversial work. Rev. Bill looked up from his desk to respond to his sixteen-year-old daughter.

"Sure, I have. Why do you ask?" he replied.

In fact, he knew a great deal about the book. It had recently been made into a movie that was causing quite a stir in the Christian community, and many pastors and church members were so upset that they had even picketed the theaters where the movie was showing.

"I was just wondering if it's a good book," Cindy answered.

"Why don't you read it for yourself, and then we will talk about it together," he suggested.

In that moment, Bill demonstrated a remarkable faith in his daughter, his own parenting, and his God. By inviting her to read and discuss this book, he showed that he trusted Cindy to think for herself.

The single greatest challenge we face as parents is that of letting go of our children in the right way and at the right time. Nowhere is this faith challenged more than in the arena of controversial ideas. Yet, we can have confidence that what we have taught them will keep them, for Scripture says, "Train a child in the way he should go, and when he is old he will not turn from it" (Proverbs 22:6).

Bill could trust Cindy because he knew that her entire life had been one characterized by learning the Word of God.

While yielding to loving parental leadership, children are also learning to yield to the benevolent leadership of God himself.

Destiny: First Chair or . . .

In all labour there is profit.
PROVERBS 14:23 KJV

What TALENT HAS GOD GIVEN ME THAT I HAVE NOT YET SHARED?

Tony's voice was marked by satisfaction as he spoke of his years in the music industry. "Oh, I could play the trumpet a little bit, and a few other instruments, but as for real talent, I didn't have any. But I do love music and this business."

Over the past thirty years he had been involved with the publication of music and the production of shows in a variety of capacities. But, according to Tony, the most important decision he ever made occurred when he was a trumpet player in a local orchestra.

"I can remember sitting in the orchestra pit looking up at this young guy who handed some papers to the conductor. They talked for quite a while, and the young guy left." The young man was a music arranger, and Tony said, "That changed my life, because I decided right then and there that I wanted to do the same thing."

Over the next several years, Tony pursued and received his undergraduate degree in music with special emphasis on arrangement. He became a successful professional working for a major music publishing company. Today he serves as a manager and leader in the company.

William Jennings Bryan once said, "Destiny is not a matter of chance, it is a matter of choice; it is not a thing to be waited for; it is a thing to be achieved."[70]

Ask the Lord to show you how to share your talents with the world. He will surely open doors for you.

Give to the world the best you have,
and the best will come back to you.

Sunrise

The sunrise from on high shall visit us.
LUKE 1:78 NASB

What TRIAL
HAVE I BEEN
THROUGH
THAT TURNED
OUT TO HAVE A
SILVER LINING?

Sunrise, shining its beams through the window on a cold winter's morning, is a welcome sight. Even if the air outside is icy cold, sunrise gives the illusion of warmth. With the rising sun, the city opens its shutters and makes preparations for the day; in the country, the farm animals are let out to pasture. Kids are off to school, adults are on their way to work, and each has a different perspective of the sunrise.

Sunrise happens whether we see it or not. Clouds may cover the sky so totally that we can't experience the beauty of the sunbeams making their way to the earth. No matter what the climate, the sun still rises in the eastern horizon and sets over the west. Sunrise is set by God's clock, and it is ours to enjoy in the early mornings when we can see it clearly. It is just as much there for us to enjoy when the cloud shadows cover it. We can trust it to be there—although it may be hidden for a while.

We can also trust God to be there every morning because He is the one, irrefutable Reality in this life, and He remains constant and true!

Life is a mixture of sunshine and rain,
Laughter and teardrops, pleasure and pain—
Low tides and high tides, mountains and
plains, triumphs, defeats and losses and
gains. But there never was a cloud
that the Son didn't shine through
and there's nothing that's impossible
for Jesus Christ to do!

I Know That Voice!

"The sheep follow him because they know his voice."
JOHN 10:4 NASB

God SPEAKS
TO ME
THROUGH . . .

A young mother had been alone with her preschoolers for a week while her husband was away on a business trip. The fourth day was particularly exasperating. After several bedtime stories, she finally got the energetic children to bed and decided to relax. She had changed into an old pair of sweats and shampooed her hair when she heard the children jumping around in their room.

Wrapping a towel around her head, she went to scold them. As she walked out of the children's room, she overheard the littlest one ask, "Who was that?"

We can be so out of practice at listening to God that we fail to recognize His voice, and then we miss out on His guidance and grace. Have you ever found yourself asking, "Who was that?" only later to realize that it was indeed your Heavenly Father?

When a sheep refuses to follow, the shepherd has no choice but to teach the sheep a lesson for its own protection. The shepherd will break one of the sheep's legs and carry the sheep around his neck until its leg heals. The animal becomes so acquainted with its master's voice and ways that it then graciously follows and obeys. Though a difficult lesson, the shepherd saves one who would otherwise be lost.

God wants us to know Him so well that we immediately recognize His voice and obey His commands. There is no better way to know the Master's voice than through an intimate relationship with Him.

If you keep watch over your hearts, and listen for the voice of God and learn of Him, in one short hour you can learn more from Him than you could learn from man in a thousand years.

The Master

*The Lord your God in your midst, the Mighty One,
will save; He will rejoice over you with
gladness, He will quiet you in His love,
He will rejoice over you with singing.*
ZEPHANIAH 3:17 NKJV

I should
EDIFY
SOMEONE
TODAY BY
SAYING . . .

The story is told of a concert appearance by the brilliant Polish composer and pianist Ignace Jan Paderewski. The event was staged in a great American music hall, where the artist was to perform for the social elite of the city.

Waiting in the audience for the concert to begin were a woman and her young son. After sitting for longer than his patience could stand, the youngster slipped away from his mother. He was fascinated by the beautiful Steinway piano awaiting the performance, and he made his way toward it. Before anyone knew what was happening, he crept onto the stage and climbed up on the piano stool to play a round of "Chopsticks."

The audience was horrified. What would the great Paderewski think? The murmurs quickly erupted into a roar of disapproval as the crowd demanded that the child be removed immediately.

Backstage, Paderewski heard the disruption and, discerning the cause, raced out to join the child at the piano. He reached around him from behind and improvised his own countermelody to his young guest's "Chopsticks." As the impromptu duet continued, the master whispered in the child's ear, "Keep going. Don't quit, son. Don't stop."[71]

We may never play alongside a master pianist, but every day in our lives can be a duet with the Master. What joy it is to feel His love wrapped around us as He whispers, "Keep going. Don't stop. I am with you!"

We are all strings in the concert of God's joy.

The Birthday Surprise

Let all that you do be done with love.
1 CORINTHIANS 16:14 NKJV

A simple ACT OF KIND- NESS THAT CHANGED MY ATTITUDE WAS . . .

It was one of those dreadful evenings every family experiences on occasion. Though it was Saturday night—and a pre-birthday celebration at that—nothing was going right. Even the ride home from the restaurant was lousy.

Dad was angry from watching too many political shows on television. The almost sixteen-year-old thought his life was over because he hadn't had driver's education classes yet, so he couldn't get his license. The eleven-year-old was yelling because the almost sixteen-year-old punched him for . . . well, no one quite knew why.

And Mom was angry that she had just spent good money on a nice restaurant meal for these ungrateful monsters.

On arriving home, she grudgingly decided to start the birthday preparations and went to the kitchen to lay out ingredients for her older son's favorite cake. Within ten minutes, almost magically, the mood of the entire family changed.

The almost sixteen-year-old walked into the kitchen, saw the task at hand, and hugged his mom for making his cake, even after his poor behavior. The eleven-year-old was excited because Mom let him help mix the cake. Dad was happy because everyone else had quit fighting.

And Mom was amazed that the whole evening turned on the baking of a cake—a small act of love.

We can never guess how important our slightest actions will be to those around us. As you go through the day, you have a choice in your interactions with everyone you meet. Choose the act of love.

The one who truly loves gives all and sacrifices nothing.

Hidden Blessings

In everything give thanks; for this is the will of God in Christ Jesus for you.
1 THESSALONIANS 5:18 NKJV

Father, I
THANK YOU
TODAY FOR . . .

It was a rough day at the office. Nancy struggled with too many meetings, too many project deadlines, and not enough time to complete anything. Her performance review was due, and she feared the raise she needed was not going to happen.

What's more, her daughter had been out of school with respiratory flu for three days with no sign of improvement. Nancy and her husband, Tom, were rotating their office leave so someone would always be home with their child.

Her phone rang. It was Tom calling, worried because their daughter's breathing was becoming labored. Nancy knew immediately that the child needed to see a doctor again.

Racing home, she wanted to cry. Why did everything have to happen at once? Suddenly, she was startled by a loud bang, as the car ahead of her blew a tire and slowly maneuvered to a nearby parking lot. Nancy took a deep breath to regain her composure and thought, *Okay, God, how bad off am I, really?*

As she picked up her daughter and sped to the emergency clinic, Nancy decided to concentrate on the things that were going right. She prayed to the Lord:

Thank You for good tires and cars that work.
Thank You for my job.
Thank You for doctors.
Thank You for insurance.
Thank You for helping my daughter to breathe.
Thank You for coming with me.
Thank You for showing me how much I have
    to be thankful for.

The finest test of character is seen in the amount and the power of gratitude we have.

Rules? What Rules?

"Blessed are the peacemakers: for they shall be called the children of God."

MATTHEW 5:9 KJV

"What do you mean, you don't have to go by rules?" Rick asked his daughter Heather, with a note of incredulity in his voice.

"Shelley said that we don't have to go by rules."

"Well, Shelley's wrong; you do have to go by rules."

"No, I don't. Shelley said so."

"Yes, you do!" he insisted.

The argument continued for a few minutes until Rick's wife, Jane, stepped into Heather's bedroom and quietly said, "Rick, do you realize that you are arguing with a three-year-old?" She then turned to their little girl and asked, "Heather, do you know what rules are?"

"No."

"When you're at school," she continued, "do you and Shelley ever need to line up so that your class can go to lunch or out to the playground?"

"Yes."

"Well, that's a rule."

"Oh, okay."

With a small smile, Jane hugged Heather and quietly left the room. With a sheepish look on his face, Rick followed. "I guess I got carried away," he mumbled.

It's pretty easy to get carried away. In fact, if we are not careful, we can find ourselves embroiled in conflict with others without ever knowing why. It took the loving voice of Heather's mother to calm the waters. We can be that voice, too, if we so desire. Remember, Jesus said, "Blessed are the peacemakers."

Gently to hear, kindly to judge.

What SITUATION HAVE I FACED WHERE I HAD A CHANCE TO BE THE PEACEMAKER?

Gentle Ripples

O God, You are my God; early will I seek You.
PSALM 63:1 NKJV

Early in the morning a lake is usually very still—no animals, no people, no noise, no boats, no cars. All is quiet.

This is the best time to skip rocks. By taking a small flat pebble and throwing it at the right angle, you can skip it across the water leaving circles of ripples every time it makes contact with the lake. The ripples form small and very defined circles at first; then they spread out and break apart until they vanish. If several people skip rocks at the same time, the ripples cross over one another and blend together to make mini-waves across the lake. The impact can be pretty amazing.

For most of us, mornings are filled with so many things that need our attention that we find it difficult to spend time alone with God. However, Christ set a marvelous example for us by rising early to listen to God. When we spend time alone with God at the beginning of each day, we become acquainted with Him and start becoming like Him. Throughout our days, the ripple effect of our time with God in the early morning will impact the lives of those with whom we have contact.

When these ripples blend with others who also spend time with God, we create mini-waves of love and joy. It all starts with a quiet time and a gentle ripple.

*It is good to be alone in the garden at
dawn or dark so that all its shy presences
may haunt you and possess you
in a reverie of suspended thought.*

Thank You, Lord

I will give thanks to the LORD with all my heart.
PSALM 9:1 NASB

A mother purchased a new violin for her son. Together they had saved for months to be able to afford this fine instrument. He had promised to care for it, but it wasn't long before the boy had forgotten his promise and left his violin out on the porch overnight. The cold night air and the heavy morning dew caused the violin to bulge, and the sound quality was no longer the same.

The boy's mother took this opportunity to teach her son a lesson for life. She decided to show him what went into the making of the violin. She took him to the store where they had made the purchase. They then visited a manufacturing company where violins were produced and went to a lumber mill where the wood had been carefully chosen for such a fine instrument. They even visited a forest where trees were being grown specifically for quality instruments. The mother and son also made trips to learn how the bow and strings were manufactured. She wanted her son to understand why he should have been thankful for the beautiful musical instrument with which he had been blessed.

It is easier to thank the Lord after we have seen His work, for we then have something to go back to and rejoice over. It is not as easy to be thankful for what we don't see or haven't experienced.

A thankful heart is not only the greatest virtue, but the parent of all other virtues.

One
BLESSING
THAT I HAVE
NOT FULLY
APPRECIATED
IS . . .

Never Give Up

*Let us not become weary in doing good,
for at the proper time we will reap
a harvest if we do not give up.*
GALATIANS 6:9

A time THAT
I THOUGHT I
SHOULD GIVE
UP, BUT DIDN'T
WAS WHEN . . .

Again, the young teacher read the note attached to the fresh green ivy: "Because of the seeds you planted, we will one day grow into beautiful plants like this one. We appreciate all you've done for us. Thank you for investing time in our lives."

A smile widened on the teacher's face as grateful tears trickled down her cheeks. Like the one leper who expressed gratitude to Jesus for healing him, the girls she had taught remembered to say thanks to their Sunday school teacher. The ivy plant represented a gift of love. For months the teacher faithfully watered that growing plant. Each time she looked at it, she remembered those special teenagers and was encouraged to continue teaching.

But after a year, something happened. The leaves began to turn yellow and drop—all but one. She started to discard the ivy but decided instead to keep watering and fertilizing it. One day as she walked through the kitchen, the teacher noticed a new shoot on the plant. A few days later, another leaf appeared, and then another. Within a few months, the ivy was well on its way to becoming a healthy plant once again.

Henry Drummond says, "Do not think that nothing is happening because you do not see yourself grow, or hear the whir of the machinery. All great things grow noiselessly."

Few joys exceed the blessings of faithfully investing time and love into the lives of others. Never, never give up on those plants!

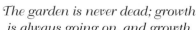

*The garden is never dead; growth
is always going on, and growth
can be seen, and seen with delight!*

Believe in Me

The Lord make you to increase and abound in love one toward another, and toward all men.

1 THESSALONIANS 3:12 KJV

What TRAIT
DO I ADMIRE
IN EACH OF
MY FAMILY
MEMBERS?

Cynthia was amazed and grateful for what she was seeing. Ms. Nelson, a fifth-grade teacher at the private school where Cynthia worked, was quietly greeting the children and their parents at the door of her classroom. Ms. Nelson spoke with pride to each parent of the work of his or her child. She took time to mention the child by name and to point out something on that child's work that was particularly noteworthy. As a result, both the parent and the child glowed with satisfaction.

This was not a special event—it was the morning of a normal school day, and Ms. Nelson made it a habit to be at the door every morning.

As Cynthia stepped into her own office, she was struck by the impact of Ms. Nelson's genuine comments and actions. She couldn't help but think of a gardener fussing over the flowers and plants of the garden—eager to provide the right nourishment and attention so that each plant grows strong and healthy.

Later that afternoon, Cynthia asked her fifth-grade son, John, how he liked being in Ms. Nelson's class. John responded, "I like it a lot. She's a really neat teacher because you always know that she believes in you. Even when you don't get everything right, she still believes in you."

What a gift—the ability to believe in others and communicate it to them daily, just as our Lord loves and believes in us without fail!

Encouragement is oxygen to the soul.

Childlike Thinking

Brethren, be not children in understanding.
1 CORINTHIANS 14:20 KJV

A truth
THAT I ONCE
MISUNDER-
STOOD WAS . . .

It had been years since the four siblings had been together, and the air was filled with laughter as they entertained their families with stories from their childhood. The three older brothers told story after story of the trials and tribulations of having three boys in one bedroom. They also told of the many practical jokes they played on one another and of the numerous fights they had had as kids. But no one could top Sherry's story of being the "baby sister."

"You know, guys," she said during a momentary lull in the conversation, "I used to think that with future generations all people were born girls and would eventually turn into boys. In fact, I used to wonder when I would become a boy just like you guys."

When she was just a child, Sherry's concept made perfect sense. She had three older brothers and no sisters, so naturally she assumed she would one day become a boy too. Of course, as she grew old enough to understand things better, this idea slipped away to become just a fond memory.

While physical growth and maturation occur independent of our control, how many times do we remain "children in our understanding" because we simply choose not to exercise our thinking abilities or because the issues we must face are just too uncomfortable? Yet we can seek God's wisdom and direction so that we might grow in our understanding of His desires for us.

❧

*If there were no difficulties
there would be no triumphs.*

Grow Up!

He will be like a tree firmly planted by streams of water, which yields its fruit in its season.

PSALM 1:3 NASB

I will
GROW MORE
MATURE
WHEN . . .

"Grow up!" is a taunt often used by teenagers to their peers who, for whatever reason, aren't acting as mature as they should at the moment. The command is given with the attitude that the immature person can simply make a choice to immediately grow up.

Commanding a friend to "grow up" doesn't do any more good than telling a tree to "grow up." There is a process that must take place, and that process takes time. Every living thing requires certain elements in order to grow—good soil, the appropriate amounts of sunshine and water, and plenty of time.

People, like trees, need a good start in order to be rooted securely. Young saplings can't mature into beautiful and tall shade trees without the right mixture of sun, water, rich soil, and space. As long as a tree is living, it never stops growing and never outgrows its need for nourishment. Most importantly, this process takes time—and lots of it.

In God's perfect timing, we will indeed "grow up." Like babies taking their first steps, so we must be willing to let nature takes its course. The growth process is a long one, and it never really is complete. Flourishing trees don't strain to grow. They merely follow the natural process God planted in them. And healthy trees don't decide to just ignore the nourishment of sun, rain, and soil. Instead, they continually draw life from these things.

Like the roots of a plant, faith must seek greater depth or be subject to the law of death.

229

Just Like Daddy

God created man in His own image,
in the image of God He created him;
male and female He created them.
GENESIS 1:27 NASB

In WHAT
WAYS DO I
LOOK LIKE MY
FATHER GOD?

The snow-covered peaks, fragrant evergreens, and a rustic lodge combined to create a picture-perfect postcard scene. Inside the adjacent condo, a grandmother kept her five-month-old granddaughter while the baby's parents took their turn skiing. After Emily had her nap, bottle, and playtime, the grandmother then zipped her into a feather-soft blue bunting and carried her toward the lobby to await the family's return.

Other guests and hotel workers began smiling when they saw the baby. They approached her, talked baby talk, and reached out to touch her chubby cheeks. Emily's flawless skin and innocent blue eyes captured everyone's attention. Big strong athletic skiers paused to coo with her. Seasoned seniors who had seen decades of history delighted in her innocence. Weary travelers paused from their hectic schedules to smile and "talk" with her.

The shuttle bus soon pulled into the driveway. As Emily's parents entered the lobby, she recognized them and squealed with delight. A lady sitting nearby commented, "Why, little girl, you look just like your daddy!" Everyone chuckled because it was true. Although only a little face peered from the bunting, anyone—even a stranger—could see the strong resemblance.

When people see us, does our joy overflow to them? Do we delight the hearts of people who cross our paths? Does the image of our Heavenly Daddy reflect in the light of our eyes? Will people recognize Him? Whom do we look like?

❧

Let each man think himself an act of God,
his mind a thought of God,
his life a breath of God.

Child's Play

*Until we all reach unity in the faith
and in the knowledge of the Son of God
and become mature, attaining to the
whole measure of the fullness of Christ.*

EPHESIANS 4:13

Professional golfer Tiger Woods is considered one of the top players with the potential to rank among the greatest of all time. Watching him line up a forty-foot downhill breaking putt, some may recall seeing him on the Tonight Show when he was about three years of age.

Tiger was already showing a talent for the game, so a small putting surface was set up for him. A ball was placed in front of him, about eight feet from the cup. He lined up the shot, putted, and missed.

Another ball was placed in the same position. He again prepared to putt—then picked the ball up, placed it six inches from the cup, and promptly sank the shot. Johnny Carson and the audience laughed and cheered to see a small child do what many adults would like to do. Of course, if he did that today, he would be ejected from the tournament.

A resident of a small town was once asked by a tourist: "Have any famous people been born here?"

He replied, "No, only babies."

We all start out as "only babies," but our Creator has placed within us the greatest power in the universe: the ability to grow, day by day, as we respond to increasing challenges.

*There are no great men in this world,
only great challenges which
ordinary men rise to meet.*

I challenge

MYSELF TO

GROW BY . . .

Texas Limestone

"Other fell on good ground, and did yield fruit."
MARK 4:8 KJV

How CAN I
PREPARE MY
HEART TO
GROW THE
FRUITS OF
THE SPIRIT?

Anita was determined to have a garden. She spent the entire hot, humid afternoon hacking away at the small plot of ground in the back of their central Texas home. In the vernacular of farmers, it was "poor" soil—incapable of sustaining even the hardiest of vegetables. After about three inches, the soil gave way to limestone. But that was not going to stop her!

Every time it seemed that she had found the last rock, sparks would fly from the blade as she again struck limestone. She was tempted to give up her garden. It seemed that nothing would grow in this place. Yet she longed for a garden filled with ripe red tomatoes, green cucumbers, tall okra, and big ears of corn.

Slowly, the soil began to turn more easily. Occasionally, she would use the garden hose to dampen the dry earth as she removed the rocks. Finally the rocks were removed. She then mixed in bags of new, rich topsoil and shaped the soil into nice smooth, parallel rows. At last, the garden was ready for her to plant the vegetable seeds.

Like her garden, Anita had to work hard to keep her heart right and free from the burdensome rocks of unforgiveness. She longed for healthy, merciful soil where seeds of God's love would yield a bumper crop of compassion and kindness. She knew that her daily choices in thought, word, and deed would determine whether her heart-garden was full of bitter rocks or joyful vegetation.

*Forgiveness is not an occasional act;
it is a permanent attitude.*

The Contest

*The child grew and became strong, filled with
wisdom; and the favor of God was upon him.*

LUKE 2:40 RSV

Stretching

MYSELF

SPIRITUALLY

WILL . . .

It was a typical day in first grade, and while their teacher was tending to other students, Sammy and Molly were engrossed in a discussion of the utmost importance: Who was taller?

Molly was one of the smaller children in the class, but that never interfered with her keen sense of competition. When Sammy declared his superior height, she responded by sitting up tall and straight. When Sammy sat up taller and straighter, Molly stood up beside her desk. When Sammy stood up across the aisle and immediately overshadowed her, Molly—after stealing a glance across the room to ensure her teacher's back was still turned—stepped up on her chair.

When the teacher finally turned to check on the commotion, the two children were standing atop their desks on their tiptoes, stretching for all they were worth!

Children are typically excited about growing bigger, and the wise adult continues to seek internal growth. Those who lose this zest die long before their funerals.

If improving in size, career, or talent is exciting, other aspects of our lives can bring even more lasting satisfaction. Growing in our relationship with God is one of them. In fact, taking our desires for growth to the Lord can result in a double blessing—gaining His strength and vision for improving our lives, while deepening our joy in knowing Him.

*A state of mind that sees God in
everything is evidence of growth
in grace and a grateful heart.*

A Garden of Hope

See, I am doing a new thing! Now it springs up;
do you not perceive it?
ISAIAH 43:19

When
SOMEONE I
LOVED DIED,
I STILL
FELT HOPE
BECAUSE . . .

As Shannon sat by her mother's bedside day by day, she observed the leaves changing to autumn splendor outside the bedroom window. And each day, she watched her mother's cancer-riddled body weaken.

As Shannon looked out the window one morning, she noticed a lone leaf hanging on tenaciously to the otherwise naked limbs of an old oak tree. The same day, her mother's pulse grew weaker, and she slipped into a coma.

Shannon longed to hear her mother's words once again—to feel the springtime of her voice and to whisper "I love you" again to her.

Outside the bedroom window, the lone leaf held on. Shannon wondered how it could keep from fluttering to the ground. An inner voice seemed to murmur the answer: *It needs to let go, and so do you.*

The next morning Shannon walked quietly into her mother's room, dreading to see her lifeless form. But her mom suddenly woke up, squeezed her daughter's hand, and said, "I love you, Shannon."

"Oh, Mom. I love you too."

And then, like a leaf that had clung too long, her mother released Shannon's hand—and she was gone.

As Shannon closed the drapes that afternoon, she realized the leaf had disappeared from the old oak tree. But in its place, a new bud was already forming. Shannon knew joy would blossom again. Like the promise of springtime, God would grow a new garden of hope in the fertile soil of Shannon's heart.

Love comforteth like sunshine after rain.

Secret Gardens

This land that was laid waste has become like the garden of Eden.

EZEKIEL 36:35

What BEAUTIFUL THING CAN I SHARE WITH SOMEONE ELSE TODAY?

The Secret Garden, by Frances Hodgson Burnett, beautifully illustrates the power of kindness and faith. Collin, the adolescent son of a rich, but grieving father who cannot rebound from his wife's death, lives his days as a demanding, selfish invalid. At first, Collin rejects the friendly gestures of Mary, his long-lost cousin. When young Mary discovers the key to a secret garden on the grounds of her uncle's estate, she also opens a hidden door to her own heart's joys. She immediately sets out to restore the garden's long-lost magic and beauty.

Little by little, Mary persuades Collin to take another step toward healing and unselfishness. Her stubborn persistence finally prevails on Collin to spend time outside in the restored garden, which had been lovingly planted by his late mother. Strength seeps back into the young boy's life and changes his saddened, bitter heart. The garden seems to work like magic on the young boy as he is restored, not only in body and spirit, but also in relationship with his distant father.

Untended souls can hide for years, as bitter thorns grow, choking out the life and obscuring the beauty that lies within. But as we gently clear away the rubble of the past and cut through the neglected gardens of people's hearts, we make a remarkable discovery—lives, sweet and beautiful, waiting to be filled with the divine fragrance of Heaven.

❦

To love abundantly is to live forever.

Black Mountain

Many are the plans in a man's heart, but it is the LORD's purpose that prevails.
PROVERBS 19:21

How CAN I
HELP RESTORE
A SPIRIT THAT
IS WOUNDED?

"I will just run away to Black Mountain!" screamed five-year-old Richard.

"Okay, if that's what you want, go ahead," responded his mother, opening the door and ushering him out to the front porch.

The silence descended on him like a cloak. The sun was long gone, and full night had settled upon the landscape. By the starlight he could just make out the dark form of Black Mountain to the north. Somewhere in the darkness, he heard the scurrying of a small animal and then the flap of wings in the night sky. Suddenly, his small heart was pounding in his chest, and his breath was coming quicker. Going to Black Mountain seemed like a really bad idea. He thought, *Why did I say that?*

He sat on the porch with his knees drawn up to his chest and arms clasped around them. A tear trickled down his cheek as he tried to fight off his fears.

From the kitchen, he heard his father ask, "Richard, would you like to come to supper with the rest of us now?"

Sometimes when we get angry with ourselves, others, circumstances, or even God, we want to run away. We stomp out our anger, and we make threats. We go out on the porch and pout. Yet, the Father waits patiently and even gently calls to us to rejoin the family. Love chases away fears, and restoration heals hurts.

Anger is quieted by a gentle word just as fire is quenched by water.

Time for Bed

Teach me thy way, O LORD.
PSALM 27:11 KJV

I am
IMPATIENT
TO BEGIN . . .

When children are around two years old, many of them decide that staying up past their regular bedtime is something worth creating havoc over. These little replicas of ourselves come up with every conceivable excuse to stay awake, no matter how tired they may actually be.

Parents read books, complain to their child's pediatrician, consult with their minister, whine to their own friends, and disagree with their spouse about the right way to handle this annoying situation. In some cases the child may gain the upper hand and stay up too late, smiling gleefully while sitting between Mom and Daddy on the sofa, watching TV, and eating popcorn.

At this stage in their lives, two-year-olds are test-driving their ability to assert their own opinions and desires, the first step to autonomy. It is the parents' responsibility to guide those desires with a balance of freedom and discipline. Physiologically, two-year-olds need more sleep than ten-year-olds or thirty-year-olds. Their growing bodies need time to rest in order to properly support each day's whirlwind of activity. The privilege of staying up later truly is something that can be earned only with time.

Like toddlers, sometimes we want something that we are not yet prepared to handle. We might not like it much, but sometimes we just have to trust God to know what is best for us. If we ask God for wisdom in balancing our lives, He is sure to help us.

Don't try to hold God's hand;
let Him hold yours. Let Him do
the holding, and you the trusting.

Let Me Do It by Myself!

Train up a child in the way he should go,
even when he is old he will not depart from it.
PROVERBS 22:6 NASB

When HAVE I
SAID TO GOD,
"LET ME DO IT,"
AND WHAT
HAPPENED?

Five-year-old Lili would often fluctuate from "Let me do it by myself" to "Mommy, help me," in a matter of moments. Tying her shoes, buttoning her sweater, pouring her milk, riding her bicycle, and brushing her hair seemed to be her rites of passage.

Her mother seldom knew whether it was all right to lend unsolicited assistance or to let the youngster work independently. When safety was an issue, the answer was obvious. "No, honey. Mommy has to help you with baking cookies (or crossing the street), because I don't want you to get hurt. When you're bigger, you can do this by yourself." Because Lili was allowed many opportunities to do the safe things on her own, it helped to take the sting out of the temporary no she got on the unsafe ones.

We say no to our children because we love them. And when the time is right, we can also say yes because we love them. It takes wisdom and knowledge to train a child. No might be the best answer to a request today, but it might change to a yes tomorrow after some instruction and practice.

From that first no-no spoken to a toddler who is about to touch a hot stove, to that moment when we reluctantly slip the car keys into our teen's hand, are tucked away years of training. If we have taught and loved our children well, we can confidently say, "Yes, you and God can do it by yourselves."

Confidence is a plant of slow growth.

What Am I Known For?

*"Every tree is known by his own fruit.
For of thorns men do not gather figs, nor
of a bramble bush gather they grapes."*
LUKE 6:44 KJV

I need TO KEEP THE PROMISE THAT I MADE TO MYSELF TO . . .

"What does it matter what other people think of me? I don't care about them anyway!" Rebecca blurted out to her mom. "Why are you so concerned that I finish the service project in Girl Scouts, anyway? I'm gonna quit Scouts next year, and besides I already have plenty of badges."

"Scouting and badges are not the issues," her mother replied. "I'm concerned with you and what you are known for. You care deeply for the welfare of others. You made a commitment to the people at the assisted living facility, and many of them look forward to your visiting them. It's just hard for me to see you not keeping a promise."

"But, I'm tired of going up there every Saturday," Rebecca said.

Her mother suggested that they find a way to reduce some of her time commitment without abandoning the promise. Before long, Rebecca felt that she could complete the commitment without giving up all of her free time.

Later she commented to a friend that she hoped she would always live up to her mom's belief in her to be caring, compassionate, and trustworthy.

We are known more by what we do than by what we say. Sometimes commitments are overwhelming, particularly during the holidays or when pressures at work, home, church, or community seem to stretch us to the limit. Setting priorities and living by them—and most importantly, asking God for wisdom—will help us keep our promises without losing our heart.

❧

*Nothing is particularly hard if you
divide it into small jobs.*

Walking in the Garden

They heard the sound of the Lord God walking in the garden.
GENESIS 3:8 NASB

My FAVORITE
TIME TO
SPEND WITH
GOD IS . . .

Sleeping in was not a common occurrence for Patti growing up on a farm, not even during summer vacation from school. But Patti's mother allowed her children to sleep in once in a great while. On those rare occasions, Patti awakened gently to the smells and sounds of her mother lovingly preparing a delicious family breakfast. The aroma of sizzling bacon frying wafted through the house. Fresh biscuits baking in the oven provided gentle nudges to help the children shake off their slumber.

One summer morning, the house was still. Patti's brothers and sisters were sound asleep, and the kitchen was void of the usual sights, sounds, and smells of meal preparation. Patti noticed that the back door was open, and she slowly eased her way out to the back porch. There she caught a glimpse of her mother weeding the garden, humming all the while. The peaceful scene wrapped itself around Patti like a cozy blanket as she watched her mother walking in the garden.

Adam and Eve lived in a perfect garden. They could commune with nature freely, and they walked and talked with the Lord face-to-face. They heard His sounds as He walked in the garden toward them. In her spirit, Patti's mother must have known the sweetness of God's presence as she walked in her garden early in the morning. Before the demands of her day busied her hands and her mind, she wisely chose the morning quiet for a peaceful walk with God in the garden.

❧

Sweet is the garden, white with bloom,
Heavy with honey, drenched with scent.

A Season of Love

Sons are a heritage from the LORD,
children a reward from him.
PSALM 127:3

If I COULD
SPEND A
DAY WITH
MY CHILD,
WHERE WOULD
I LIKE TO GO?

In his book *Fatherhood,* Bill Cosby shares his humorous views on parenting:

We . . . did not have (children) because we thought would be fun to see one of them sit in a chair and stick out his leg so that another one of them running by was launched like Explorer I.

After which I said to the child who was the launching pad, "Why did you do that?"

"Do what?" he replied.

"Stick out your leg."

"Dad, I didn't know my leg was going out. My leg, it does that a lot."

Cosby says, "If you cannot function in a world where things like this are said, then you better forget about raising children and go to daffodils."[72]

In fact, raising children is a lot like growing daffodils. Children, like those colorful bulbs, will bloom where they are planted. But they only bloom for a season.

Just ask Bill Cosby. In spite of his tongue-in-cheek tales about parenting, he loved his son Ennis dearly but was granted only a season in which to enjoy him. An apparent robber killed Ennis in the prime of his youth.

Our children are God's gifts to us. Though they move out of our homes, they will never grow out of the garden of our hearts. Like spring daffodils, the memories of their childhood reappear continually.

Enjoy them while you can.

Love every day. Each one is so
short and they are so few.

Holy Laughter

*He will yet fill your mouth with laughter
and your lips with shouts of joy.*
JOB 8:21

When I HEAR
CHILDREN'S
LAUGHTER,
IT MAKES
ME FEEL...

The air was filled with peals of laughter along with giggles of delight and chortles of joy. Just hearing it made Ron's day better. His mother, Irene, had run a licensed day-care facility in their home for as long as he could remember, and dozens of children from single-parent households benefited from her unconditional love. In fact, it was easy to think of their home as an oasis of love in a world lacking in it.

Ron remembered the December morning when four-year-old Louis came in from the cold and quite seriously said, "It's winter out there, Reen (short for Irene)!" as he struggled to pull his arms free from his heavy coat.

Or there was the time when Jeffrey came by to visit and hand-deliver an invitation to his high school graduation. "Grandma Reen" had cared for him throughout his elementary school years. Ron remembered Jeffrey coming from school each day of third grade. He and his best friend would exit the school with their arms draped around one another's shoulders, and they would walk that way all the way to the car.

Many, many other memories existed. But the best, without a doubt, was that of the joyous laughter of the children as they played together. There was something so natural and carefree about the sound that anyone who heard it would know that this place was a world of safety and love—thanks to "Grandma Reen."

*Laughter is the most beautiful and beneficial
therapy God ever granted humanity.*

Nights with Mom

I have been reminded of your sincere faith,
which first lived in your grandmother
Lois and in your mother Eunice.

2 TIMOTHY 1:5

Saturday evenings had a special, even magical quality to them for young Kevin. In fact, he could hardly wait for them to come. The routine was nearly always the same, and it made his world safe and predictable.

First, the family would share a casual supper together. This meal would nearly always be home-made hamburgers, French fries, and cold pork and beans. The table would include condiments for the hamburgers, napkins for the milk mustaches, and conversation for the heart. It was a time of love and closeness. To this day, homemade hamburgers remind Kevin of his childhood.

After supper, he would polish everyone's Sunday dress shoes at one end of the kitchen table, while at the other end his mother prepared her Sunday school lesson for the next day.

She taught a class for young children, so she used flannel-graph characters to tell the Bible stories. As she cut out the characters and rehearsed the lessons, Kevin would listen in; the stories seemed to come alive. He saw David slay Goliath, Joseph sold into slavery by his brothers, Moses leading the Israelites across the Red Sea, and many more great events so vital to the Christian heritage and faith.

It is simply amazing how much of Kevin's own faith story was learned right there as he polished shoes and listened to his mother. To this day, the smell of shoe polish brings back warm memories and bolsters his faith.

Faith is not belief without proof,
but trust without reservations.

A smell
FROM MY
CHILDHOOD
THAT BRINGS
BACK A SWEET
MEMORY IS . . .

Growing in Wisdom

*A wise man will hear and increase in learning, and
a man of understanding will acquire wise counsel.*
PROVERBS 1:5 NASB

A skill
I WOULD LIKE
TO LEARN IS . . .

After their wedding, the young couple prepared for their move from Ireland to America. It meant leaving their families behind and starting from scratch in a new country, but they were committed for the long haul. Although many from their village came and settled close to them, it didn't take long for the newlyweds to realize that the man's trade would not allow him to provide for his family. What could have been the justification for a speedy retreat back to Dublin was, instead, the fuel that fired the determination to learn a new skill and prove he could provide for his family against all odds.

He and his wife agreed that Christ would be their Strength and Guide for the uphill battle that lay ahead. They decided that until a new skill was mastered, everything else had to take a backseat to their love and devotion to God and to each other.

The man bought a used typewriter, an adding machine, and several textbooks. After his regular job ended every day, he would sit until the wee hours of the next morning, studying, pecking away at both machines until he had taught himself how to type proficiently and how to do the work of a master accountant.

His work became so well-known that for the rest of his life he was in constant demand. He left a legacy to his children and others of a man who was willing to listen, learn, and grow in wisdom.

*True wisdom consists not only
in seeing what is before our eyes,
but in foreseeing what is to come.*

Field of Dreams

Hope deferred makes the heart sick, but a longing fulfilled is a tree of life.
PROVERBS 13:12

I would LIKE TO BE ABLE TO HELP . . .

There was nothing special about Randy. Each year his teachers repeated the same words: "You don't want Randy in your class. He's a loser."

But that was before he entered Miss Jewel's sixth-grade art class. Miss Jewel saw the sparkle in Randy's eyes when he watched her demonstrations. His huge, rough fingers took to a paintbrush like an athlete to sports. Charcoals, clay, watercolor, oils—whatever the project, he excelled beyond any student Miss Jewel had ever seen.

She challenged him to take private lessons and suggested the names of several artists she knew. Randy made excuses for not pursuing the lessons, but she suspected it was because of his family's poverty.

The teacher decided to make Randy her special project. On his graduation from high school, she sent him an anonymous check to cover his college tuition—and the name of an artist who agreed to teach him in the summers.

One day about ten years later, she received a package in the mail—a beautiful oil painting of herself and a note with these words: "I will never forget you. I have dedicated my life to helping others grow their dreams like you did for me. Thank you, Randy."

God may give each of us "Randys" to nurture—perhaps children, friends, students, or coworkers. Our words, our time, even our belief in their abilities could help produce a crop of doctors, musicians, presidents, or simply loving Moms and Dads who will rise in their own "field of dreams."

Quality is never an accident; it is always the result of intelligent effort.

Garden-Variety Players

Now you are the body of Christ,
and each one of you is a part of it.
1 CORINTHIANS 12:27

As a TEAM
MEMBER,
HOW CAN I
HELP OUR
TEAM WIN?

Daron dreamed of playing basketball. He practiced daily. His dad bought a backboard and goal, and together they shot hoops. In his freshman year, Daron didn't make the team. Discouraged, but refusing to quit, he kept practicing. He hung around after school and watched the guys practice. In his sophomore year, he made the team but sat on the bench most of the year.

As a junior, Daron finally became a regular on the starting lineup. Although he could hit 75 percent of his shots, the coach rarely changed the rules: "Get the ball to Jim—as much as you can." Jim was the star of most games. He won the Most Valuable Player every year for three years and received a complete scholarship to a nearby college.

Daron expected no scholarship. After all, he was just a garden-variety player. One day a coach from a prestigious university out of state called him, offering him a full scholarship.

"Why would you want me?" Daron asked.

"We've watched videos of you and your team in action, and we're impressed with your team skills. Lots of guys can be a star. But it takes a team—and a team player—to win successive games."

We may feel like "garden variety" Christians, being used in only small ways. We wonder how we could be making a difference. But God is not in the business of recruiting "star" players. What He wants is a faithful heart, willing to serve Him as Heaven's team player.

Faithfulness in little things is a big thing.

The Art of Cultivation

The secrets of his heart will be laid bare.

1 CORINTHIANS 14:25

What GOOD
THINGS IS
GOD WAITING
TO PLANT IN
MY HEART? IS
MY HEART'S
SOIL READY?

"What's this, Grandpa?" asked ten-year-old Samantha. She was exploring the contents of the garage and had come across a very strange device. It had a long handle like a rake or shovel, but on the end was a round rubber wheel with a funny attachment consisting of two interlocking circles of steel teeth. When she tried to roll it on the concrete floor, the steel teeth prevented the rubber wheel from touching the floor, and it made an awful racket.

Turning from his workbench, Grandpa Bill smiled. "Sweetheart, that's a cultivator, and it's used in our garden. Those teeth break up the surface of the soil and uproot weeds, allowing water and nutrients to get to the roots of our vegetables."

"Wow, Grandpa, that's neat. Our Sunday school teacher was telling us the story of how a man's enemy put bad seeds in his wheat, and then weeds grew up. If they would have had a cultivator, they could have removed the weeds without waiting until the harvest."

"Yes, you're right," Bill replied. "The hard soil and weeds in my life need cultivating too. Sometimes I have to clean 'spiritual weeds' out of my life."

"I never thought of it that way before, Grandpa. When I do wrong and then I feel bad, is God just getting my attention now so I can do it better next time?"

"Yes," Grandpa Bill replied. "He uproots the bad weeds in our hearts and breaks up the soil so He can plant good things."

God wills us free, man wills us slaves,
I will as God wills, God's will be done.

Freedom to Dance

It is for freedom that Christ has set us free.
Stand firm, then, and do not let yourselves
be burdened again by a yoke of slavery.
GALATIANS 5:1

God HAS
GIVEN ME
FREEDOM
TO DO . . .

As a child, Ellen loved her Uncle Merrill's garden. The plants that captured her attention most were the hundreds of white gladioli planted in long, straight rows just like Uncle Merrill's sweet corn. It frustrated Ellen, however, when a breeze forced the tall, slender flowers to sway out of position. She preferred to see them standing tall and erect instead of dancing in the breeze.

As Ellen grew into adulthood, she tried to make her life perfect like Uncle Merrill's rows of sweet corn instead of his dancing gladioli. She tried with all her might to march a narrow, straight line, but she constantly swayed out of the rigid position.

One day in utter frustration, she cried out to God, "I can't do it! These rules are too heavy a burden." After a good cry, she decided to go see Uncle Merrill.

Ellen sat in her car a long time watching Uncle Merrill's white gladioli weave back and forth in the breeze. Slowly she began to see that although the flowers freely danced in the sunshine, they remained firmly rooted in the soil. Those stalks of glorious white blossoms proclaimed to her a joyous message. If her heart is firmly rooted in Christ, she is free to rejoice in her faith. When Ellen attempted to abide by a lengthy list of harsh rules, she realized she was choosing slavery when God had already set her free.

Love is never satisfied with doing
or giving anything but the best.

Planting for a Lifetime

"You are the light of the world."
MATTHEW 5:14

Eight-year-old Ray looked with open adoration and love at his pastor. He was an unremarkable man in many ways—small and thin, with a wisp of hair on top of his head. To Ray, though, Pastor Majors was right next to God in holiness. He was gentle, with a kind, loving heart, and with his eyes closed, he now played hymns on his harmonica.

Pastor Majors could recite any verse in the entire Bible. God had blessed him with a "photographic memory" of the Holy Scripture. He never read aloud from the Bible; he only recited it. One Sunday evening he shared a story from his own youth that planted seeds of faith and courage in Ray's heart—seeds that would grow in his heart for a lifetime.

"I was in high school when I broke my neck," the pastor said. "I was on the top of a school bus packing the band instruments to leave on a trip when I fell off and landed on my head. It was my faith in God that allowed me to recover and play music again."

The story of his pastor's faith as a teenager helped Ray grow faith in his own heart over the course of his lifetime.

We never know when what we say will have a life-lasting impact. Henry George said, "Let no man imagine that he has no influence."[73] We cannot stop our influence, but we can choose which types of seeds we will plant.

Faith is power to believe and power to see.

I want TO SHARE THE STORY OF WHEN I . . .

The Birthday

The righteous shall flourish.
PSALM 92:12 KJV

I have
PROGRESSED
OVER THE
SPIRITUAL
OBSTACLE
OF . . .

Eleven-year-old Will hurried ahead of the rest of the party as they arrived at the restaurant for dinner to celebrate his mother's birthday. When everyone else came through the door, he had already spoken to the hostess, informing her that they would need a table for a party of seven in the nonsmoking section. The table was waiting, and the group quickly sat down. Throughout the dinner, Will, seated between his two grandfathers, was engaging and polite. He and his grandfathers seemed to share a secret as they whispered to each other off and on during dinner. He smiled often at his mother and winked knowingly.

Finally, as dinner came to a conclusion, the waiter arrived at the table with a serving of cheese-cake topped with fresh berries for Will's mother. Coffee cups were refilled and fresh forks provided as she shared the wonderful dessert with her family. Will, grinning, giggling, and outright laughing, clapped his hands and said, "Now you know why I was winking, don't ya, Mom!"

Later Will's parents commented on what a delightful young man he was becoming. It hardly seemed possible that this was the same little boy who, just a few short years earlier, had been so shy and withdrawn that you could barely get him to say hello to a waiter.

Spiritual growth is just like that too. When we surround ourselves with other believers, study God's Word, attend worship, and pray faithfully, we cannot help but grow in the Lord.

❧

*We can never be lilies in the garden
unless we have spent time as
bulbs in the dark, totally ignored.*

Faulty but Familiar

In all the travels of the Israelites,
whenever the cloud lifted from above
the tabernacle, they would set out.
EXODUS 40:36

"The Israelites had this cloud, Mom," Ellie's six-year-old exclaimed as the children tumbled into the car after Sunday school. "It was bigger than a thunderhead."

"Yeah, and at night it had fire in it brighter than a streetlight, so no one had to be afraid of the dark," echoed Ellie's timid four-year-old as she recalled the details of the Bible story they had heard.

"Every time the cloud moved, the people had to move," the six-year-old continued. "That would be great. You wouldn't be stuck in the same camp-ground for forty years!"

Their spirited chattering continued on the short drive home as they shared that the Israelites never knew how long they would be in one campsite. Whenever God's cloud began to move, the Israelites were required to pack up and move too.

As Ellie walked into her kitchen that day, she took a close look at the linoleum that was gouged in places and the cupboards that were in need of another coat of paint. The contents of the over-filled trash can formed a precarious pyramid. The faucet still dripped annoyingly, and the dishes from breakfast sat piled on the counter. Yet with all its faults and peculiarities, it was home.

As her family bustled off to their rooms, Ellie sat down quietly at the kitchen table. "Thank You, God, for my kitchen," she said aloud. "I don't care if it does have drips and gouges and flaws. At least it's a kitchen that stays in one place!"

Home, the spot of earth supremely blest,
A dearer, sweeter spot than all the rest.

Father,
TODAY I
WANT TO
THANK YOU
FOR . . .

Everyone's a Critic

Let those also who suffer according to the will of God entrust their souls to a faithful Creator in doing what is right.

1 PETER 4:19 NASB

Father,
I NEED
COURAGE
TO GO
AGAINST MAN'S
OPINION
TO ACCOM-
PLISH . . .

Winston Churchill exemplified integrity and respect in the face of opposition. During his last year in office, he attended an official ceremony. Several rows behind him two gentlemen began whispering, "That's Winston Churchill. They say he is getting senile. They say he should step aside and leave the running of the nation to more dynamic and capable men."

When the ceremony ended, Churchill turned to the men and said, "Gentlemen, they also say he is deaf!"[74]

Most people find it difficult to ignore the brunt of public opinion. It's easier to do things they don't want to do, or not do what they feel is right, rather than stand up for their own desires and convictions. One writer called it "worshipping the god of other people's opinion."

In the words of Ralph Waldo Emerson:

Whatever you do, you need courage. Whatever course you decide upon, there is always someone to tell you, you are wrong. There are always difficulties arising that tempt you to believe that your critics are right. To map out a course of action and follow it to an end requires some of the same courage that a soldier needs. Peace has its victories, but it takes brave people to win them.

Ignoring the god of other people's opinion requires strength and focus. Fortunately, we know the God who can grant us that strength and stand with us as we pursue the paths we feel are right. His opinion is the only one that counts.

❧

Take courage. We walk in the wilderness today and in the Promised Land tomorrow.

A Package or a Gift?

*The gift of God is eternal life
in Christ Jesus our Lord.*
ROMANS 6:23

What GIFT
HAS GOD
GIVEN ME
THAT I HAVE
NOT BEGUN
TO USE?

A gaily-wrapped package rested on the kitchen counter. Having spent several days looking for just the right birthday present, Leslie knew her daughter would be pleased with the contents of the box. As she and her friends streamed through the back door after school, Leslie heard their exclamations—"Open it, Steph! It must be for you!"

She joined the excited girls and smiled at the surprised look on her daughter's face. "It's so pretty; I almost hate to open it," her daughter said. "Maybe I should wait until later."

"No!" her friends cried, urging her to open the package immediately to see what was inside.

Armed with their encouragement, Stephanie grinned and tore off the wrappings. Prying open the small box, she gasped and quickly gave her mother a kiss. "It's just what I wanted!" she cried as she pulled the stuffed animal out of the tissue paper and showed the cuddly canine to her friends.

Stephanie's reaction reminded Leslie of the way she had been approaching God lately—hesitant to open the packages He wanted to give her every day. God offers us so many gifts—the gift of grace, the gift of peace, the gift of talents and abilities, the gift of love, the gift of eternal life. All too often we stand and stare at His packages and comment on how nice they are. Isn't it time to start opening those packages and enjoying the gifts inside?

A joy that's shared is a joy made double.

SEPTEMBER 2

*Trust in the Lord with all your heart and
lean not on your own understanding;
in all your ways acknowledge him, and
he will make your paths straight.*
PROVERBS 3:5-6

A small
MIRACLE IN
MY LIFE
HAPPENED . . .

Jocelyn didn't look like the average person who used food stamps. She was dressed for an office job in a nice dress and heels. She felt people staring at her as she paid for her groceries, but she also knew that the stamps were God's provision. Without them, she would not be able to feed her family. She worked hard at the best job she could get but it just wasn't enough.

That same year, she had needed emergency surgery for an ovarian cyst. The doctors were afraid it was cancerous, while she was more afraid of the hospital bill. Explaining her dilemma to the doctor, she learned that the welfare system would cover her unexpected expenses.

The same week that Jocelyn needed surgery, one of her sons was hospitalized with what appeared to be spinal meningitis. The doctors thought it would be dangerous to put off her surgery. So she and her eleven-year-old son ended up in hospitals some fifteen miles apart. And because they were new to the area, there was no one to talk to, or visit, her young son—not even her.

"Lord," Jocelyn prayed, "please help me to talk to my son."

When she told her doctor about her situation, he had her moved to a semi-private room, where a phone waited beside her bed—all at the doctor's expense.

Put your trust in your loving Father, and boldly ask Him for help. He will take care of you.

❦

*If we love Christ much,
surely we shall trust Him much.*

Soul Hunger

The city has no need of the sun nor of the moon to give light to it, for the splendor and radiance (glory) of God illuminate it, and the Lamb is its lamp.

REVELATION 21:23 AMP

Despite endless cloudy days this spring, the columbines still managed to bloom. Blue, scarlet, and gold bell-shaped flowers with delicate dangling spurs towered over lacy foliage. They danced gracefully in the breeze, their bright colors attracting hummingbirds. Yet, without God's sun, they didn't seem as radiant as in previous springs.

It is the same with humans. Although we follow our genetic codes and grow into healthy people physically, we have no radiance without the Son of God. The windows of our souls appear cloudy, and God's love cannot shine through us.

Just as columbines hunger for the sun's warm rays, our souls hunger for the loving presence of Jesus. Unlike the columbines, however, we can find the Son even on cloudy days of despair.

We can take action to find the Son by simply reading or listening to His Word and obeying it. We can meet Him in a flower garden, where each stem and blossom appears like a signpost to His presence. We can hear His praises being sung by the rustle of leaves held in the tree's uplifted branches.

Getting to know Him in a personal way enlightens our souls. His radiance fills our hearts and enlivens our spirits with hope for eternal life with Him in Heaven.

In Heaven, the sun will not be needed because God himself will be our Light. Perhaps Heaven's columbines will always dance with radiance from the glow of God's glory.

If I COULD NOT HAVE THE WRITTEN BIBLE, I WOULD FIND GOD IN . . .

❧

The glory of God, and, as our only means to glorifying Him, the salvation of human souls, is the real business of life.

Tending His Flock

He tends his flock like a shepherd: He gathers the lambs in his arms and carries them close to his heart; he gently leads those that have young.
ISAIAH 40:11

I know I CAN
TRUST GOD
BECAUSE . . .

Eight-year-old Jonathan was always tempting fate. His mother often held her breath when she heard him call, "Hey, Mom, watch me!"

One day, Jonathan was riding his bike at breakneck speed downhill beside the house. At the bottom of the hill was his swing set, minus the swings. His mother watched in disbelief as her son raced down the hill, stood on the bicycle seat, then grabbed the top bar of the swing set.

She stifled a scream as he quickly flipped over the top of the bar and landed flat on his back on the cold, hard ground. It seemed to take forever for her to reach her son, who was uncharacteristically quiet. Gently, she lifted him in her arms, carried him back to the house.

Jonathan was breathing hard after having the breath knocked out of him. His mother wasted no time in dialing the doctor's office. While the pediatrician's phone rang, Jonathan said, "Mom, I'm not hurt. I'm all right."

Looking over his arms and legs, she was surprised to see where Jonathan had circled, with a ballpoint pen, every hurt, scar, scrape, and bruise.

"What's all this?" she asked.

Jonathan sat up on the sofa, beaming. "That's all my hurts. I put a circle around all of them," he said.

We may never know how many times God's providential hand has prevented an injury, either physical or emotional, in our lives. What a blessing to know He is ever tending His flock and protecting His lambs!

If God maintains sun and planets in bright and ordered beauty, He can keep us.

Send in the Clowns

Whatever you do, work at it with all your heart,
as working for the Lord, not for men.
COLOSSIANS 3:23

The FUNNI-
EST THING
THAT HAS
HAPPENED TO
ME WAS . . .

Sheila noticed posters going up all over town, announcing that the circus was coming. Lion tamers, wire-walkers, trapeze artists and of course, those most anticipated performers—the clowns—were on their way!.

Clowns work hard at their profession. In fact, in order to travel with the Ringling Brothers Circus, clowns must successfully complete clown college—an intense course of study that covers everything from makeup to pratfalls, costuming to making balloon animals, juggling to sleight of hand.

As Sheila stood at the stove sautéing vegetables for supper, she sensed a connection to this group of performers in the circus. Though she didn't wear a clown costume or clown makeup, she worked hard at juggling—balancing her time among home, family, work, friends, and church. She wasn't skilled at card tricks or sleight of hand, but she could work "magic," transforming everyday grocery items into flavorful meals seven days a week. And while she might not know the ins and outs of balloon-animal art, she made lots of other things, from costumes for school plays to crafty Christmas gifts and decorated birthday cakes. And she had taken many a fall—not pratfalls, but real falls—when she'd gone in-line skating with the children or walked the dog on icy sidewalks.

God's Word says that we are to work at whatever we do with all our hearts, whether we're clowns or cooks, minstrels or mothers. And when we do, we might just provide our friends and families with some laughter along the way!

Lord, turn the routines of work
into the celebrations of love.

Perfect Landing

She is clothed with strength and dignity;
she can laugh at the days to come.
PROVERBS 31:25

Am I ABLE
TO LAUGH AT
MY OWN
MISTAKES?

Betty was normally a pretty good cook. She could prepare some delicious meals for her family, as long as they didn't want anything too difficult. One day, however, her husband asked her to make biscuits for dinner. She had never attempted such a feat before, but with determination as her guide, she went to the grocery store to buy the ingredients. Luckily, there was a recipe on the flour bag. As she gathered all the ingredients, she dreamed of the lightest, fluffiest biscuits ever.

When she arrived home, she placed the ingredients before her, and began the process of biscuit preparation. The biscuits even smelled great as they cooked. Betty called her starving family to dinner before she removed the biscuits from the oven. While she stirred the stew, she asked her husband to take the pan out of the oven and place it on the table.

The kids looked at one another in disbelief as their father followed his wife's instructions and placed the pan of biscuits on the hot pad. The biscuits were as flat as pancakes. Her family's eyes focused on her as she reached down and picked up a biscuit.

"What's that, Mom?" her youngest daughter asked.

"A Frisbee!" she shouted, and she sailed the biscuit across the room. Laughter broke the tense silence. The ability to turn a disaster into a comical situation is one we could all learn. There's enough in life to be serious about, so learn to laugh as often as you can!

Laughter is the joyous universal
evergreen of life.

Kitchen Sabotage!

God is not a God of disorder but of peace.

1 CORINTHIANS 14:33

Kathleen's kitchen cupboards and drawers were a mess. Cupboards overflowed with mismatched dishes, receipts, expired prescriptions, and empty bottles of cough medicine. Twist ties, clothespins, and rubber bands cluttered the silverware drawer. There was no doubt about it—her kitchen had been sabotaged by the excesses of daily life!

When her husband announced an upcoming camping trip, Kathleen sensed an opportunity to undo some of the damage to the kitchen. She helped pack food, swimming supplies, sleeping bags, flashlights, toys, and the clothes needed for a weekend in the woods. But when the time came for the car and camper to pull out of the driveway, she was not aboard. She turned back to the house to face the kitchen-clutter monster!

Armed with cleaning supplies, trash bags, and new shelf paper, Kathleen went to work. Soon she had unloaded the contents of the cupboards onto the kitchen table and the hallway floor. Time flew by, and she barely stopped to eat. But the interiors of those cupboards smelled fresh and clean, and the only items allowed back were things that were supposed to be there. Then she tackled the drawers.

When Kathleen finished, the cupboards were done. The drawers were organized. The counters were clear. Her body ached, but it felt good. She had taken a disorganized mess and made it into a useful kitchen once again.

Is there an area of your home or life that has been sabotaged by the excesses of life?

Our life is frittered away by detail . . . simplify, simplify.

I can
IMPROVE MY
OUTLOOK
BY ORGAN-
IZING . . .

Penny Bear

*They will lay up treasure for themselves
as a firm foundation for the coming age.*
1 TIMOTHY 6:19

How COULD
I SAVE SO AS TO
HAVE TO
SHARE WITH
OTHERS?

In the 1950s, a honey distributor packaged its honey in a glass bottle shaped like a baby bear. Grandma used this brand of honey in her cooking, and she quickly used up the contents. The bottle was too pretty to throw away, so she put the bottle to use as a penny jar.

Her grandchildren loved to count the pennies in Grandma's "penny bear." They'd pour the penny bear's contents onto the kitchen table and make neat stacks of pennies. Then they'd write the date and the total amount of pennies on a small slip of paper and tuck it into the penny bear's lid. Whenever the penny bear was full, Grandma took it to the bank and put the pennies into a savings account. The empty penny bear reappeared on the kitchen counter with a clean slip of paper in its lid.

When Grandma's oldest granddaughter began preparations for college, she noticed a piece of paper sticking out of the top of the empty penny bear. She picked up the bottle and discovered that the paper was a check for the total cost of her books for her first semester at college. Because of Grandma's penny-saving habits, there was enough money in the penny bear account to buy her college textbooks for that first semester and for several more years.

Now whenever her granddaughter finds a penny on the ground, she thanks God for Grandma's faithful stewardship.

❧

Whoever is capable of giving is rich.

Volcano Stew

Rejoice in the Lord always.
I will say it again: Rejoice!
PHILIPPIANS 4:4

I could SAVE
TIME IF I
SLOWED
DOWN
ENOUGH
TO . . .

Candy was running late getting home from work again. She finally stumbled into the house muttering apologies and grabbed the pot of leftover stew from the refrigerator. Slamming it on the stove, she flipped on the burner and rushed to change into some comfortable clothes while hollering, "Someone please set the table!"

A few minutes later when she rushed back into the kitchen, her nose sensed disaster. The stove! The pot of stew she had placed on the burner was a bubbling imitation of Mount Vesuvius. Tall columns of tomato-red sauce spurted into the air above the pot. Pieces of vegetables spewed over its sides.

Candy shrieked, and her family hurried into the kitchen. The pot was boiling so furiously that it was impossible to turn the burner off without being spattered by the tomato-sauce columns. The foaming vegetables were spilling over so quickly that no one could grab the pot's handles without getting burned. But someone had to try. Amid exclamations of "Ouch!" "Hey, that's hot!" and "Yeow!" hands reached from all directions and eased the pot from its heat source.

Quickly Candy switched the burner off and surveyed the kitchen. Stew had splattered everywhere, and everyone's hands were covered with the sticky red goo. Her oldest child broke the silence. With a glint in her eye, she licked the stew from her hands and said, "Good dinner, Mom."

The laughter that accompanied the cleanup that night echoed with the Bible's admonition to always rejoice.

A good laugh is sunshine in a house.

Teenage Trauma

*Charm can be deceptive and beauty
doesn't last, but a woman who fears
and reverences God shall be greatly praised.*
PROVERBS 31:30 TLB

A topic THAT
MY TEENAGER
IS INTERESTED
IN IS . . .

"But, Mom, all the girls are wearing black lipstick!" her teenage daughter cried.

"I don't care if they're wearing blue lipstick," Carol screamed. "You are not going out of this house dressed like a witch!"

Rachel stomped her foot and flounced out of the kitchen, and Carol winced as she heard her daughter slam the bedroom door. First it was miniskirts and a pierced nose, and now this.

Remember when you wore miniskirts and white go-go boots? the still, small voice of God reminded her. *Remember pale pink lipstick and bare midriffs?*

Yes, Lord, she argued inside, *but You don't approve of her rebellion, do You?*

God seemed to answer, *I loved you even when you were yet in sin.*

Carol did love her daughter, despite Rachel's outrageous behavior . . . and she had to admit, she had done some stupid things when she was a teenager.

"Rachel," she said, tapping at the door. "Can we talk?"

"Go away!" her daughter sobbed.

"Please?" Gently, Carol opened the door and sat down on the bed beside her daughter. "I love you, you know. That's why I care so much."

Rachel rolled away from her mother and said, "All you care about is what your friends will say!"

"Right now, all I care about is what you have to say. Talk to me."

Every teenager is unique and special, yet every teenager needs the same things: love, discipline, and understanding. Start a dialogue with your teenager today.

The first duty of love is to listen.

Let's Try It Again!

A heart at peace gives life to the body.
PROVERBS 14:30

Misty held her big brother's hand in a vise-like grip. Her eyes widened as she took in the incredible scene playing out before her. There, atop the best sledding hill in all of Connecticut, her eighty-year-old grandmother was preparing for the ride of her life.

Poised on the toboggan, she sat as royalty, her long fur coat wrapped around her legs and her fur cap pinned perfectly into place. A small push on the snow with her elegant gloved hand . . . and she was off.

Halfway down the hill, the toboggan toppled to the side, and Misty watched in horror as her grandmother did an amazing acrobatic move through the snow, tumbling three times before sliding to a halt midway. Running full tilt to the rescue, Misty arrived breathless before a disheveled lump of fur.

Rosy cheeks appeared beneath a fur cap that was relocated to cover one ear. Snow was encrusted in the hair surrounding her face, and her bright, mischievous eyes met Misty's fearful gaze. With the confident laugh of one who loves God and knows of His care, Grandmother grabbed hold of Misty's hand and said, "Again! Let's try it again!"

If you ask, God will give you the confidence to step into life's adventures, knowing that His hand will always be there to catch you.

❧

*Confidence in the natural world
is self-reliance, in the spiritual
world it is God-reliance.*

It would TAKE A BIG DOSE OF COURAGE FOR ME TO TRY . . .

Realistic Expectations

The Lord has compassion on those who fear him;
for he knows how we are formed.
PSALMS 103:13-14

I want TO BE
MORE LIKE
JESUS. WHO
ALWAYS
SEEMS . . .

"Watch out! Can't you be more careful?" It seemed lately like Jackie had been saying those words far too often to her six-year-old, Katie. This time her daughter's love of ketchup had resulted in a large tomato stain on a brand-new tablecloth. It had been a long day already, and Jackie's temper flared as the angry words escaped her lips. But as the words tumbled out, she saw Katie's quivering lip and a tear slip out of the corner of her eye.

Jackie felt terrible. Sure, the bottle had fallen over, but her daughter had not intentionally made a mountain of ketchup on the table. It was an accident. Jackie had responded inappropriately and barked an angry response without thinking.

She stopped wiping the stain and reached across the table to give her child a hug. And then she looked her straight in the eye and said, "I'm sorry I yelled at you. Will you forgive Mommy?"

Her daughter's tear-stained face nodded a reply, and they sat locked in a soggy embrace for several seconds.

Later, while finishing the dishes, Jackie thought about how easy it was to forget that Katie was only six years old. She often expected her to behave as if she were nine or ten.

Thankfully, God isn't like that. He remembers how He made us. And in His compassion, He never expects more from us than He knows we can do or be.

Have a heart that never hardens,
a temper that never tires, and
a touch that never hurts.

Peace at Last

"Peace I leave with you; my peace I give you. I do not give to you as the world gives. Do not let your hearts be troubled and do not be afraid."

JOHN 14:27

With a throbbing headache, Diane prepared breakfast for her children and made a mental note of all the people she needed to contact. Her aunt in the nursing home. Her single neighbor down the street. But she just didn't have the time! Diane thought of a friend who had just lost her mother. A simple card could say so much.

Her thoughts were interrupted by the telephone. Her prayer partner told her that a man in their church had just suffered a heart attack. So many needs, and so little time!

"If only I had time to take care of all these things, Lord," she whispered.

In a few minutes, the kids were gone, and silence filled the house. Finally, she could rest. She turned on the television, then it dawned on her that this would be the perfect time to address a few cards and make some calls. After a few minutes of prayer, Diane wrote out the notes and dropped them in the mail on her way to visit her aunt. Then she returned home and had the entire afternoon to clean house and prepare dinner. After dinner there was enough left over to take a plateful of food to a lonely neighbor.

When she got home, Diane thought she had never felt better. God had given her the time she needed to take care of all the things that had weighed so heavily on her heart. And in giving, she had received far more than she ever expected.

God takes life's pieces and gives us unbroken peace.

If I HAD AN EXTRA HOUR EACH DAY THIS WEEK, I WOULD . . .

Spiritual Physics

He who walks with the wise grows wise.
PROVERBS 13:20

If I COULD
CHOOSE A
SPIRITUAL
MENTOR, IT
WOULD BE . . .
BECAUSE . . .

"Mama!" Josh's voice carried through the quiet house.

"Yes, Josh?"

"Mama! Come bounce me!"

Mary looked out the kitchen window to the trampoline that seemed to take up half the yard. With a smile that dimpled her cheeks, she grasped her youngest son's hand and went out to bounce him. It was an odd sort of pride she took in being able to skyrocket her son's little body into the air. She outweighed him by a number of pounds, and her weight caused him to go higher than any of his friends could take him. It was just a simple matter of physics, really; the heavier your partner, the higher you go.

It's no different spiritually. The people you surround yourself with will either send you skyrocketing into spiritual understanding and maturity or leave you grounded and struggling.

When you look at those in your life today, who is it that stands out as wise? Who walks with that quiet charisma and peace that you find yourself craving? What would it take to call that person? Keep it simple and comfortable. Plan a casual lunch at home, invite her over for coffee, or simply spend an afternoon talking. Or perhaps you can find an activity you both enjoy. Surround yourself with people who will encourage your spiritual growth.

The Bible says in James 1:5, "If any of you lacks wisdom, he should ask God." Ask God to expand your wisdom and your world.

Wisdom is seeing life from God's perspective.

Hide-and-Seek

Then Barnabas went to Tarsus to look for Saul.
ACTS 11:25

I would
LIKE A NEW
FRIEND WHO
WAS . . .

When Lucille's children were young, they enjoyed playing hide-and-seek in the dark. The old country kitchen with its cavernous cupboards and deep recesses contained many good places to hide. On one such occasion, one of their cousins—the smallest one, in fact—curled up into the back of the cupboard where Lucille kept her baking pans. With the pans arrayed in front of him, he was virtually invisible. It was an ideal hiding place.

With a shout of "Ready or not, here I come!" the game started. One by one, the hiding places and hidden children were found. But the littlest cousin, curled up in the baking pan cupboard, evaded discovery. An older child would have been thrilled. But this child didn't see things that way. Sipping a cup of tea in the darkened kitchen, Lucille heard a tiny voice whimper, "Isn't anyone going to come looking for me?" That little voice was all it took for the rest of the children to locate their cousin. Though the others congratulated him on his hiding place, he was just glad someone had found him.

Though we may not play hide-and-seek anymore as grown-ups, we can sometimes feel buried under responsibilities and schedules that close in on us and hide us from time with friends and family. Do you know someone who needs to be found? Reach out—with a note, a phone call, a prayer, or a visit—and do a little seeking, not hiding, today.

Kindness is love in work clothes.

Cardinal Grace

Give me a sign of your goodness, that my enemies
may see it and be put to shame, for you,
O LORD, have helped me and comforted me.
PSALM 86:17

The MOST
COMFORTING
THING THAT
EVER HAP-
PENED TO ME
WAS WHEN . . .

While her six-year-old granddaughter fought the cancer that had invaded her brain, Donna often was amazed at Jennifer's faith. Jenny had no doubt that God loved her and watched over her. Donna always accompanied her daughter and Jennifer to the hospital for the chemotherapy treatments, and when they returned home, they would always stop by the park for a few minutes. Jenny liked to watch the robins, blue jays, and cardinals. The cardinals were her favorite, she said, because red was her favorite color.

After her last treatment, the doctor confirmed what they feared most of all. She had only a short time to live. When she was not in a drug-induced sleep, she would tell her grandmother about the cardinal that frequently perched on her windowsill. No one but Jenny ever saw it.

Several months after Jenny passed away, Donna stood crying at her sink, feeling as cold and barren as the winter landscape. Her grief clung to her like a shroud. Just then, a flash of red startled her. A cardinal! Donna watched as the beautiful bird perched on the kitchen windowsill and cocked its head at her. Her tears stopped, replaced by the warmth and assurance of God's love. A moment later, the cardinal took flight and disappeared.

God wants you to know that He loves you and He sees your tears. Let Him comfort you today.

God is closest to those
whose hearts are broken.

Do You Promise?

The LORD is my light and my
salvation—whom shall I fear?
PSALM 27:1

Samantha had to have the promise. Every night at bedtime, she always called out to her mother as she walked away from her closed bedroom door: "Mom? Do you promise?"

"Yes, Honey, I promise."

Every night, she and her mother said the same words. Their ritual began with Samantha's fear of tornadoes, then dogs, then the green-eyed slime monster that she had glimpsed on a television show she wasn't supposed to be watching. Fear of snakes, the boogeyman, thunderstorms, fire ants (her mother is still not sure what brought that one on!), winged creatures of every sort, and fires followed one after another.

But later, the promise was no longer specific . . . just the general promise that Sam would wake up whole, unscathed by alien dream creatures and free from wounds inflicted by nature.

Her mother took a risk every night, promising that no harm would come to her young daughter. The truth was, a thunderstorm could occur, a fire ant could crawl into her bed, and even a tornado was not beyond the realm of possibility.

But in another sense, there was no risk. The Bible says that when God is on your side, there is absolutely nothing to fear! When your heart rests with Him, there is no one who can break it. When your aching body cries for help, He is there to grant you peace. Cast off your fear; He will take it and tame it. For His promises can never be broken!

⊱❧⊰

The wise man in the storm prays to God, not
for safety from danger, but for deliverance
from fear. It is the storm within which
endangers him, not the storm without.

God's MOST
SPECIAL
PROMISE TO
ME IS . . .

A Soothing Lotion

As a mother comforts her child,
so will I comfort you.
ISAIAH 66:13

When HAS A
PERSON WHOM
I SHOULD
HAVE BEEN
SERVING
SERVED ME
INSTEAD?

Anne felt bloated. The pain from her incision was excruciating, worsened by the hacking cough she could not seem to shake. Her husband was at work, and her new daughter was sleeping soundly in her crib. In the moment of silence, she tried to absorb the peace that seemed to surround her.

Anne's mother sat beside her—there to help out while she recovered from the emergency caesarean section. Anne barely noticed as her mother knelt before her and gently removed the socks from her swollen, hurting feet. Her mother took one foot in her hands and began to rub it in a smooth, rhythmic motion. The pain lessened.

As Anne watched her mother's aging hands soothing her swollen ankles, applying lotion to the dry areas, and massaging the calluses, she marveled. Her mother's hands were strong and tenacious, characteristic of a woman who had held her own in every aspect of life. Anne glanced down at her own tender hands. They didn't have the marks of wisdom, the edges of strength, or the grasp of one who labors. She realized that the one she should serve was serving her.

Just like Jesus washed the feet of His disciples before the Last Supper, He assures us that He will be there to comfort us in the midst of life's chaos, even more than a mother comforts her own child. Rest in that knowledge today. Let it be a soothing lotion to the dry and barren patches of your soul.

God does not comfort us to make us
comfortable, but to make us comforters.

Playful Joy

[There is] a time to weep and a time to laugh.

ECCLESIASTES 3:4

Grandma Lu watched her grandson, a bit perplexed by his actions. Benjamin, in all his six-year-old glory, was spinning. Not for any apparent reason, he was simply spinning, around and around and around. His little arms were stretched out on either side of his body, and his head was thrown back as a deep belly laugh escaped from his rosy lips. It didn't seem that he was doing much . . . hardly anything amusing or interesting. Grandma Lu paused.

Was there something fun about spinning? she wondered. She glanced around the lobby of the hotel where she sat. There were only a few people nearby, and they were buried deep in magazines and newspapers. She stood up and set her purse on the seat, blushing even as she walked toward her spinning grandson. She wasn't sure if there was any special technique, so she watched him for a moment before spreading out her own arms. She began slowly at first, careful not to bump into anything, worried she might slip and fall. Then she threw caution to the wind and began to speed up. She threw her head back and laughed, as she felt the momentum of her own body carry her in circles. What fun!

Benjamin began to laugh, and she laughed with him. They made quite a pair in that hotel lobby—disheveled, flushed, spinning grandmother and grandson. But people smiled because their joy was real.

Take that time today, and revel in the abandonment of playful joy.

~∞~

Laughing is the sensation of feeling good all over and showing it principally in one spot.

The SIMPLEST FUN I EVER HAD WAS WHEN I . . .

Monster Hugs

Our mouths were filled with laughter,
our tongues with songs of joy.
PSALM 126:2

"That's thirty-four monster hugs, Mommy!" Sandy said as she tugged on her mother's shirt and pointed to the chart on the refrigerator. "Yup! Since I did my room, that's three, and then I was nice to our guests, that's five . . . and then I get an extra five for being your favorite daughter!"

"You're my only daughter, Sandy!" her mom laughed.

"Yes, but that should be worth at least five!"

Sandy smiled at her mother in that mischievous way and wrote "34" at the far end of the chart. Her mother didn't stop her. Why begrudge her five monster hugs? They were a pleasure to give. She picked up her daughter, who at age seven was getting harder to lift, dropped her on the couch, and kissed, giggled, and cuddled—each monster hug lasting about thirty seconds. Not only were they a pleasure for Sandy, but they also were a joy for her mother, an incentive that tied their love together.

How much more does our Father in Heaven wish to reward us for steps in the right direction! He knows our greatest pleasures and our deepest desires, and as we remain faithful, He, like a loving father, envisions the fun He will have in giving us our reward.

Even when it seems difficult, even when the task is hard, stay faithful. Right now, your Father is planning for the best monster hugs ever, with you as the giggling recipient.

Laughter is the music of life.

Revolving Door

"Come to me, all you who are weary and burdened, and I will give you rest."

MATTHEW 11:28

The MOST
PEACEFUL
SCENE I CAN
IMAGINE
WOULD BE . . .

Aimee felt like her life was caught in a revolving door. Each day she pulled herself out of bed and headed to the kitchen. After preparing lunches and cooking breakfast, she dropped the kids off at school and battled traffic on the way to work. By the time she reached her office, it felt as though she had already done a day's work.

Then there were telephone calls to return and a mountain of paperwork to tackle. Problems crowded out the pleasure her career was supposed to bring.

Dinner was just as much of a routine as the rest of her life. *What will it be tonight?* she wondered. *Chicken, pork, or beef?* She had to find a better way of getting through the day! Aimee realized that the only thing she could change was her attitude.

The next morning when she woke, she prayed first—the first step out of that revolving door. She kissed and hugged her children, sang in the shower, dressed, and hurried to her car, slowing down for a moment to notice the flowers in bloom. When she got to the office, she thanked God for the opportunity to work for such a good company. The revolving door began slowing down. That night, she transformed the same old beef into beef stroganoff.

If your life is stuck in a revolving door, step out and enjoy the peace that God offers. He'll be with you all along the way as you change your tune.

True peace is found by man in the depths of his own heart— the dwelling-place of God.

The Hand of Friendship

"This is my command: Love each other."
JOHN 15:17

What
PERSON FROM
MY PAST DO I
WISH I HAD
TAKEN TIME
TO REACH
OUT TO?

It's not always easy to love. Growing up, Ben and Mary constantly fought. As brother and sister, they were inseparable, but they were interested only in tormenting each other—a push here, a shove there, stolen cookies, disappearing toys.

One spring afternoon, their mother reached her limit. She sat down both her young children and looked from one to the other. "I've had enough of your fighting. For the rest of the day, I want you to play nicely, love each other, and be kind. Period. End of story. Just do it." She got up, brushed herself off, and went back to her tasks.

Ben and Mary sat and looked at each other. Love each other? How could they love each other? Just by being told? Especially when the sight of the other was enough to bring mud bombs and hair-pulling to mind? But they had never seen their mother quite so angry.

A few moments passed in silence until Ben finally reached out, took Mary's hand, and asked, "Want to build a fort?"

Mary smiled and said, "Okay."

Of course, it's not always quite as easy as grabbing someone's hand and playing soldier, but it's also not as hard as we might think. Sometimes loving each other is simply a matter of letting go, starting anew with a fresh page before you, and deciding that the past is gone and all you have is the future to mold. It's a matter of extending your hand in friendship.

Love is most divine when it loves according to needs, and not according to merit.

Adopted for Life

He chose us in him before the creation of the world to be holy and blameless in his sight. In love he predestined us to be adopted as his sons through Jesus Christ, in accordance with his pleasure and will.

EPHESIANS 1:4-5

Some years ago, Jack brought Susie home from a "foster home" because his wife wanted a basset hound. At first, Helen wanted to return the dog. Susie wasn't a show dog; she had no pedigree; and from what the woman could see, she wasn't even very special. After a week, however, she and the dog bonded.

Susie became a protective member of the family, barking at strangers and routinely following Helen's children to school. And as the years passed, Susie developed quite a character. Then one day, Helen received a desperate phone call from a boy in her neighborhood. "You need to come over right away," he told her. "Your dog is here, and she's not moving." Fearing the worst, she and her older boys drove down the street.

When they arrived, they saw Susie's still form lying in the crabgrass. Helen leaned out the car window and called to her. The animal didn't move. She opened the car door and walked slowly toward the motionless body. She saw one lazy ear perk up. "Thank goodness," she whispered, "she's still alive!"

Just as Helen leaned down to see how badly she was hurt, Susie jumped up and gave her the sloppiest dog kiss ever. Throwing her arms around the dog, she realized Susie was as much a part of her family as any of her children.

When we are adopted into the family of God, we become part of a heavenly family that serves a sovereign Lord.

The love we give away is the only love we keep.

A pet THAT WAS A SPECIAL PART OF MY FAMILY WAS . . .

A Bubbly Challenge

Like arrows in the hands of a warrior are sons born in one's youth. Blessed is the man whose quiver is full of them.
PSALMS 127:4-5

Children
HAVE BEEN
USED BY GOD
TO TEACH
ME . . .

One dreary winter day, Barbara, the mother of two toddlers, felt discouraged as she swept up cookie crumbs and wiped up spilled juice. She was exhausted from trying to prevent her two little ones from getting into one thing after another.

While she answered the doorbell, her daughter slipped into a white eyelet dress to parade around the kitchen in bare feet. Barbara picked up her unhappy child and marched her into the bedroom to change.

After putting shoes on the children, she left them in front of the television for a moment, while she went into her bedroom to get dressed. Before she could zip her jeans, she heard an earsplitting shriek from outside. She dashed out the back door and heard her three-year-old son squalling. He was lying facedown on the other side of a three-foot-high brick wall. Through his tears, he said, "Sissy pushed me."

After fussing at her children for their disobedience, the woman felt a tug at her angry heart. "Please, Lord," she prayed, "give me peace and patience with my children."

Later that evening, as the kids were taking their bath, Barbara heard giggling and laughing, so she peeked in on her little "angels." To her dismay, the room was filled with bubbles. Not a bit of bubble bath was left. Then she discovered that her bottle of peach-scented shampoo—her favorite—was completely empty. But the impatience she had felt earlier that day was replaced by a joyful, laughing heart.

Children need love, especially when they don't deserve it.

Run with Perseverance

Since we are surrounded by such a great cloud of witnesses, let us throw off everything that hinders and the sin that so easily entangles, and let us run with perseverance the race marked out for us.

HEBREWS 12:1

Jenny Spangler won the women's marathon at the United States Olympic Trials in February 1996, earning the right to compete at the Summer Olympic Games in Atlanta, Georgia.

At the time of the trials, Spangler was qualifier number 61, which meant that sixty runners had entered the race with faster times than hers. No one had ever heard of her—and no one thought she could maintain a winning pace when she passed the leaders at the sixteen-mile mark.

Spangler had few successes to her credit. She had set an American junior record in the marathon during college, but then she left the sports scene after a stress fracture dashed her hopes in the Olympic Trials of 1984. Abandoning the sport after she ran poorly in 1988, she returned to school and earned a master's degree in business administration. She ran only two marathons between 1988 and 1996.

The favorites in February's race expected Spangler to fade, but she never did. Somewhere inside herself, she found the courage and stamina to finish strong. Not only did she make the Olympic team, but she also took home first prize—forty-five thousand dollars.

Does the day ahead of you look as grueling as a marathon? Run the race God has marked out before you. Keep moving! You can end each day with the satisfaction of knowing you are that much closer to the goal!

*Today, whatever may annoy,
the word for me is Joy, simple Joy.*

I find IT EASIER TO KEEP RUNNING WHEN . . .

God Is Good

"'Friend, go up higher.'"
LUKE 14:10 KJV

I can TRUST
GOD'S PLANS
FOR ME
BECAUSE I
KNOW . . .

An ancient legend of a swan and a crane tells us about God's goodness—which may be different from what we believe to be good.

A beautiful swan came to rest by the banks of a pond where a crane was wading, seeking snails. For a few minutes the crane looked at the swan and then asked, "Where do you come from?"

The swan replied, "I come from Heaven!"

"And where is Heaven?" asked the crane.

"Heaven!" replied the swan, "Heaven! Have you never heard of Heaven?" And the beautiful swan went on to describe the splendor and grandeur of the eternal city. She told the crane about the streets of gold and the gates and walls made of precious stones. She told about the river of life which was as pure as crystal. On the banks of this river stood a tree with leaves for the healing of the nations of the world. In great and eloquent language, the swan described the hosts of saints and angels who lived in the world beyond.

Somewhat surprisingly, the crane didn't appear to be the least bit interested in this place the swan described. Eventually he asked the swan, "Are there any snails there?"

"Snails!" declared the swan "Of course there aren't!"

"Then you can have your Heaven," said the crane. "What I want are snails!"[75]

How many of us turn our backs on the good God has for us in order to search for snails?

*Our love for God is tested by the question
of whether we seek Him or His gifts.*

Prayer for Harried Moms

He will take great delight in you,
he will quiet you with his love,
he will rejoice over you with singing.
ZEPHANIAH 3:17

Financial hardship had forced Valerie to take a part-time job delivering newspapers. The route took two hours, and she had to take her two young children along with her. After sitting at the kitchen table stuffing papers in plastic bags, Valerie started out with her two toddlers, a box of crackers, two apples, and seven stacks of newspapers.

While she had gotten used to dodging large trucks, commercial buses, and a herd of goats, she was not used to her daughter repeatedly asking, "Mom, what can I eat?"

"Eat an apple," Valerie answered.

From the backseat came the reply, "They're all gone." The distraction caused Valerie to miss a mailbox, and she had to go back.

"Then eat a cracker," she said, biting her lip. Turning around, Valerie saw half the box of crackers littering the backseat. Then Amy started whining. "I've got to go to the bathroom."

Valerie turned the car around and headed for the nearest fast-food restaurant. With only forty minutes left, Valerie and her helpers arrived back on the paper route. Just as she stuffed the last paper in a box, she heard singing coming from the back seat. "Jesus loves me, this I know."

The Lord loves us whether we're about to scream in exasperation or ready to shout for joy from a rooftop. When we know God is in ultimate control of everything, we can turn our circumstances over to Him and feel His love surround us.

How things look on the outside of us depends
on how things are on the inside of us.

The PROBLEMS IN MY LIFE THAT I NEED TO SEEK GOD ABOUT ARE . . .

The Plaster Solution

A man hath joy by the answer of his mouth:
and a word spoken in due season, how good is it!
PROVERBS 15:23 KJV

I can
IMPROVE THE
WAY I HANDLE
DISAGREE-
MENTS BY . . .

Disagreements are a natural part of working together—and different points of view are critical to creative and problem-solving processes. Still, the friction caused when differing opinions arise can cause needless pain and waste valuable time and energy. Occasionally, the best way to convince someone of your point of view while maintaining clear lines of communication is just to keep quiet and "start plastering."

Benjamin Franklin learned that plaster sown in the fields would make things grow. He told his neighbors, but they did not believe him, arguing that plaster could be of no use at all to grass or grain.

After a little while, he allowed the matter to drop. But he went into the field early the next spring and sowed some grain. Close by the path, where people would walk, he traced some letters with his finger and put plaster into them.

After a week or two, the seed sprang up. His neighbors, as they passed that way, gasped at what they saw. Brighter green than all the rest of the field, sprouted Franklin's seeded message in large letters, "This has been plastered."

Benjamin Franklin did not need to argue with his neighbors about the benefit of plaster any longer!

The answer to some disagreements may be to stop talking and try out several solutions together, measure them against like standards, and then resume the selection process. Meanwhile, tempers cool, objectivity returns, and new options can surface.

The best way to keep people from
jumping down your throat is
to keep your mouth shut.

Step Right Up

*Blessed are those who hear the joyful
blast of the trumpet, for they shall
walk in the light of your presence.*
PSALM 89:15 TLB

"Getting away from it all" takes on a whole new meaning when you decide, as a young Scottish girl did, to walk around the world. A troubled home life convinced her she needed a change of scenery, as well as a challenge that would test her mettle.

How does one go about walking around the world? In Ffyona's case, she spent eleven years and covered more than nineteen thousand miles walking from northern Scotland to southern England; New York to Los Angeles; Sydney to Perth, Australia; and South Africa to Morocco. Along the way, she fought disease, poisonous insects, bad weather, blisters, stonings, and loneliness.

To keep herself going, she had to come up with a way to motivate her often-tired feet. She quickly discovered that if she could focus her mind on doing what had to be done to make it through each phase of the walk, her body would do the rest. The stronger her mind, the better her body performed.

Another of Ffyona's important discoveries was that she needed to take one day at a time. Building in breaks and small rewards along the way made it much easier for her to stay committed to her bigger goal.[76]

Oh, the power of a walk! Even when we have no particular destination, our feet can take us to a new place and give us both a physical and a psychological break from where we've been.

∞

*When we are obedient,
God guides our steps and our stops.*

Where
WOULD I LOVE
TO GO FOR A
WALK? WHAT
MIGHT I SEE
THERE?

Sensitivity

Do not touch My anointed ones.
PSALM 105:15 NASB

I want TO BE
MORE SENSI-
TIVE TOWARD
GOD'S VOICE.
I CAN DO
THIS BY . . .

On the Big Island of Hawaii grows a delicate little plant called sensitivity, a member of the mimosa family. Its name is derived from the movement it makes when anything, including a change in the wind, comes near or across it. This minute, spiny-stemmed tropical American plant grows close to the ground. Unless you are directly upon it, you can't distinguish it from grass or weeds in the same area, and it can easily be crushed underfoot.

As the sun rises in the South Pacific, the tiny sensitivity plant opens itself as wide as it can and reaches upward toward the warmth of the early morning sunbeams shining down from heaven. This wee drooping plant has a built-in mechanism that causes it to quickly fold itself over and withdraw from anything that might cause it harm. However, sensitivity can't distinguish between a lawn mower rolling toward it to cut it down or the man coming by to make certain it is protected.

We all have the built-in need to protect ourselves from danger. God gave us His Word as a manual to equip us to be aware of the ways of the enemy and to prepare us to know how to protect ourselves.

We can reach up every morning, even when it's raining or snowing, and receive His warmth, love, protection, and anointing for the day ahead of us. God has blessed us with His sensitivity, but we must be alert and use the tools He has provided for us.

*God's way becomes plain
when we start walking in it.*

You Are One of Us

Be ye kind one to another, tenderhearted,
forgiving one another.
EPHESIANS 4:32 KJV

I can
DEVELOP A
FORGIVING
ATTITUDE BY
TAKING THIS
FIRST STEP . . .

"It's all right; sometimes I don't know why I do things either. You are part of our group, and we support you." With that one statement, the tension evaporated from the room, and other teens expressed their support to Sara.

The setting was a community meeting of adolescents in a mental health treatment facility. Sara suffered from chronic schizophrenia, and she often did not comprehend her actions or control them. The previous evening, upon returning from a visit home, she had promptly set a small fire in her bathroom that created major problems for the unit, including an evacuation as well as the canceling of evening activities.

The next morning, the staff and patients met to work through the problems of Sara's actions and the anger it created among the other teens. For nearly an hour she sat mute in the group, refusing to look into anyone's eyes.

But when Sam, another patient, came across the room, knelt down before her, looked up into her face, and expressed his support for her, she responded. Sara told how her mother had become angry with her and screamed at her, "Why don't you just stop being schizophrenic?"

"I just wanted to die; that's why I started the fire," Sara said in a barely audible voice.

Sam's willingness to forgive her in spite of this error in judgment made it safe for Sara to share her heart with the group.

Forgiveness is not an occasional act,
it is a permanent attitude.

Think on These Things

Whatever is true, whatever is noble, whatever is right, whatever is pure, whatever is lovely, whatever is admirable—if anything is excellent or praiseworthy—think about such things.
PHILIPPIANS 4:8

A situation
WHEREIN I
NEEDED
SOMEONE'S
GRACE WAS . . .

Irene Harrell, author or coauthor of more than two dozen books, once wrote about an argument she had with one of her teenage sons. She recalled clenching her fists and gritting her teeth in anger. The teen had spared no expense in irritating his mother, and she was ready for a verbal fight. But the boy was saved by the bell—the telephone. By the time Irene had finished the call, her son was nowhere in sight.

Later that day as Irene went about her household chores, she complained to her younger son, James, about her older son's transgressions. After finishing a load of dishes, she found her young son deep in thought.

"I think I know what would help you with Tommy," James said. Not knowing what to do with her teenager, she listened carefully to her son's advice. "Just don't think about it," he said matter-of-factly.

While she swept the kitchen floor, this childlike suggestion rolled around in her mind. Then she turned her thoughts to God, concentrating on His grace and mercy.

Later, when her teenage son came home, she was able to treat him with mercy and grace. Instead of spouting angry words, Irene offered him an ice-cream float before he went to bed. To her great surprise, the boy washed his glass and spoon that evening and mumbled, "Thanks, Mom," as he shuffled off to bed.

Is there someone who needs your grace? Today, think on these things—whatever is noble, right, pure, lovely, or admirable![77]

Mercy comes down from heaven to earth so that man by practicing it may resemble God.

Joy in the Morning

*Weeping may remain for a night,
but rejoicing comes in the morning.*

PSALM 30:5

The CUTEST
THING I
EVER HEARD
A CHILD
SAY WAS . . .

"It's a kitty," whispered four-year-old Donnie. A smile played around his mouth. Hesitantly, he stroked the orange tabby's head. "What's his name?"

"He kind of reminds me of a ball of sunshine," his mother said. "Why don't we call him Sunny?" Recently divorced, Grace hoped the new kitten would help her son with his loneliness for his father.

But as evening shadows crossed the room, Grace felt depression stalking her again. How would she ever raise her son without any help? The divorce had not been easy, and the emotional battering had taken its toll. Later that night, she lay in bed, still battling the sadness.

The next morning, Donnie crawled into bed with her and the kitten. With sunlight streaming through slatted blinds, they cuddled and watched Sunny swat at dust balls. It was easy to smile at the kitten's antics, but she wondered if she would ever be happy again.

Donnie picked up the kitten and put him on his lap. Gently, the boy patted his head, and then rubbed the kitten behind his ears. Soon the cat began to purr—loudly. Donnie leaned down and listened, his eyes widening in surprise. "Mom, my kitty's swallowed a motorcycle!" he said. Grace burst into laughter.

Sometimes, we all sink into a well of discouragement. When that happens, thank God for the small things of life, even when you're walking in the valley of shadows. Let Him turn your weeping into joy.

❧

*To get the full value of a joy, you must
have somebody to divide it with.*

The Tattered Bible

*Let the word of Christ dwell in you
richly as you teach and admonish
one another with all wisdom.*
COLOSSIANS 3:16

What IS
MY FAVORITE
PART OF
THE BIBLE?

Sarah's worn and tattered cookbook sat on a desk in the corner of the kitchen. Some of its pages were stuck together with drops of cake batter or cookie dough. Practically every page was stained, but it was obvious which recipes were her favorites. Those pages were barely readable. Between the leaves of the book were recipes from newspapers and store packages that she had carefully cut out over the years.

Sarah couldn't get along in the kitchen without her trusted cookbook. Not only did it provide a list of ingredients needed and instructions for preparing her favorite dishes, it also provided many useful facts to enable her to run her kitchen efficiently.

"Learning to read a recipe correctly is the most important part of cooking," she told her daughter many times.

Sitting close beside that trusted cookbook was her Bible. Like the cookbook, its pages were worn. It held clippings of memorable events that had taken place in her life and the lives of her family members over the years. Ink spots dotted the pages of her favorite Scripture passages. After many years of use, certain verses were difficult to read.

"Learning to understand the Bible and using it as a guideline for life is the most important part of living," she told her daughter. "This is God's instruction book designed especially for us. Everything that you will ever need to know about life is written on these pages."

The Bible is the cornerstone of liberty.

Coming Home

No eye has seen, no ear has heard,
no mind has conceived what God
has prepared for those who love him.

1 CORINTHIANS 2:9

Amanda trudged through the snow on the Connecticut hillside. It had been a great afternoon of sledding, playing, and throwing snowballs. She had thrown the perfect snowball at her teenage son, Cody. He'd grinned, looked at her through snow-covered eyelashes, and shouted, "Nice shot, Mom! But look out! I'll get you back!" Amanda had attempted to run but didn't get far before her mischievous son had helped her land face first in the soft snow.

Now they made their way back on the seemingly endless snow-covered path. By the time Amanda opened the front door to their home, she could barely feel her nose, ears, or fingertips. "We're back!" she called to her mother.

Amanda and the children peeled off their frozen layers and settled into the warmth of the living room couches. Grandmother bustled in with cups of steaming hot cocoa, and the smell from the kitchen indicated warm cookies were on the way. There was nothing like it! Nothing eclipsed the feelings of home, of warmth, of coming in from the cold to the waiting hot chocolate.

God is preparing for us. He watches from the window as we make our way across the cold and barren landscape. The minute we walk through the door of Heaven, we will be overwhelmed with the love of a gracious, waiting Father. It will be a celebration of peace, of coming home—the feelings of pleasure and joy more intense than we can even imagine.

I think
THAT HEAVEN
WILL BE LIKE
WHAT SPECIAL
PLACE?

The knowledge that we are never alone
calms the troubled sea of our lives
and speaks peace to our souls.

287

Future Father

"Whoever welcomes a little child like this in my name welcomes me."
MATTHEW 18:5

A time WHEN A GROWNUP MADE A DIFFERENCE IN MY LIFE AS A CHILD WAS . . .

June surveyed the crowd before her. The noise seemed almost overwhelming as everyone tried to speak at once. It was Sunday dinner, and all the family was gathered around the large table.

Down near the end of the table sat Daniel, a friend of June's youngest child, Nate. Daniel was only eight years old and looked flustered and nervous as people passed food around and over him. June watched as one of the other children noticed and attended to him, asking, "Would you like some of these potatoes, Daniel?"

The small boy nodded and smiled a simple grin of appreciation. The others seemed to take notice of him then and began asking him questions about school and friends. June knew that Daniel had a difficult home life. She was proud of her children as they focused on his hopes and dreams and seemed genuinely interested. "What do you want to be when you grow up?" asked one of the children.

Daniel hesitated, looked around at the family, then said, "I want to be a Dad. With lots of kids, like this family."

Is there a little one you can love on today—someone in your home, your church, or your neighborhood? Just a few small words of encouragement, a pair of listening ears, or an afternoon in the midst of your family can make a difference in the life of a child.

There is a grace of kind listening, as well as a grace of kind speaking.

Leave It to Me

Cast your burden on the Lord [releasing the weight of it] and He will sustain you.
PSALM 55:22 AMP

A problem
THAT WAS
SOLVED WHEN
I GAVE IT TO
GOD WAS . . .

Many people find it easier to commit their future into the Lord's hands than to commit the problems and concerns of the day. We recognize our helplessness in regard to the future, but we often feel as if the present is in our own hands.

A Christian by the name of Mary Ellen once had a great burden in her life. She was so distraught she could not sleep or eat. She jeopardized her physical and emotional health and was on the verge of a nervous breakdown. She recognized, however, that there wasn't anything she could do to change her circumstances.

Then Mary Ellen read a story in a magazine about another woman, Connie, who also had major difficulties in her life. In the account, a friend asked Connie how she was able to bear up under the load of such troubles. She replied, "I take my problems to the Lord."

Connie's friend replied, "Of course, that is what we should do."

Then Connie added, "But we must not only take our problems there. We must leave our problems with the Lord."[78]

The Lord wants you to cast your burdens on Him—and leave them there! He desires for you to give Him the full weight of your problems as well. Then you can go on with life in full confidence He will take care of those things you have entrusted to Him.

We ought never to bear the burden of sin or doubt, but there are burdens placed on us by God, which He does not intend to lift off. He wants us to roll them back on Him.

Quality Time

Thou wilt shew me the path of life:
in thy presence is fulness of joy.
PSALM 16:11 KJV

I love MY
FATHER
BECAUSE . . .

In his book *Unto the Hills,* Billy Graham tells a story about a little girl and her father who were great friends and enjoyed spending time together. They went for walks and shared a passion for watching birds, enjoying the changing seasons, and meeting people who crossed their path.

One day, the father noticed a change in his daughter. If he went for a walk, she excused herself from going. Knowing she was growing up, he rationalized that she must be expected to lose interest in her Daddy as she made other friends. Nevertheless, her absence grieved him deeply.

Because of his daughter's absences, he was not in a particularly happy mood on his birthday. Then she presented him with a pair of exquisitely worked slippers, which she had handmade for him while he was out of the house walking.

At last he understood and said, "My darling, I like these slippers very much, but next time buy the slippers and let me have you all the days. I would rather have my child than anything she can make for me."[79]

Is it possible our Heavenly Father sometimes feels lonely for your company? Are we so busy doing good deeds that we forget—or are too weary—to spend some quiet time with Him?

Take a walk with your Heavenly Father as the sun sets. Spend some quality time, talking to Him about anything and everything. You will be blessed, and so will He!

Time is the deposit each one has in the bank
of God, and no one knows the balance.

Come Home

> *"'This son of mine was dead and is alive again;*
> *he was lost and is found.'"*
>
> LUKE 15:24

What PLACE
DO I THINK
OF AS A
TRUE HOME?

Once there was a widow who lived in a miserable attic with her son. Years before, the woman had married against her parents' wishes and had gone to live in a foreign land with her husband. Her husband had proved irresponsible and unfaithful, and after a few years he died without having made any provision for her and their child. It was with the utmost difficulty that she managed to scrape together the bare necessities of life.

The happiest times in the child's life were when the mother took him in her arms and told him about her father's house in the old country. She told him of the grassy lawn, the noble trees, the wild flowers, the lovely paintings, and the delicious meals. The child had never seen his grandfather's home, but to him it was the most beautiful place in all the world. He longed for the time when he would go to live there.

One day the postman knocked at the attic door. The mother recognized the handwriting on the envelope, and with trembling fingers she broke the seal. There was a check and a slip of paper with just two words: "Come home."[80]

Like this father—and the father of the Prodigal Son—our Heavenly Father opens His arms to receive us back into a place of spiritual comfort and restoration at the end of a weary day.

Nor can we fall below the arms of God,
how lowsoever it be we fall.

Everyday Needs

*This is the confidence we have in approaching God:
that if we ask anything according to his will, he hears
us. And if we know that he hears us—whatever we ask—
we know that we have what we asked of him.*
1 JOHN 5:14-15

What SORTS
OF DETAILS IN
MY WORLD IS
GOD INTER-
ESTED IN?

"Oh, no! We're going to have to run for the ferry again!" Elaine cried. "And, unless we find a parking place in the next minute or two, we're never going to make it!"

As Elaine and her daughter, Cathy, struggled through the downtown Seattle traffic, she thought back to when they had moved to Bainbridge Island four years earlier. They had thought it to be a perfect, idyllic place. Her daughter was in high school, and Elaine could work part-time at home.

Now college bills had made full-time work a necessity for Elaine. She, her husband, and Cathy were obliged to make the daily commute to Seattle via the ferry. With a car parked on both sides of the water, praying for parking spaces had become a daily event.

"I told you we needed to get away from your office sooner," Cathy chided.

"God knew about that last-minute customer I had, and He knows we have to make this ferry in order to get home in time to fix dinner and make it to the church meeting," Elaine assured her. Then she prayed aloud, "Lord, we'll circle this block one more time. Please have someone back out, or we're not going to make it."

"Mom, there it is!" Cathy shouted, as they rounded the last corner. "Those people just got in their car. I have to admit—sometimes you have a lot more faith than I do. Who'd think God would be interested in whether or not we find a parking place?"[81]

The Lord knows all the circumstances of your day—and your tomorrow. Trust Him to be the "Lord of the details."

❧

*You may trust the Lord too little, but
you can never trust Him too much.*

Fragments

One day Jesus was praying in a certain place.
When he finished, one of his disciples said to him,
"Lord, teach us to pray."

LUKE 11:1

Margaret Brownley tells of her son's first letters from camp:

When my oldest son went away to summer camp for the first time, I was a nervous wreck. Although he was nine years old, he hadn't as much as spent a night away from home, let alone an entire week. I packed his suitcase, making sure he had enough socks and underwear. I also packed stationery and stamps so he could write home.

I received the first letter from him three days after he left for camp. I quickly tore open the envelope and stared at the childish scrawl, which read: "Camp is fun, but the food is yucky!" The next letter offered little more: "Jerry wet the bed." *Who's Jerry?* I wondered. The third and final letter had this interesting piece of news: "The nurse said it's not broken."

Fragments. Bits of information. It made me think of my own sparse messages to God. "Dear Lord," I plead when a son is late coming home, "keep him safe." Or, "Give me strength," I pray when faced with a difficult challenge. "Let me have wisdom," is another favorite prayer of mine. "Thank-you, God," I say before each meal or when my brood is tucked safely into bed.

Fragments. Bits and pieces. Are my messages to God as unsatisfactory to Him as my son's letters were to me? With a guilty start, I realized that it had been a long time since I'd had a meaningful chat with the Lord.[82]

Cultivate the thankful spirit!
It will be to you a perpetual feast.

I want
TO TAKE TIME
TO TALK TO
THE LORD
ABOUT . . .

All the Details

*"Do not let your hearts be troubled.
Trust in God; trust also in me."*
JOHN 14:1

I hope
WITH GOD'S
HELP TO
IMPROVE IN . . .

Andrea stewed over a mounting pile of pressures. Just-bought groceries for tomorrow's dinner guests sprawled across every bit of counter space. Buried under them was a Sunday school lesson to be prepared. A week's worth of laundry spilled out of the laundry room into the kitchen, and an upsetting letter from a faraway friend in need lay teetering on the edge of the sink.

In the midst of this turmoil, Steven's Sunday school teacher called. "We'll be leaving for the carnival about noon. If Stephen didn't bring home his permission slip, just write the usual information on a slip of paper and send it along with him."

Andrea heard the doorbell ring, followed by an awful commotion. Rushing to the living room, she found two little girls waving pink slips of paper at her crying son. "What's the matter?" she asked as she gently put her arms around him.

"I can't go!" he wailed. "I don't have one of those pink papers!"

"Oh, yes, you do. Only yours happens to be white," she said as she dried his tears, stuffed the paper in his pocket, and sent him out the door.

Back in the kitchen Andrea wondered, *Hasn't he been my child long enough to know I'd have a solution?*

Suddenly a tiny smile crept across her face as she surveyed the chaos around her—and she could almost hear her Heavenly Father say, "Haven't you been My child long enough to know that I have it taken care of?"[83]

*Trust God where you cannot trace him.
Do not try to penetrate the cloud he brings
over you; rather look to the bow that is on it.
The mystery is God's; the promise is yours.*

Heaven's Spot Remover

*It is of the Lord's mercies that we are not consumed,
because his compassions fail not. They are
new every morning: great is thy faithfulness.*

LAMENTATIONS 3:22-23 KJV

"Let it snow; let it snow; let it snow." That's the cry of school-aged children everywhere when winter weather finally arrives.

First, there's catching those early snowflakes on your tongue. After a few more flakes hit the ground, you can start making snowballs and have some terrific battles. Several inches later, it's time to build the snowmen and snow forts. And when the blanket of snow reaches a hefty thickness, the best thing to do is make snow angels.

Remember snow angels? You find a good patch of untouched snow, stand with your arms stretched out to the side, and fall backward onto what feels like a cold, wet cloud. Flap your arms and legs as if you're doing jumping jacks. Then, carefully get up and look at your handiwork.

Have you noticed though that by the end of the day, every square inch of clean snow has been used up. Patches of dead grass show through where someone dug down deep to roll a snowman's head.

But something magical happens overnight. The snow falls again. You look out your window in the morning to find another clean white blanket covering all of the previous day's blemishes. All that was ugly is once again beautiful.

The God who turned the humiliation and shame of His Son's death on the Cross into the gift of salvation for all who believe in Him can take the tattered rags of our daily lives and make them like new again—every morning.

*When God's goodness cannot be seen,
his mercy can be experienced.*

The VIVID MEMORY THAT COMES TO MIND WHEN I THINK ABOUT SNOW IS . . .

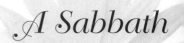

A Sabbath

Be glad and rejoice for ever in that which I create.
ISAIAH 65:18 RSV

I would
DESCRIBE
THE PERFECT
RESTFUL
PLACE AS . . .

What is it that gives you that warm fuzzy feeling inside?

To Oscar Hammerstein, that warm, fuzzy, everything-is-going-to-be-okay feeling came from "whiskers on kittens and warm, woolen mittens." What are some of your favorite things? When was the last time you gave yourself permission to be "nonproductive" and enjoy some of life's simple pleasures—like the beauty of a sunset?

Logan Pearsall Smith wrote, "If you are losing your leisure, look out! You may be losing your soul." When we don't take time for leisure or relaxation, when we give our discretionary time away to busyness and relentless activity, we are living in a way that says, "everything depends upon me and my efforts."

Consequently, God prescribed a day of rest, the Sabbath, to enjoy His creation and to give us time to reflect and remember all He has done for us and all He is. The Sabbath is time to remember God is God—and we're not!

The Sabbath doesn't have to be Sunday. You can take a Sabbath rest anytime you relax and turn your focus to God and His creation. Sometimes you have nothing better to do than relax. You may have something else to do, but you don't have anything better to do.

Relax and just enjoy God's creation. After all, He created it for you to enjoy.

*Jesus knows we must come apart
and rest awhile, or else
we may just plain come apart.*

Shalom

"Peace I leave with you, my peace I give unto you."
JOHN 14:27 KJV

A word that appears throughout the Old Testament is shalom. It is often translated "peace," but shalom means far more than peace in the aftermath of war or peace between enemies. Shalom embodies an inner peace that brings wholeness, unity, and balance to an individual's life. It describes a harmonious, nurturing environment with God at its center.

In creation, God brought order and harmony out of chaos. He created shalom. It was people's sin that destroyed shalom, but it has always been God's plan that it be restored—first to the human heart and then, flowing from that, to heart-to-heart relationships.

God has given us many promises for peace in His word. Meditate on His promises of shalom, and as you do, they will flood your heart and mind with peace.

- *Since we have been justified through faith, we have peace with God through our Lord Jesus Christ* (Romans 5:1).
- *Great peace have they who love your law, and nothing can make them stumble* (Psalm 119:165).
- *When a man's ways are pleasing to the Lord, he makes even his enemies live at peace with him* (Proverbs 16:7).
- *May the God of hope fill you with all joy and peace as you trust in him, so that you may overflow with hope* (Romans 15:13).
- *The peace of God, which transcends all understanding, will guard your hearts and your minds in Christ Jesus* (Philippians 4:7).

❧

First keep the peace within yourself, then you can also bring peace to others.

I can MAKE MY HOME A PEACEFUL PLACE BY . . .

Five Minutes

*In peace I will both lie down and sleep; for thou
alone, O LORD, makest me dwell in safety.*
PSALM 4:8 RSV

Tonight,
BEFORE I
FALL ASLEEP, I
WILL THINK
ABOUT . . .

If you wake up as weary as you were when you went to bed the night before, try to recall what you were thinking about the last five minutes before you went to sleep. What you think about in that five minutes impacts how well you sleep, which determines what kind of day tomorrow will be.

When you sleep, your conscious mind is at rest, but your subconscious mind remains active. Psychologists call the subconscious the "assistant manager of life." When the conscious mind is "off duty," the subconscious mind takes over. The subconscious carries out the orders that are given to it, although you are not aware of it.

For example, if the last minutes before going to sleep are spent in worry, the subconscious records and categorizes that as fear, and acts as if the fear is reality. Thus muscles remain tense, nerves are on edge, and the body's organs are upset, which means the body is not really at rest.

However, if those last five minutes are spent contemplating some great idea, an inspiring verse, or a calm and reassuring thought, it will signal to the nervous system, "All is well," and put the entire body in a relaxed, peaceful state. This helps you to wake up refreshed, strengthened, and confident.

You can input positive, healthy thoughts into your conscious mind and pave the way for quiet, restful sleep by simply meditating on God's Word as you drop off to sleep.

*Our pursuit of God is successful
just because He is forever
seeking to manifest himself to us.*

Serenity

I have [expectantly] trusted in, leaned on,
and relied on the Lord without
wavering and I shall not slide.
PSALM 26:1 AMP

Many people are familiar with the *Serenity Prayer*, although most probably think of it as a prayer to be said in the morning hours or during a time of crisis. Consider again the words of this prayer: "God, grant me the Serenity to accept the things I cannot change, Courage to change the things I can, and Wisdom to know the difference."

Can there be any better prayer to say at day's end? Those things that are irreversible or fixed in God's order, we need to relinquish to Him. True peace of mind comes when we trust that God knows more about any situation than we could possibly know.

Those things we can change, we must have the courage to change. Furthermore, we must accept the fact that in most cases we cannot change things until morning comes! We can rest in the interim, knowing the Lord will help us when the time comes for action.

The real heart of the *Serenity Prayer* is revealed in its conclusion: that we might know the difference between what we need to accept and what we need to change. That takes wisdom. James tells us, "If any of you is deficient in wisdom, let him ask of the giving God [Who gives] to everyone liberally and ungrudgingly, without reproaching or fault-finding, and it will be given him. Only it must be in faith that he asks with no wavering" (James 1:5-6 AMP).

Ask the Lord to give you true serenity tonight!

The invariable mark of wisdom is
to see the miraculous in the common.

What SITUATION DO I NEED COURAGE TO CHANGE?

What Do You Want?

I thank You and praise You, O God of my fathers,
Who has given me wisdom and might and has
made known to me now what we desired of You.
DANIEL 2:23 AMP

Father, I
HAVE A NEED
TO BRING
TO YOU . . .

Children are quick to respond to their environment. Babies immediately cry when they are hungry, thirsty, tired, sick, or wet. Toddlers are not at all bashful in communicating what they do and do not want. However, as we grow older, maturity teaches us to use discernment in making our desires known and to give way to the needs of others in many situations.

The Lord nevertheless tells us we are wise to always come to Him as little children—telling Him precisely what we need and want. While looking directly at a man whom He knew was blind, Jesus asked him, "What do you want Me to do for you?" Without hesitation he replied, "Master, let me receive my sight" (Mark 10:51 AMP).

Jesus could see he was blind, yet He asked him to make a request. In like manner, God knows what you need "before you ask Him" (Matthew 6:8 AMP). Yet He says in His Word, "by prayer and petition (definite requests) . . . continue to make your wants known to God" (Philippians 4:6 AMP).

Why pray for what seems to be obvious? Because in stating precisely what we want, our needs and desires become obvious to us.

State your requests boldly before the Lord tonight. He'll hear you. He'll respond to you. And just as important, you'll hear yourself and respond in a new way to Him.

Our prayers must mean something to us
if they are to mean anything to God.

Shining Through

> *"Let your light so shine before men, that they may see your good works and glorify your Father in heaven."*
> MATTHEW 5:16 NKJV

A little girl was among a group of people being given a guided tour through a great cathedral. As the guide explained the various parts of the structure—the altar, the choir, the screen, and the nave—the little girl's attention was intently focused on a stained glass window.

For a long time she silently pondered the window. Looking up at the various figures, her face was bathed in a rainbow of color as the afternoon sun poured into the transept of the huge cathedral.

As the group was about to move on, she gathered enough courage to ask the tour conductor a question. "Who are those people in that pretty window?"

"Those are the saints," the guide replied.

That night, as the little girl was preparing for bed, she told her mother proudly: "I know who the saints are."

"Oh?" replied the mother. "And just who are the saints?"

Without a moment's hesitation the little girl replied: "They are the people who let the light shine through!"[84]

As you look back over your day, did you let God's light shine through? Sometimes we pass these opportunities by, saying, "It will just take too much out of me." But the Bible lets us know that everything we give will come back to us—multiplied. (See Luke 6:38.)

Remember, the light of your life gives those around you a glimpse of Jesus, the Source of eternal and constant light. As you let your light shine, it will grow brighter!

I can LET GOD'S LIGHT SHINE THROUGH ME BY . . .

Should first my lamp spread light and purest rays bestow The oil must then from you, my dearest Jesus, flow.

Like a Child

"Truly I tell you, whoever does not receive and accept and welcome the kingdom of God like a little child [does] positively shall not enter it at all."
MARK 10:15 AMP

The MOST WONDERFUL THING ABOUT A CHILD IS . . .

Many parents have stood in awe by the beds of their sleeping children, amazed at the miracle of their lives, captured by their sweet expressions of innocence, and bewildered by their ability to sleep peacefully regardless of the turmoil that may be around them.

Those same parents have also felt great frustration earlier in the day when their children were willful or disobedient, and they marveled at their children's ingenuity, energy, curiosity, or humor. Children seem to embody all of life's extremes.

What did Jesus mean when He said we must receive and welcome the kingdom of God as a little child? Surely He meant we must welcome the Lord's will; not with debate, question, worry, or fear; but with a sense of delight, expectation, and eagerness.

Andrew Gillies has written a lovely poem to describe the childlikeness the Lord desires to see in us.

Last night my little boy confessed to me
Some childish wrong;
And kneeling at my knee,
He prayed with tears—
"Dear God, make me a man like Daddy—
Wise and strong; I know you can!"
Then while he slept I knelt beside his bed,
Confessed my sins,
And prayed with low-bowed head—
"O God, make me a child like my child here—
Pure, guileless,
Trusting Thee with faith sincere."[85]

Be content to be a child, and let the Father proportion out daily to thee what light, what power, what exercises, what straits, what fears, what troubles He sees fit for thee.

Think On These Things

*His delight is in the law of the Lord, and
on his law he meditates day and night.*

PSALM 1:2

A scripture
THAT I LOVE
TO MEDITATE
ON IS . . .
BECAUSE . . .

In a recent study, twenty-two women experiencing "high anxiety" were hooked up to heart monitors and told to spend ten minutes watching the beat of their pulses on special wristwatches. After twelve weeks of this, all of the women had definite improvement in their anxiety levels.

One of the doctors involved in the study said that when you sit and focus on these steady rhythms, you are forced to remain in the moment. Dedicating yourself to this task for ten minutes takes your mind off both the past and the future—the two hobgoblins of modern life.

There are 960 working minutes in a day (if you allow eight hours for sleep). This doctor points out that all of us can find ten minutes for this simple form of "meditation"—especially when the payoff is less stress.[86]

In the Bible, God commanded Joshua to engage in a different kind of exercise: "Do not let this Book of the Law depart from your mouth; meditate on it day and night" (Joshua 1:8).

When Joshua meditated on God's Word, he was focusing on something that would help him live a righteous life at that moment. Foremost in his mind was the question, "What does God want me to do right now? How can I keep my finger on God's pulse?"

Ask Jesus what He would like you to be thinking about as you fall asleep.

*Who brought me hither will bring me hence;
no other guide I seek.*

Home Fires

Teach the young women to be sober, to love their husbands, to love their children.
TITUS 2:4 KJV

If I COULD
CHANGE ANY
ASPECT OF MY
HOME, IT
WOULD BE . . .

Ernestine Schuman-Heink is not the first to ask, "What is a home?" But her answer is one of the most beautiful ever penned:

A roof to keep out the rain. Four walls to keep out the wind. Floors to keep out the cold. Yes, but home is more than that. It is the laugh of a baby, the song of a mother, the strength of a father. Warmth of loving hearts, light from happy eyes, kindness, loyalty, comradeship. Home is first school and first church for young ones, where they learn what is right, what is good and what is kind. Where they go for comfort when they are hurt or sick. Where fathers and mothers are respected and loved. Where children are wanted. Where the simplest food is good enough for kings because it is earned. Where money is not so important as lovingkindness. Where even the teakettle sings from happiness. That is home. God bless it.[87]

God asks us to call Him "Father," and family life is at the heart of the Gospel. Through Jesus Christ, God the Father has forged a way to adopt many children. As a result, the Scriptures have much to say about what a happy home should be like. Good family life is never an accident, but an achievement by those who share it.

Keeping the home fires burning is letting God's Word and presence guide your way and keeping the love of God ablaze in the hearts of your family.

The home is a lighthouse that has the lamp of God on the table and the light of Christ in the window to give guidance to those who wander in darkness.

The Dinner Table

*He took bread, gave thanks and
broke it, and gave it to them.*
LUKE 22:19 NKJV

Elton Trueblood has written eloquently about family dinnertime. Perhaps it's time we reinstitute this practice in our lives! She writes:

The table is really the family altar! Here those of all ages come together and help to sustain both their physical and their spiritual existence. If a sacrament is "an actual conveyance of spiritual meaning and power by a material process," then a family meal can be a sacrament. It entwines the material and the spiritual in a remarkable way. The food, in and of itself, is purely physical, but it represents human service in its use. Here, at one common table, is the father who has earned, the mother who has prepared or planned, and the children who share, according to need, whatever their antecedent participation may have been.

When we realize how deeply a meal together can be a spiritual and regenerating experience, we can understand something of why our Lord, when He broke bread with His little company toward the end of their earthly fellowship, told them, as often as they did it, to remember Him. We, too, seek to be members of His sacred fellowship, and irrespective of what we do about the Eucharist, there is no reason why each family meal should not take on something of the character of a time of memory and hope.[88]

When was the last time your family gathered together for a meal?

*The family circle is the supreme
conductor of Christianity.*

For A SPECIAL MEAL, I WOULD PREPARE . . . AND SERVE IT IN AN ATMOS-PHERE OF . . .

Stargazing

He brought [Abram] outside and said, "Look now toward heaven, and count the stars if you are able to number them." And He said to him, "So shall your descendants be."
GENESIS 15:5 NKJV

The LAST TIME I LOOKED AT THE STARS IN THE SKY, I THOUGHT . . .

A father decided to take his young daughter for an evening walk along a country road. The family lived in a large city, where walking at night was not the custom or considered safe. The father could hardly wait to see how his daughter would respond to a star-filled sky.

As dusk turned into dark, the little girl became fearful and clung to her father's hand. Then suddenly, she looked toward the sky and exclaimed with surprise, "Daddy, somebody drew dots all over the sky!"

Her father smiled. His young daughter had never seen a night sky away from the city lights. He was glad the moon had not yet risen so the stars appeared even closer and more distinct. "Daddy," she continued in her enthusiasm, "if we connect them all, will they make a picture?"

What an interesting notion, the father thought. "No," he replied to his daughter, "the dots are there for another purpose. Each one is a hope God has for your life. God has lots of hopes that your life will be filled with good things. In fact, there are more hopes than you or I can ever count!"

"I knew it!" the little girl said. "The dots do make a picture." And then she added more thoughtfully, "I always wondered what hope looked like."

Stargazing is one of the best ways to get your earthy life back into perspective and realize that in God's infinite universe, He has a specific plan for you.

Eternity is the divine treasure house, and hope is the window, by which mortals are permitted to see, as through a glass darkly, the things which God is preparing.

Family Devotions

"When you pray . . . pray to your Father who is in the secret place; and your Father who sees in secret will reward you openly."
MATTHEW 6:6 NKJV

Bedtime prayers are often limited to reciting a poem or saying a little memorized prayer. However, bedtime prayers can become family devotions if the entire family gathers at the bedside of the child who retires first.

Each member of the family says a heartfelt prayer that is spontaneous and unrehearsed. A verse or two of Scripture might be read prior to prayer. The point of such a devotional time is not that children are obedient to say a prayer before sleep, but that the children's hearts are knit to the heart of God and to the hearts of other family members.

Albert Schweitzer once commented on the need for parents to provide an example in devotion:

From the services in which I joined as a child I have taken with me into life a feeling for what is solemn, and a need for quiet self-recollection, without which I cannot realize the meaning of my life. I cannot, therefore, support the opinion of those who would not let children take part in grown-up people's services till they to some extent understand them. The important thing is not that they shall understand but that they shall feel something of what is serious and solemn. The fact that a child sees his elders full of devotion, and has to feel something of devotion himself, that is what gives the service its meaning for him.[89]

Give family devotions a try soon!

When I am with God My fear is gone;
In the great quiet of God
My troubles are as the pebbles on the road,
My joys are like the everlasting hills.

A prayer
THAT I
REMEMBER
ASKING OF
GOD AS A
CHILD WAS
ABOUT . . .

God Is Awake

He will not let your foot slip—he who watches over you will not slumber; indeed, he who watches over Israel will neither slumber nor sleep.
PSALMS 121:3-4

When I FEEL AFRAID I REMIND MYSELF OF THE FACT THAT . . .

Anna was alone in her new home for the first time. Jake's new job meant they would someday be able to buy a home of their own in a safer part of town. But for now, they could afford only a rental in a less secure area.

Jake left on a business trip, admonishing her to be sure all the windows and doors were locked before she and their daughter, Daisy, went to bed. "We'll be okay," she assured him. "God has always taken care of us."

Later, however, as she checked the last door lock, Anna thought she heard people yelling somewhere down the street.

When she reached Daisy's room, she found her sitting in a little ball in the middle of her bed. Her wide eyes told Anna that she had heard the yelling too.

"Mom, do we have to turn out the lights tonight?" Daisy pleaded. Anna had not left the lights on for Daisy since she was four. The bright country moon had provided enough light to wean her away from the night-light. But God's lamp, as they had called it, was nowhere to be seen in this smoggy city atmosphere.

"Sweetie, God never sleeps. Even when you can't see His lamp, He's up there watching over you."

"Well," Daisy replied, "as long as God is awake, there is no sense in both of us staying awake!"

God is awake! He's always watching over you, ready to protect you from harm.

God is protecting because He is proactively detecting!

Night Sounds

I will bless the Lord who counsels me; he gives me
wisdom in the night. He tells me what to do.
PSALM 16:7 TLB

The night seems to have different sounds and rhythms than the day. It is at night that we seem to hear certain sounds more clearly. Sounds like:

- the ticking of a clock
- the creak of a stair
- the chirp of a cricket
- the barking of a dog
- the scrape of a twig against the window
- the clatter of a loose shutter
- the deep call of a foghorn
- the wind in the trees
- the croaking of a frog
- the opening of a door
- the strains of music down the hall
- the whimper of a child
- the whispers of a spouse

It is also at night that we are more prone to listen with our spiritual ears. Frederick Buechner has suggested, "Listen to your life. See it for the fathomless mystery that it is."[90]

- Listen to the moment.
- Listen to your thoughts and feelings.
- Listen to your impulses and desires.
- Listen to your longings and fears.
- Listen to the beat of your own heart.
- Listen to God's still small voice in the innermost recesses of your being.

Night is for listening. Listen—and learn—with your spiritual ears, as well as your natural ones.

God has given human beings
one tongue but two ears that we may
hear twice as much as we speak.

In THE LAST
FIVE MINUTES
SOME OF
THE SOUNDS
I HEARD
WERE . . .

Praying Grandmothers

The eyes of the Lord run to and fro throughout the whole earth, to shew himself strong in the behalf of them whose heart is perfect toward him.
2 CHRONICLES 16:9 KJV

In MY OWN LIFE GOD HAS SHOWN HIMSELF STRONG TO HEAL . . .

For fifty years Sister Agnes and Mrs. Baker had prayed for their nation of Latvia to be freed from Soviet oppression. Most of all, they prayed for the freedom to worship in their Methodist Church in Leipaja. When the atheistic Soviet regime came to power, the enemy invaders took over their church building and turned the sanctuary into a sports hall.

Their prayers were answered in 1991, when the oppression came to an end. The Soviets left, and the tiny nation was free. But it needed to be rebuilt, and Sister Agnes and Mrs. Baker were determined to help.

The two women, now past eighty, talked to a local minister. They said if he would agree to be their pastor, they would be his first members. A church was reborn!

Next they had to get the church ready for worship services. One of the church members undertook painting the twenty-five-foot-high walls. The tall Palladian windows were cleaned to a bright, gleaming shine, and the wood floor was restored to a rich luster.

The church pews were found in storage out in the country. They were returned and put in place. Sister Agnes had kept the church pump organ safe in her own home, so she returned it to the sanctuary.

God had been faithful!

God wants to show himself strong on your behalf, just as He did for Mrs. Baker and Sister Agnes. Jesus said, "I will build my church; and the gates of Hades will not overcome it" (Matthew 16:18).

Faith is the eye that sees Him, the hand that clings to Him, the receiving power that appropriates Him.

In His Eyes

The eyes of the Lord are upon the righteous.
PSALM 34:15 KJV

In *The Upper Room*, Sandra Palmer Carr describes a touching moment with one of her sons. When her younger son, Boyd, was four years old, she was rocking him in a high-backed wooden rocking chair, as was her habit. But this time he was facing her, straddling her lap with his knees bent.

Suddenly, he sat up straight, lifted his head, and stared intensely into her eyes. He became very still, and Sandra stopped rocking. He cupped her face in his little hands and said in a near-whisper, "Mommy, I'm in your eyes."

They stayed that way for several long moments, staring into one another's eyes. The rocking stopped, and the room grew quiet. Then Sandra whispered back, "And I'm in yours." Boyd leaned his head against her contentedly, and they resumed their rocking.[91]

How can we be assured we are always in God's eyes? The Bible has many, many verses to indicate He is continuously thinking of us, attending to us, and doing all He can to bless us. Certainly, Jesus' death and resurrection are constant reminders of how dear and precious we are to Him.

Your Heavenly Father desires to comfort you with His love, letting you stop now and then to call to mind a verse of Scripture that tells you how much you mean to Him.

You should never doubt you are the focus of God's tender care and attention. You can have a grateful and confident heart knowing you are always in His eyes.

◦◦◦◦

*The only important decision
we have to make is to live with God;
He will make the rest.*

I think
THAT GOD
SEES ME AS . . .

After the Uproar

*After the uproar was ceased, Paul called
unto him the disciples, and embraced them.*
ACTS 20:1 KJV

My HUG
IN RETURN
TO JESUS
TELLS HIM . . .

For a small child, the most comforting place in the world is in the secure arms of his mother or father. It's not really very different for grown-ups. The embrace of caring arms is a wonderful place to be. Even a brief hug from a casual friend can lift one's spirits.

At the end of a busy or frustrating day, "after the uproar has ceased," grown-ups may long for a pair of loving parental arms to assure them everything's going to be all right—to hear a voice that says soothingly, "I'm here, and I'll take care of you."

Take this little poem as a "hug" this evening from One who loves you without measure, and who watches over your every move with tenderness and compassion:

> When the birds begin to worry
> And the lilies toil and spin,
> And God's creatures all are anxious,
> Then I also may begin.
> For my Father sets their table,
> Decks them out in garments fine,
> And if He supplies their living,
> Will He not provide for mine?
> Just as noisy, common sparrows
> Can be found most anywhere—
> Unto some just worthless creatures,
> If they perish who would care?
> Yet our Heavenly Father numbers
> Every creature great and small,
> Caring even for the sparrows,
> Marking when to earth they fall.
> If His children's hairs are numbered,
> Why should we be filled with fear?
> He has promised all that's needful,
> And in trouble to be near.

—Author Unknown

*Our ground of hope is that God
does not weary of mankind.*

Tea for at Least Two

He leadeth me beside the still waters.
He restoreth my soul.
PSALM 23:2-3 KJV

Praising

GOD SPONTA-
NEOUSLY
USUALLY
HAPPENS
WHEN I . . .

The brief respite known as afternoon tea is said to have been the creation of Anna, Duchess of Bedford, in the nineteenth century. At that time the English customarily ate a hearty breakfast, paused for a light lunch at midday, and didn't return to the table until late evening. Understandably hungry long before dinner, the duchess asked to have a small meal served in her private quarters in the late afternoon. Eventually, she invited close friends to share the repast. The sensible custom was quickly adopted throughout England.

While the Duchess's initiation of teatime was aimed at nourishment of her body, she and the rest of England soon discovered that adding beautiful china and good friends to the occasion also nourished the soul.

In fact, the real value of formal teatime lies in its ability to enrich and brighten the everyday routine by stressing the importance of courtesy and friendship.[92]

We are wise to recognize our need for a "spiritual teatime" each day. Even if we have a "hearty breakfast" in the Word each morning, there may be times when the pressures of the day come to bear in late afternoon. Our spirits long for a little peace and refreshment in the presence of our loving Savior. Just as enjoying a muffin with a few sips of tea can give something of a lift to our lagging physical energy level, a quick prayer or the voicing of praise can give our spirit a lift.

Gratitude is born in hearts that
take time to count up past mercies.

That Loving Touch

*He hath said, I will never leave thee,
nor forsake thee.*
HEBREWS 13:5 KJV

God HAS
ENCOURAGED
ME IN BLEAK
TIMES BY . . .

A minister told of a certain family in his church who had waited a long time for a child. The couple was overjoyed when at last a son was born to them, but they were crushed when they learned he had a severe handicap. He would go into extremely violent seizures without warning. Nevertheless, as he grew, they tried to make his life as normal as possible.

Whenever the church doors were open, this family could be found in attendance. As time passed, the child developed a deep love for the same Jesus his parents loved, and he counted on Him to bring him through each of his life-threatening episodes.

The minister tells of the father's love as reflected on one particular Sunday:

I remember the father always holding the little boy during worship at our church. I remember one particularly hard seizure when the father gently but firmly held the little guy and went to the back of the sanctuary. There he held him to his chest, gently whispering into his ear. There was no hint of embarrassment or frustration on that father's face. Only calm, deep, abiding love.

That is a picture of our Heavenly Father's love for us. In spite of our deep imperfections, He is not embarrassed to call us His children. He tenderly holds us through the deepest, hardest part of our struggles and whispers words of assurance and encouragement while He clutches us to himself and supports us with His loving care.

*He prayeth best, who loveth best, All things
both great and small; For the dear God
who loveth us, He made and loveth all.*

The Sympathetic Jewel

> *"I say unto you, Love your enemies,*
> *bless them that curse you, do good to them*
> *that hate you, and pray for them which*
> *despitefully use you, and persecute you."*
> MATTHEW 5:44 KJV

What OPPORTUNITY HAVE I HAD TO REACH OUT TO ANOTHER?

Have you ever noticed that those who reject you often seem to lack joy? Have you ever considered that they could be guarded and standoffish because they have been rejected themselves?

Sometimes your warm attitude toward them can make all the difference. This is illustrated by the story of a man who visited a jewelry store owned by a friend. His friend showed him magnificent diamonds and other splendid stones. Among these stones the visitor spotted one that seemed quite lusterless. Pointing to it, he said, "That stone has no beauty at all."

His friend put the gem in the hollow of his hand and closed his fingers tightly around it. In a few moments, he uncurled his fingers.

What a surprise! The entire stone gleamed with the splendor of a rainbow. "What have you done to it?" asked the astonished man.

His friend answered, "This is an opal. It is what we call the sympathetic jewel. It needs only to be gripped with the human hand to bring out its full beauty."

People are very much like opals. Without warmth, they become dull and colorless. But "grasp" them with the warmth and love of God, and they come alive with personality and humor.

It's difficult to embrace those who have rejected us. However, if we can see beyond the facade they have erected to the potential inside them, we can be the healing hands of Jesus extended to them . . . and bring healing to ourselves in the process.

Nobody will know what you mean
by saying that "God is love"
unless you act it as well.

A Time for Everything

There is a right time for everything.
ECCLESIASTES 3:1 TLB

Today
IS THE BEST
TIME TO . . .

Most Christians are familiar with the passage in Ecclesiastes that tells us, "To everything there is a season." Consider this modern-day version of the same message:

To everything there is a time . . .
A time to wind up, and a time to wind down;
A time to make the call, and a time to unplug the phone;
A time to set the alarm, and a time to sleep in;
A time to get going, and a time to let go.
A time for starting new projects, and a time for celebrating victories;
A time for employment, and a time for retirement;
A time for overtime, and a time for vacation;
A time for making hay, and a time for lying down on a stack of it to watch the clouds go by.
A time for making plans, and a time for implementing them;
A time for seeing the big picture, and a time for mapping out details;
A time for working alone, and a time for involving others.
A time for building morale, and a time for growing profits;
A time for giving incentives, and a time for granting rewards;
A time for giving advice, and a time for taking it.

No matter what your situation or environment, the Lord has designed a rhythm for life that includes rest and exertion. If you maintain this balance, you'll likely find there is plenty of "time for everything" that is truly beneficial to you!

Time to do well, Time to live better,
Give up that grudge, answer that letter,
Speak the kind word to sweeten a sorrow,
do that kind deed you would
leave 'till tomorrow.

Rewards

Surely there is a reward for the righteous.
PSALM 58:11 NKJV

I have
STRESS IN
MY LIFE CON-
CERNING . . .

The writer of Hebrews encourages us to believe two things about God: First, He exists, and second, He is a "rewarder of those who diligently seek Him" (Hebrews 11:6 NKJV). Among those rewards are reconciliation to God, forgiveness of sins, peace of heart and mind, provision and help, and power to overcome evil. All of these are wonderful rewards—but they are also intangible ones.

Like children who live in a material world, we often desire a "God with skin on." We long to see, feel, and touch our rewards. We long to feel appreciation, to be hugged and kissed, and to receive tangible gifts from our loved ones.

Is there a link between the intangible rewards that come from God and the tangible rewards of the "real world"? There may be! Research has revealed that those who have less stress in their lives—a by-product of peace, forgiveness, reconciliation, and spiritual power—enjoy these rewards:

- Fewer illnesses, doctors' appointments, need for medication, and overall health care expense.
- Fewer repairs on appliances and machinery. Apparently when we are at peace on the inside, we use machines with more precision and patience. We break things with less frequency.
- Fewer automobile accidents. When we are feeling peace and harmony with God and people, we are less aggressive and more careful in driving.

Diligently seek the Lord today. Make your relationship with Him your number one concern. And enjoy the rewards He will bring your way!

God is never found accidentally.

Coping Skills

My times are in your hand.
PSALM 31:15 NRSV

I want
PEOPLE TO BE
PATIENT WITH
ME, BUT WHEN
I HAVE TO
WAIT I FEEL . . .

How we handle delays tells us a lot about ourselves.

Consider how one man handled a delay. Just as the light turned green at the busy intersection, his car stalled in heavy traffic. He tried everything he knew to get the car started again, but all his efforts failed. The chorus of honking behind him put him on edge, which only made matters worse.

Finally he got out of his car and walked back to the first driver and said, "I'm sorry, but I can't seem to get my car started. If you'll go up there and give it a try, I'll stay here and blow your horn for you."

Things rarely go as smoothly as we would like, and we don't usually schedule ourselves any extra time just in case something goes wrong.

The ability to accept disappointments, delays, and setbacks with a pleasant, generous spirit is a gift of graciousness that comes from one who has received grace from others in pressured circumstances. Life is a series of choices, and no matter what situation we are in, we always have the freedom to choose how we are going to respond.

Refuse to get out of sorts the next time your schedule gets interrupted or turned upside down. Pray for strength to remain calm, cheerful, relaxed, and refreshed in the midst of the crisis. And always remember: God's plans for you are not thwarted by delays!

Sometimes God's appointments
come from life's disappointments!

Seventy Times Seven

"Forgive, and you will be forgiven."
LUKE 6:37 NKJV

When one boy hit another during Sunday school class, the teacher's aid took the offending child outside for discipline. She then assigned a crafts project to the rest of the class so she could talk to the child who had been hit. "You need to forgive Sam for hitting you, Joey," she said.

"Why?" Joey asked. "He's mean. He doesn't deserve any forgiveness."

The teacher said, "The disciples of Jesus may have felt that same way. They asked Jesus how many times they had to forgive someone who was mean to them, and Jesus said seventy times seven." (See Matthew 18:21-22.) Joey sat thoughtfully, and the teacher continued, "Do you know how many times that is, Joey?"

Joey had just learned how to multiply, so he took a nearby pencil and piece of paper and worked this math puzzle. Upon getting his answer, he looked up at the teacher and said in shock, "Do you mean to tell me that Sam is going to hit me 489 more times! I'm going to be black-and-blue for forgiving him all year!"

To forgive does not mean another person's behavior has not hurt us or that they were justified in their actions. But forgiving means saying, "I choose to let you go. I will not hold the memory of this inside me. I will not seek revenge." We may have to "let go" 490 times. But in the end, we will be free, and the other person will be in God's hands.

"I can forgive, but I cannot forget," is only another way of saying, "I cannot forgive."

If SOMEONE HURTS ME, HOW CAN I FORGIVE AND STILL PROTECT MYSELF?

Lightening Up

Blessed be the LORD, for He has made marvelous
His lovingkindness to me in a besieged city.
PSALM 31:21 NASB

I can LOOSEN
UP MY DAILY
SCHEDULE TO
MAKE ROOM
FOR THINGS
LIKE . . .

When it comes to your daily schedule, are you strict or loose? Do you refuse to deviate from your to-do list, or are you easygoing enough to shift gears when opportunity knocks at your door?

A young mother with four small children had given up on ever finding time for a break. Her husband frequently worked overtime, which meant she was totally responsible for taking care of the house and the children. She had decided the only way to make it all work was to be as rigid as a drill sergeant.

Certain chores had to be performed at a set time each day and on certain days of the week. If not, she felt pressured to make up for lost time by staying up later or getting up earlier . . . which drained her energy, made her cranky, and resulted in getting less done the following day.

One afternoon, her five-year-old daughter came into the kitchen, where she was planning dinner. "Come to my tea party," she said, a big smile on her face. Normally, Mom would have said, "Not now; I'm busy." But that day she had a flashback to her own five-year-old self inviting her mother to a tea party and being turned down.

Instead of saying no, she helped her daughter put together a tea party. The two oldest children were at school. The youngest was napping. The house was quiet, and the young mother couldn't remember when she'd enjoyed a cup of tea so much.

Drop thy still dews of quietness,
Till all our strivings cease;
Take from our souls the strain and stress,
And let our ordered lives confess
The beauty of thy peace.

Fire!

Be pleased, O LORD, to deliver me:
O LORD, make haste to help me!
PSALM 40:13 NKJV

It's usually about teatime when we realize that the clock's been moving faster than we have. So we break into a mental sprint to see if we can beat the clock to the day's finish line. It's usually about this time of day when everyone and everything needs immediate attention. Sometimes we end the day thinking all we did for the last few hours was "put out brush fires." Consequently, the primary objectives of the day stand waiting for attention.

With the usual candor of children, one kindergartner shed some light on this late-afternoon dilemma. He was on a class field trip to the fire station to take a tour and learn about fire safety. The fireman explained what to do in case of a fire. "First, go to the door and feel it to see if it's hot. Then, if you smell or see smoke coming in around the door, fall to your knees. Does anyone know why you ought to fall to your knees?"

The little boy piped up and said, "Sure! To start praying to ask God to get you out of this mess!"

What a good idea for those brushfires that break out in the heat of the day! If we mentally and spiritually fall to our knees, we move our thoughts to God's presence around us and His authority over the circumstances we are facing.

Sometimes your teatime becomes a "falling on your knees" time!

Speak to Him thou for He hears,
and spirit with spirit can meet—
Closer is He than breathing,
and nearer than hands and feet.

Putting MY DAY IN GOD'S HANDS WILL HELP ME . . .

The Key Ingredient

This is the day the LORD has made;
Let us rejoice and be glad in it.
PSALM 118:24

DO I HAVE ALL THE INGREDIENTS FOR A FULFILLED LIFE?

Caroline's son, Brad, had left home for college a few months earlier, leaving her home much too quiet and empty. The phone hardly ever rang, and the doorbell remained silent. Now he was coming to visit.

Excitedly, Caroline changed the sheets on Brad's bed, fluffed his pillow, and straightened up his bedroom. Then she breezed into the kitchen to bake his favorite dessert—a buttermilk pound cake.

All the ingredients were on hand, and she almost had the recipe memorized. She measured them out carefully and made every effort to mix it as directed, but before all the flour was mixed in, the phone rang. After a brief conversation, she returned to the cake. She poured the batter into the baking pans and hurriedly placed them in the pre-heated oven.

About halfway through the baking time, she looked into the mixing bowl. Oh, no! She had left out a large portion of the flour! A quick glance into the oven confirmed her fears; the cake was not rising. She was so disappointed. Despite her good intentions, she had left out most of an important ingredient. The cake might have tasted okay, but it was flat and gooey.

Life is a lot like that cake. Some experiences may seem to be good and offer happiness, but without Christ, the most important element of life is missing.

Be simple; take our Lord's hand
and walk through things.

The Person in the Mirror

Looking unto Jesus the author and finisher of our faith; who for the joy that was set before him endured the cross, despising the shame, and is set down at the right hand of the throne of God.

HEBREWS 12:2 KJV

As Christ's nature grows within us, the selfish nature with which we were born begins to recede into the background. Our attitudes toward others change along with our behavior.

Some years ago, when I was away on a preaching appointment, my wife and little daughter stayed at the home of a friend. On the bedroom wall just over the head of the bed in which they slept there was a picture of the Lord Jesus, which was reflected in the large mirror of the dressing table standing in the bay of the bedroom window.

When my little daughter woke on her first morning there, she saw the picture reflected in the mirror and exclaimed, "Oh, Mummy, I can see Jesus through the mirror!" Then she quickly kneeled up to take a better look, but in doing so brought her own body between the picture and the mirror, so that instead of seeing the picture of Jesus reflected, she now saw herself.

So she lay down again, and again she saw the picture of Jesus. She was up and down several times after that with her eyes fixed on the mirror.

Finally, she said, "Mummy, when I can't see myself, I can see Jesus; but every time I see myself, I don't see Him."

When self fills our vision, we do not see Jesus. This afternoon, when the events of the day and your personal concerns are heavy on your mind, turn your eyes to Him.

Before us is a future all unknown, a path untrod; beside us a friend well loved and known—that friend is God.

I want TO SEE JESUS IN MY LIFE BECAUSE . . .

What Shape Are You In?

The inward man is being renewed day by day.
2 CORINTHIANS 4:16 NKJV

Why WOULD
I REQUIRE THE
INSIDE OF MY
DISH TO BE
CLEANER THAN
THE OUTSIDE?

Clay pots were valuable tools in ancient households. Large jars were used to store water and olive oil; jugs were used to carry water; and small terra-cotta vials held perfume. Clay storage jars were filled with grain and other foods. Homemakers used clay pots for cooking. At mealtime, shallow pottery bowls were used as platters and dishes. In the evening the homes were lit by clay lamps.

The potters who supplied these much-needed pots were important to the economic life of ancient villages. A modern potter described her craft like this:

Both my hands shaped this pot. And, the place where it actually forms is a place of tension between the pressure applied from the outside and the pressure of the hand on the inside. That's the way my life has been. Sadness and death and misfortune and the love of friends and all the things that happened to me that I didn't even choose. All of that influenced my life. But, there are things I believe in about myself, my faith in God and the love of some friends that worked on the insides of me. My life, like this pot, is the result of what happened on the outside and what was going on inside of me. Life, like this pot, comes to be in places of tension.[93]

Throughout the day we may be buffeted by stress, but remember, your inner life gives you the strength you need to become a useful vessel in the household of God.

The best time to relax is when you don't have time to relax.

Hold On!

Preserve me, O God, for in You I put my trust.
PSALM 16:1 NKJV

A crisis
THAT GOD
BROUGHT
ME THROUGH
WAS . . .

A little girl was very nervous at the prospect of her first horseback ride, although she was to be perched behind her grandfather, who was an excellent rider. As her parents helped her onto the horse, she cried, "What do I do? I don't know how to ride a horse! I haven't done this before! What do I do?"

Her grandfather said in a reassuring tone, "Don't worry about the horse or about how to ride it. Just hold on to me, Darlin', just hold on to me."

What good advice for us today! We thought our day was going to be a "tired old nag" sort of day, but it turned out to be a "bucking bronco" day instead. On days like that, we need to "just hold on" to our faith in the Lord and stay in the saddle.

The Lord knows the end from the beginning of each day, and He knows how long the current upheaval in your life will last. Above all, He knows how to bring you safely through each "wild ride."

Harriet Beecher Stowe offered this advice:

When you get in a tight place and everything goes against you, till it seems you could not hold on a minute longer, never give up then, for that is just the place and time that the tide will turn.

Always remember that you don't "ride" the beasts of this life alone. The Lord is with you, and He has the reins firmly in His grasp. Just hold on!

Whatever God calls us to do,
He also makes possible for us to accomplish.

Energy Crisis

The joy of the Lord is your strength.
NEHEMIAH 8:10 KJV

One OF MY
ROUTINES
THAT I WOULD
LIKE TO
CHANGE IS . . .

Most of us have a daily routine—a series of repetitious chores, errands, and tasks that demand our time and are required to maintain life at its most basic level. "Routine," says Jewish theologian Abraham Heschel, "makes us resistant to wonder." When we let our sense of wonder and awe drain away, we lose the sense of our preciousness to God.

Jesus recognized our preoccupation with these duties in His Sermon on the Mount. He said, "Do not worry about your life, what you will eat or drink; or about your body, what you will wear. Is not life more important than food, and the body more important than clothes?" (Matthew 6:25).

But how do we apprehend the life that is "more important than food" when so much of our time and energy are spent providing and maintaining the essentials of food, clothing, and shelter? The "daily grind" can cause us to lose our sense of God's purpose and presence. We may feel like Job, who despaired, "When he passes me, I cannot see him; when he goes by, I cannot perceive him" (Job 9:11).

If life's routines are wearing down your enthusiasm and joy, take time to seek out His love, majesty, and goodness revealed in creation. Be renewed in your joy of who God is—and who you are to Him—and find His strength and purpose in even your most routine tasks.

People need joy quite as much as clothing.
Some of them need it far more.

Easy as A, B, C

In the day of trouble he will keep me safe
in his dwelling; he will hide me in the shelter
of his tabernacle and set me high upon a rock.
PSALM 27:5

You never want to hear the words, "We need to run some tests" from a doctor. Our first inclination is to expect the worst. Especially intimidating are the machines used to diagnose our disorders. The Magnetic Resonance Imager (MRI), with its oh-so-narrow magnetic metal tunnel, can bring out the claustrophobia in all of us.

A test like this causes a real break in our daily routine. While we might never reach the point where we look forward to such "breaks," we can do what one woman did to use the time constructively.

Once inside the tube, she found herself on the verge of panic. Then she remembered some advice her pastor had given her: "When things are going badly for you, pray for someone else."

To simplify things, she decided to pray alphabetically. Several friends whose names began with A immediately came to mind. She moved on to B and continued through the alphabet. By the letter D she was totally oblivious to her environment.

Thirty minutes later, she was only halfway through the alphabet, and the test was done. A day later, she used a short "break" in her doctor's office to complete her prayers while she waited for the test results, which showed no abnormalities.

When you find yourself taking a break that would not be your chosen activity, turn it over to your Father God and watch Him transform it into a special time for the two of you.

Faith is the capacity to trust
God while not being able to
make sense out of everything.

Three PEOPLE
THAT I
SHOULD
REMEMBER TO
PRAY FOR
TODAY ARE . . .

Balm

Is there no balm in Gilead,
Is there no physician there?
JEREMIAH 8:22 NKJV

My FAVORITE
SONG OF
WORSHIP IS . . .

In centuries past, groves of balsam trees were planted on terraces in the hills south of Jerusalem. They were also planted in fields east of the Jordan River, in the area known as Gilead. The sap from the trees was harvested to create a balm that was considered to have great medicinal value in helping wounds to heal. The balm was used especially to treat scorpion stings and snake bites. Since scorpions and snakes abounded in the wilderness regions of Judea and throughout the Middle East, the balm was extremely valuable and was an important export item along ancient trade routes.[94]

The "balm of Gilead" is identified with Jesus. He is the One who heals our wounds.

Every day holds the potential for us to experience stings and bites, both literal and figurative. While not always life-threatening, these "jabs" from the enemy are hurtful nonetheless. How can we apply the balm of Jesus Christ to them?

The foremost way is through praise. Any time we find ourselves under attack or wounded, we can turn our minds and hearts to Him with a word, a thought, or a song of praise.

For example, if we feel attacked by a swarm of stinging problems, we can say, "Praise You, Jesus, You are my Deliverer, my Rescuer, my sure Help."

As you praise Jesus, you will find the pain associated with an incident or situation soothed. He is the Lord of Lords—including anything that tries to "lord" it over you!

We increase whatever we praise.
The whole creation responds to praise,
and is glad.

Holy Humor

He who sits in the heavens shall laugh.
PSALM 2:4 NKJV

The FUNNI-
EST STORY I
CAN THINK OF
IS THE ONE . . .

In Umberto Eco's novel *The Name of the Rose,* a villainous monk named Jorge poisoned anyone who came upon the one book in the monastery library that suggested that God laughed. Jorge feared if the monks thought God laughed, God would become too familiar to them, too common, and they would lose their awe of Him. Jorge probably never considered the idea that laughter is one of the things that sets us apart as made in God's image.

In *Spiritual Fitness,* Doris Donnelly tells us that humor has two elements: an acceptance of life's incongruities and the ability not to take ourselves too seriously. The Christian faith is filled with incongruities—the meek inherit the earth, the simple teach wisdom, death leads to life, a virgin gives birth, a King is born in a stable. And many of life's incongruities are humorous.[95]

"Lighten up" can be good spiritual advice! How can we renew our sense of humor?

- Be on the lookout for humor. Almost every situation contains some element of humor.
- Spend time with people who have a sense of humor—their perspective will be contagious.
- Practice laughing. Take a five- to ten-minute laugh break every day.

You can benefit from laughing. Humor requires a sense of honesty about yourself—without arrogance or false humility. Humor has also been proven to be good for your health. Take time to laugh each day—it is good for the soul as well as the body.

*Laughter is an inexpensive way
to improve your health.*

Encumbrances

Let us lay aside every weight, and the sin which so easily ensnares us.
HEBREWS 12:1 NKJV

I can SERVE
GOD FREELY IF
I CUT . . .

In Jules Verne's novel *The Mysterious Island*, he writes of five men who escape a Civil War prison camp by hijacking a hot-air balloon. As they rise into the air, they realize the wind is carrying them over the ocean. Watching their homeland disappear on the horizon, they wonder how much longer the balloon will stay aloft.

As the hours pass and the surface of the ocean draws closer, the men decide they must cast some of the weight overboard because they have no way to heat the air in the balloon. Shoes, overcoats, and weapons are reluctantly discarded, and the uncomfortable aviators feel their balloon rise.

However, they soon find themselves dangerously close to the waves again, so they toss their food overboard. Unfortunately, this, too, is only a temporary solution, and the craft again threatens to lower the men into the sea. One man has an idea: they can tie the ropes that hold the passenger car and sit on them. Then they can cut away the basket beneath them. As they do this, the balloon rises again.

Not a minute too soon, they spot land. The five jump into the water and swim to the island. They are alive because they were able to discern the difference between what was really needed and what was not.

Ask God to show you how your life could improve if you made some changes and dropped some things that are weighing you down.

✦

*It's not enough to be busy.
The question is:
What are we busy about?*

Stop and Think

*God . . . richly furnishes us
with everything to enjoy.*
1 TIMOTHY 6:17 RSV

Have you ever noticed that when we're in a hurry, we hit nothing but red lights? Although they are annoying when we're racing to an appointment, stoplights are there for our protection.

We need stoplights throughout our day too. Hard work and busy schedules need to be interrupted with time for leisure and reflection. Without it we can become seriously sick with stress-induced illnesses. Time set aside for recreation or relaxation can rejuvenate our spirits. This poem by W. H. Davies tells us to take time to "stop and stare":

> What is this life if, full of care,
> We have no time to stand and stare.
> No time to stand beneath the boughs
> And stare as long as sheep or cows.
> No time to see, when woods we pass,
> Where squirrels hide their nuts in grass.
> No time to see, in broad daylight,
> Streams full of stars, like stars at night.
> No time to turn at Beauty's glance,
> And watch her feet, how they can dance.
> No time to wait till her mouth can
> Enrich that smile her eyes began.
> A poor life this if, full of care,
> We have no time to stand and stare.[96]

There are two ways of making it through our busy life. One way is to stop thinking. The second is to stop and think. Take time to contemplate what life is for and to what end you are living. The word Sabbath literally means, "stop doing what you are doing."

A happy life consists of tranquility of mind.

I can SEE SEVEN WONDERFUL THINGS OUT MY WINDOW. WHAT ARE THEY?

God's Promise

"I am with you all the days (perpetually, uniformly, and on every occasion), to the [very] close and consummation of the age."
MATTHEW 28:20 AMP

I can
SAFELY TRUST
GOD BECAUSE
HE HAS . . .

A person who conducted an informal survey about the prayers of people in his church found that most people pray one of two types of prayers. The first was an SOS—not only "Save Our Souls," but also "O God, help us now."

The second was SOP—"Solve Our Problems." People asked the Lord to eliminate all needs, struggles, trials, and temptations. They wanted carefree, perfect lives, and they fully believed that is what God had promised them. He concluded from his survey: "Most people want God to do it all."

God has not promised, however, to live our lives for us—but rather, to walk through our lives with us. Our part is to be faithful and obedient; His part is to lead us, guide us, protect us, and help us. Annie Johnson Flint recognized the true nature of God's promise in this poem:

"What God Hath Promised"

God hath not promised
Skies always blue,
Flower-strewn pathways
All our lives through;
God hath not promised
Sun without rain,
Joy without sorrow,
Peace without pain.
But God hath promised
Strength for the day,
Rest for the labor,
Light for the way,
Grace for the trials,
Help from above,
Unfailing sympathy,
Undying love.[97]

You cannot control the length of your life, but you can control its width and depth.

Do what you know you can do today—and then trust God to do what you cannot do!

Knowing Your Worth

*Let your yea be yea; and your nay, nay;
lest ye fall into condemnation.*
JAMES 5:12 KJV

In his book *Up from Slavery,* Booker T. Washington describes an ex-slave from Virginia:

I found that this man had made a contract with his master, two or three years previous to the Emancipation Proclamation, to the effect that the slave was to be permitted to buy himself, by paying so much per year for his body; and while he was paying for himself, he was to be permitted to labor where and for whom he pleased.

Finding that he could secure better wages in Ohio, he went there. When freedom came, he was still in debt to his master some 300 dollars. Notwithstanding that the Emancipation Proclamation freed him from any obligation to his master, this black man walked the greater portion of the distance back to where his old master lived in Virginia and placed the last dollar, with interest, in his hands.

In talking to me about this, the man told me that he knew that he did not have to pay his debt, but that he had given his word to his master, and his word he had never broken. He felt that he could not enjoy his freedom till he had fulfilled his promise.[98]

The man Washington described knew that as a free child of God, his word should be trustworthy. We live in a world where giving our word is not taken seriously. God wants us to walk in blessing and sleep in peace, and that's why He exhorts us to stand by our word.

❧

*Self-respect is the noblest garment
with which a man may clothe himself.*

When HAS ANOTHER PERSON KEPT HIS WORD TO ME AND HOW DID IT AFFECT MY LIFE?

Wayside Stops

Jesus . . . withdrew again to a mountain by himself.
JOHN 6:15

My MOST
MEANINGFUL
WAY OF
COMMUNING
WITH MY
FATHER IS
BY . . .

A sanctuary is a place of refuge and protection—a place where you can leave the world behind.

Attending a worship service on a weekend does not usually provide everything we need to see us through an entire week. As inspiring as the service may be, we need something more to keep us going until the next service. We need stopping places during the week, intimate sanctuaries here and there where we can stop and let God refresh our soul with His presence.

What are some sanctuaries you might find to get away and find restoration?

- Reading Scripture is one such stopping place. Immerse yourself in a favorite passage or Psalm.
- A little book of devotion—such as the one you are reading now—is a good way to restore energy.
- A trusted Christian friend with whom you can be yourself is a type of sanctuary. You can gain a great deal from the faith, encouragement, and insight of others.
- Your own communion service during the week gives you a chance to take part in the nourishment of the Lord's Supper.
- Going to a park or sitting in your own backyard and reading gives you a chance to rest while enjoying God's creation.
- Singing aloud a great hymn or praise song helps to restore your joy.

Jesus is your Example, and He often went away to a quiet place to gain strength from His Heavenly Father. Establish your own personal sanctuaries today!

What sweet delight a quiet life affords.

What Do You Know?

*I consider everything a loss compared
to the surpassing greatness of
knowing Christ Jesus my Lord.*
PHILIPPIANS 3:8

"Knowledge is of two kinds," said Samuel Johnson. "We know a subject ourselves, or we know where we can find information upon it."

There's also a third area of knowledge: the unknowable. Try as we might to uncover all the secrets of the universe, there are simply some things we will never discover or comprehend. As the apostle Paul told the Corinthians, "Now I know in part; then [in the afterlife] I shall know fully, even as I am fully known" (1 Corinthians 13:12).

We must face the hard fact that we can never know everything there is to know about anything. We can never achieve perfection of skill to the point where we never make mistakes. In fact, the more we know about something, the more we realize how much we don't know. The more proficient our skills, the more we are aware that accidents happen, some days are "off" days, and everyone has a slump now and then.

If we choose, we can become obsessed with our own perfection and potential, spending all our available time reading, studying, and taking courses. A wiser way might be to spend more time knowing God. The more you know Him, the easier it is to trust Him, hear His voice, and show His love to your family, friends, neighbors, and coworkers. What we know and can do is never as satisfying or meaningful as knowing God and serving others.

Instead of trying to become a bank of information, become a channel of blessing!

How CAN
I BLESS MY
FRIEND
TODAY?

*Teach me, my God and King,
in all things thee to see; And what I do
in anything, to do it as for thee!*

Shortsighted

As we have therefore opportunity, let us do good unto all men, especially unto them who are of the household of faith.
GALATIANS 6:10 KJV

Today I
WILL FOLLOW
CHRIST BY . . .

A fellow approached a cab driver in New York and said, "Take me to London." The cab driver told him there was no possible way for him to drive across the Atlantic. The customer insisted there was. "You'll drive me down to the pier; we'll put the taxi on a freighter to Liverpool; and you'll drive me to London, where I'll pay you whatever is on the meter."

The driver agreed, and when they arrived in London, the passenger paid the total on the meter, plus a thousand dollar tip.

The driver roamed around London, not quite knowing what to do. Then an Englishman hailed him and said, "I want you to drive me to New York." The cab driver couldn't believe his good luck. How often can you pick up a person in London who wants to go to New York?

When the passenger began to say, "First, we take a boat . . . " the driver cut him off.

"That I know. But where to in New York?"

The passenger said, "Riverside Drive and 104th Street."

The driver responded, "Sorry, I don't go to the west side."

Look for God-given opportunities to serve Him by serving others. Don't allow your daily routines, personal biases, or shortsightedness to cause you to miss what the Lord wants to do in you and through you today.

∽

A good deed is never lost; he who shows courtesy reaps friendship, and he who plants kindness gathers love.

Giving Thanks

Do not be anxious about anything, but in everything, by prayer and petition, with thanksgiving, present your requests to God.

PHILIPPIANS 4:6

The Thanksgiving table stood ready, a plump turkey in the center and a myriad of side dishes that seemed to cover every remaining square inch. The aroma of stuffing wafted from the oven door as Susan set out the deviled eggs.

The combined smells brought back memories of the first Thanksgiving that Susan could remember. She had been a five-year-old then. That year she had contracted strep throat, which developed into rheumatic fever. She was sick for days. Her mother handled the sickness matter-of-factly, although she probably knew the risk of heart damage. Throughout the day and night, Susan would hear her mother slip into her room to check on her.

Standing at the stove, Susan stirred the gravy. Other Thanksgivings came to mind—seasons when she'd lost loved ones. Although those were the hardest, she was thankful that God had blessed her with people who had made a difference in her life. And a smile graced her lips when she thought of the Thanksgivings when her children were toddlers. She could almost hear the kids sitting on the floor banging on pots and pans with wooden spoons.

Susan brought her mind back to the present as her family began arriving. Her grandchildren burst through the back door, and she hugged each one. And looking Heavenward, she thanked God for all the memories yet to be made.

Thanksgiving . . . invites God to bestow a second benefit.

My MOST MEMORABLE THANKSGIVING DAY WAS . . .

Form and Substance

"When you pray, go into your room, close the door and pray to your Father, who is unseen. Then your Father, who sees what is done in secret, will reward you."
MATTHEW 6:6

Father,
TODAY I NEED
TO TALK TO
YOU ABOUT . . .

A devout Christian spent several minutes each day at prayer and meditation in his bedroom. He came to cherish this quiet time in his bedroom, but his cat came to like it too. She would cozy up to him, purr loudly, and rub her furry body against him. This interrupted the man's prayer time, so he put a collar around the cat's neck and tied her to the bedpost whenever he wanted to be undisturbed while at prayer.

Over the years, the daughter of this man noted how much his devotional time meant to him. When she began to establish some routines and patterns for her own family, she decided she should do as her father had done. Dutifully, she tied her cat to the bedpost and then proceeded with her devotions. But in her generation, time moved faster, and she couldn't spend as much time at prayer as her father did.

The day came when her son was grown up. He also wanted to preserve some of the family tradition that had meant so much to his mother and his grandfather. But the pace of life had quickened all the more, and there simply was no time for elaborate devotional proceedings. So he eliminated the time for meditation, Bible reading, and prayer. But in order to carry on the tradition, each day while he was dressing, he tied the family cat to the bedpost!

He who ceases to pray ceases to prosper.

Window on the World

> *O Lord, I pray, open his eyes that he may see.*
>
> 2 KINGS 6:17 NASB

I can

CHANGE MY

SURROUND-

INGS BY

ADDING . . .

A story from England called "The Wonderful Window" tells about a London clerk who worked in drab and depressing circumstances. But that ordinary clerk was not about to let his outlook on life be determined by the dreariness of his surroundings. So one day he bought a beautiful, multi-colored Oriental window painted with an inspiring scene.

The clerk took his window to his workplace and had it installed high up on the wall in his office. When he looked through his window, he did not see the familiar slum scenes, with dark streets and dirty marketplaces. Instead he saw a fair city with beautiful castles and towers, green parks, and lovely homes on wide tree-lined streets. On the highest tower of the window there was a large white banner with a strong knight protecting the fair city from a fierce and dangerous dragon. This wonderful window put a "halo" on his everyday tasks.

Somehow as he worked long hours at tedious book work and accounting, trying to make everything balance, he felt he was working for that knight on the banner. This feeling produced a sense of honor and dignity. He had found a noble purpose helping the knight keep the city happy, beautiful, prosperous, and strong.

You don't have to let your circumstances or surroundings discourage you, either. God has sent you to your place of work—whether it is at home, in an office, at a school, or in a factory—to do noble work for Him.

❧

It is our best work that God wants,
not the dregs of our exhaustion. I think
He must prefer quality to quantity.

The Trouble with Being Right

"Take heed to yourselves: If thy brother trespass against thee, rebuke him; and if he repent, forgive him."
LUKE 17:3 KJV

The KINDEST
THING
ANOTHER HAS
EVER SPOKEN
TO ME WAS . . .

A passenger on a dining car looked over the luncheon menu. The list included both a chicken salad sandwich and a chicken sandwich. He decided on the chicken salad sandwich but absent-mindedly wrote chicken sandwich on the order slip. When the waiter brought the chicken sandwich, the customer angrily protested.

Most waiters would have immediately picked up the order slip and shown the customer the mistake was his. This waiter didn't. Instead, expressing regret at the error, he picked up the chicken sandwich, returned to the kitchen, and a moment later placed a chicken salad sandwich in front of the customer.

While eating his sandwich, the customer picked up the order slip and saw that the mistake was his. When it came time to pay the check, the man apologized to the waiter and offered to pay for both sandwiches. The waiter's response was, "No, sir. That's perfectly all right. I'm just happy you've forgiven me for being right."

By taking the blame initially and allowing the passenger to discover his own mistake, the waiter accomplished several things: he allowed the passenger to retain his dignity, reminded him to be more cautious before blaming others, and created a better atmosphere for everyone in the dining car. Next time people blame you for their mistakes, don't get defensive, but instead find a creative way to make things right.

It is not who is right, but what is right, that is of importance.

Prayer Pause

Uphold me according to Your promise,
that I may live.
PSALM 119:116 AMP

When we pray at the outset of our day, our prayer is often for general guidance and help from the Lord. When we pray in the midst of our day, our prayer is much more likely to be specific and aimed at immediate needs and concerns. By the time a coffee break rolls around, we have a much better idea of what our day holds, including what particular dangers, difficulties, or temptations we are going to face! It is with that knowledge, born of experience, that this prayer of Saint Patrick takes on even greater meaning:

> May the wisdom of God instruct me,
> The eye of God watch over me,
> The ear of God hear me,
> The word of God give me sweet talk,
> The hand of God defend me,
> The way of God guide me.
> Christ be with me.
> Christ before me.
> Christ in me.
> Christ under me.
> Christ over me.
> Christ on my right hand.
> Christ on my left hand.
> Christ on this side.
> Christ on that side.
> Christ in the head of everyone to whom I speak.
> Christ in the mouth of every person who speaks to me.
> Christ in the eye of every person who looks upon me.
> Christ in the ear of everyone who hears me today.
> Amen.[99]

Take time in the middle of your day to ask the Lord for His wraparound presence, His unending encouragement, and His all-sustaining assistance. And in return, be a vessel that carries His presence, encouragement, and assistance to others.

My "COFFEE BREAK" PRAYER TODAY WILL BE ABOUT . . .

Do not look upon the vessel,
but upon what it holds.

God Knows!

"Even the very hairs of your head are all numbered."
MATTHEW 10:30 AMP

If JESUS
THINKS OF ME
TODAY, I HOPE
HE THINKS
I AM . . .

Do you ever wonder if God has lost your address? Do you ever think perhaps He has lost track of you or even forgotten you altogether? God's Word answers those thoughts with a resounding, "Not so!"

The psalmist recognized God's thorough and intimate knowledge of us. Read these words from Psalm 139, and be encouraged. The Lord not only knows, but He knows precisely what you are facing and experiencing today.

O Lord, you have examined my heart and know everything about me. You know when I sit or stand. When far away you know my every thought. You chart the path ahead of me, and tell me where to stop and rest. Every moment, you know where I am. You know what I am going to say before I even say it. You both precede and follow me, and place your hand of blessing on my head.

This is too glorious, too wonderful. . . . I can never be lost to your Spirit! I can never get away from my God!

You saw me before I was born and scheduled each day of my life before I began to breathe. Every day was recorded in your Book!

How precious it is, Lord, to realize that you are thinking about me constantly! I can't even count how many times a day your thoughts turn towards me. And when I waken in the morning, you are still thinking of me!

—Psalms 139:1-7,16-18 TLB

*Before God created the universe,
he already had you in mind.*

Whose Strength?

When I am weak, then I am strong.
2 CORINTHIANS 12:10 NKJV

The MOST
STRETCHING
EXPERIENCE
OF MY LIFE
HAS BEEN . . .

In the springtime, it's fun to watch tiny baby birds with downy crowns begin to find their way around. They make their way to the edge of their nest and take a peek over to view the very large, unexplored world around them.

At first they may look into the abyss and then shrink back to the familiar security of their nest. Perhaps they imagine the strength of their own untried wings is all that will save them from a fatal fall—and they know how weak and unproven those little wings are! Yet, when they are either pushed out of the nest or gather courage to launch out on their own to try that first flight, they find the air supports them when they spread their wings.

How often do we allow unfamiliar situations and circumstances to loom large and threatening in our imagination? Sometimes when we look at circumstances that lie outside our familiar "nest" we may feel just like a baby bird. We take a look at our own weakness, and we may want to turn around and head back to safety.

In times of crisis—either real or imagined— what is it that God has called us to do? He may be trying to push us out of our nest and "stretch our wings," so we can grow in our faith.

Let us not pray for lighter burdens,
but for stronger backs.

Knowing God's Will

I pray You, if I have found favor in Your sight,
show me now Your way.
EXODUS 33:13 AMP

Some of
GOD'S PLANS
FOR ME
INCLUDE...

Saint Ignatius of Loyola saw the doing of God's will as not only our command in life, but also our reward:

Teach us, good Lord, to serve thee as thou deservest: to give and not to count the cost; to fight and not to heed the wounds; to toil and not to seek for rest; to labor and not to ask for any reward save that of knowing that we do thy will.[100]

It is as we know we are doing God's will that we find true meaning in life and a deep sense of accomplishment and purpose.

How can we know that we are doing God's will? One of the simplest approaches is this:

1. Commit yourself to the Lord each day, and periodically throughout the day, by simply saying, "Lord, I put my life in Your hands. Do with me what You will."

2. Trust the Lord to send you the work and the relationships you need for His purpose in your life to be accomplished.

As Roberta Hromas, a noted Bible teacher, once said: "Simply answer your door, answer your phone, and answer your mail. The Lord will put in your path the opportunities that He desires for you to pursue."

God's will is not a mystery you try desperately to unlock. The key is to seek His will, to listen to the Holy Spirit, and to read and study His Word. Then you can know what He has planned for you!

A man's heart is right when
he wills what God wills.

The Ripple Effect

"[The mustard seed] indeed is the least of all seeds: but when it is grown, it is the greatest among herbs, and becometh a tree, so that the birds of the air come and lodge in the branches thereof."

MATTHEW 13:32 KJV

A century and a half ago a humble minister lived and died in a small village in Leicestershire, England. He lived there his entire life and never traveled far from home. He never attended college and had no formal degrees, but he was a faithful village minister.

In his congregation was a young cobbler to whom he gave special attention, teaching him the Word of God. This young man was William Carey, later hailed as one of the greatest missionaries of modern times.

The village minister also had a son—a boy whom he taught faithfully and encouraged constantly. The boy's character and talents were profoundly impacted by his father's life. That son grew up to be a man many considered the mightiest public orator of his day: Robert Hall. Widely admired for his saintly character, his preaching was powerful, and his sermons influenced the decisions of statesmen.

It seems the village pastor accomplished little in his life as a preacher. There were no spectacular revivals, great miracles, or major church growth. But his faithful witness and godly life had much to do with giving India its Carey and England its Robert Hall.

When you think you are having no impact in the world by teaching a Sunday school class or visiting those who are homebound, remember the little country preacher who influenced two nations for the Lord.

How CAN I REACH THE WORLD THROUGH MY CHILDREN?

∽≫↷

We never know what ripples of healing we set in motion by simply smiling on one another.

In Progress

He who has begun a good work in you will complete it until the day of Jesus Christ.
PHILIPPIANS 1:6 NKJV

TO BE
CHRISTLIKE I
WILL HAVE TO
CHANGE . . .

A sign in a hotel lobby that was being remodeled stated, "Please be patient. Renovation in progress to produce something new and wonderful." Perhaps we all need to wear a sign like that! We are all unfinished projects under construction, being made into something wonderful. Being mindful of this, we might have greater grace and patience for others, as well as for ourselves, while the work is underway.

Hope is the anticipation of good. Like the hotel lobby in the disarray of renovation, our hope is often in spite of our present circumstances. What is the basis for our hope?

For the Christian, hope is not simple optimism or a denial of reality. The Reason for our hope is Jesus Christ, the solid Rock of our faith. As the hymn writer wrote, "My hope is built on nothing less than Jesus' blood and righteousness." We are never without hope for our lives if we know the Lord Jesus.

The focus of our hope is to be like Jesus. This goal may seem too great and way beyond our ability to achieve, and it is.

The Scriptures tell us it is "Christ in you" that is our hope. (See Colossians 1:27.) The transformation of our lives into Christlikeness is a goal that is larger than life. As Paul wrote to the Corinthians, to have hope only for this life is to be miserable. (See 1 Corinthians 15:19.) The Christian hope is for this life and for eternity.

Our hope lies, not in the man
we put on the moon, but in
the Man we put on the cross.

Do-It-Yourself Misery

Deceit is in the heart of them that imagine evil:
but to the counsellors of peace is joy.
PROVERBS 12:20 KJV

My
RECIPE FOR
HAPPINESS
CALLS FOR . . .

Some people just can't figure out why life has dealt them such a miserable hand. They see others around them enjoying life, and that only adds to their misery. They're convinced their horrible lot in this world is a plot by others to keep them down. In truth, misery is always self-concocted. Here's a sure-fire recipe for misery printed in the Gospel Herald:

- Think about yourself.
- Talk about yourself.
- Use "I" as often as possible.
- Mirror yourself continually in the opinion of others.
- Listen greedily to what people say about you.
- Be suspicious.
- Expect to be appreciated.
- Be jealous and envious.
- Be sensitive to slights.
- Never forgive a criticism.
- Trust nobody but yourself.
- Insist on consideration and the proper respect.
- Demand agreement with your own views on everything.
- Sulk if people are not grateful to you for favors shown them.
- Never forget a service you may have rendered.
- Be on the lookout for a good time for yourself.
- Shirk your duties if you can.
- Do as little as possible for others.
- Love yourself supremely.
- Be selfish.[101]

This recipe is guaranteed to work. In fact, you don't even need all the ingredients to achieve total misery.

On the other hand, if misery's not your idea of a good time, do just the opposite. If you do, you'll have a hard time feeling even a little blue!

For most men the world is centered
in self, which is misery; to have one's
world centered in God is peace.

A "Body of Work"

Christ Jesus . . . gave Himself on our behalf that
He might redeem us (purchase our freedom) from
all iniquity and purify for Himself a people
(to be peculiarly His own).
TITUS 2:13-14 AMP

A close
FRIENDSHIP
THAT I HAVE
MADE
THROUGH MY
WORK IS . . .

Sixty-five years has within it exactly 569,400 hours. If you subtract the number of hours that a person spends growing up and receiving a basic high-school education, and then subtract the hours that a person normally spends eating, sleeping, and engaging in recreation, you will still have 134,000 hours for work between the ages of eighteen and sixty-five.

That's a lot of time! Yet, many people reach retirement age, look back over their years, and conclude: "I was only putting in time and drawing a paycheck."

Take a different approach, starting today. Choose to create a "body of work" with the time that you have!

A body of work is more than a career or a pile of achievements, awards, and accomplishments. A "body" of work is just that—physical and human. A body of work is people.

Get to know the people with whom you work. Spend time with them. Value them. Share experiences with them. Be there when they face crises and when they celebrate milestones. Count your colleagues—and also those above and below you on the organizational ladder—among your friends, and treat them as friends. Build relationships that endure through the years, regardless of who is transferred, promoted, or laid off. People are what will matter to you far more than possessions when you reach your retirement years.

See everything; overlook a great deal;
correct a little.

Make Hay while the Sun Shines

This is what the Lord says: "Stand at the crossroads and look; ask for the ancient paths, ask where the good way is, and walk in it, and you will find rest for your souls."

JEREMIAH 6:16

Medicine—what a glamorous profession! High salaries, prestige, respect, travel, speaking engagements, curing the sick, and discovering new drugs.

Medicine—occasional tedium, exposure to a host of diseases, making an incorrect diagnosis, watching patients die, long hours, no sleep, no family time, and malpractice suits.

Medicine—maybe not so glamorous after all.

When doctors spend most of the year trying to help their patients sort out various physical and mental ailments, while trying not to become emotionally involved, where do they go to heal their own wounded spirits?

One doctor in Michigan goes back home to Vermont to help her father and brother with the haying. "It's elegantly simple work," she says. The job has a set of basic steps that, when followed, result in neatly bound bales of hay that are then trucked off the fields and sold the following winter. Haying is hot, sweaty, tiring work, but it has a satisfying beginning, middle, and end . . . unlike medicine.[102]

All of us need an activity that is the antithesis of what we do all day. We need a cobweb-clearer, a routine-shaker. Crafts and hobbies for those in mental work. Puzzles or reading for those who perform manual labor. Gardening for workers with high stress. People activities for those who work alone.

We each need to be completely out of our normal work mode for a little while every day— and for a week or two when we can manage it. It's a crucial part of living a balanced life!

✥

Take rest; a field that has rested gives a bountiful crop.

I would LIKE TO TRY . . .

DECEMBER 7

We do not have a High Priest who cannot sympathize with our weaknesses, but was in all points tempted as we are, yet without sin.
HEBREWS 4:15 NKJV

I feel
CLOSEST TO
GOD WHEN I
AM IN . . .

When Jesus instituted the Last Supper, He told His disciples to "do this in remembrance of me" (Luke 22:19). Remembering someone is to allow them to shape and influence our lives. Jesus was asking His disciples to remember Him in the Lord's Supper so that even when He was no longer physically present with them, He would still be shaping and guiding their lives. When we go to the Lord's Table, we give witness to the fact we are depending upon Jesus.

As we remember Jesus, we have the picture of Him giving himself to us to nurture and feed our souls. A song written by Arden Autry describes how He lovingly gave—and continues to give—His life for us:

As you eat this bread, as you drink this cup,
Let your heart give thanks and be lifted up.
Your soul can rest in this truth secure:
As you eat this bread, all I am is yours.
All I am is yours. All I am I gave,
Dying on the cross, rising from the grave,
Your sins to bear and your life restore:
As you eat this bread, all I am is yours.
In delight and joy, in the depths of pain,
In the anxious hours, through all loss and gain,
Your world may shake, but my Word endures:
As you eat this bread, all I am is yours.[103]

Throughout your day, remember Jesus. Let Him direct your thoughts and ways.

The mind grows by what it feeds on.

Morning by Morning

O GOD, thou art my God; early will I seek thee.
PSALM 63:1 KJV

Great is Thy faithfulness, Oh God my Father!
Morning by morning, new mercies I see.
All I have needed, Thy hands hath provided.
Great is Thy faithfulness, Lord, unto me.

—Traditional Hymn

I could
SPEND MORE
TIME WITH
GOD IF I . . .

There's something fresh and new about the beginning of each day. As sun filters through the trees, as birds begin their morning song, as day dawns, there is a new awareness of God's hand at work in our hearts and lives. Yesterday is past; tomorrow is still a day away. But today offers a new beginning—here and now.

"In the morning, O LORD, you hear my voice; in the morning I lay my requests before you and wait in expectation" (Psalm 5:3).

Throughout Scripture, the Lord invites us to spend time with Him before we face the demands of our lives. He urges us to seek Him first, to give our best to Him first, and to ask Him first.

Why? Because we need Him. And knowing that we need Him is always a good place to start any day.

Just as a good night's sleep refreshes the body, so a quiet moment with God at daybreak revitalizes our spirit before the day's responsibilities descend upon us. Starting the day with a holy hush before the morning rush can make the difference between a day wasted and a day well lived.

"Rejoicing comes in the morning" (Psalm 30:5).

All the troubles of life come upon us because we refuse to sit quietly for a while each day in our rooms.

Holy Hush

You, O LORD, are a compassionate and gracious God, slow to anger, abounding in love and faithfulness.
PSALM 86:15

A piece OF GOD'S ARTWORK THAT I ADMIRE IS . . .

All is still as a man sits at his dining room table, allowing the pages of a well-worn Bible to slip slowly through his fingers and basking in the peace of the moment. The pages have a comfortable feel, and the soft plop they make as they fall barely disturbs the quiet. Early morning always brings with it a hush of holiness for him. In his mind's eye he remembers another such morning.

The new dawn air is tangy and sharp as he and his brother turn onto a gravel road bordered by wheat fields. Early in the growing season the wheat is about two feet high and a brilliant green. Suddenly the boy catches his breath. From the edge of the wheat field, a ring-necked pheasant comes into view just as a bright ray of sunshine creates a natural spotlight. As if showing off for God himself, the pheasant stops and strikes a pose.

Time stands still, sound ceases, and God paints an image on the young boy's mind that will remain for a lifetime. The beautiful hues of the pheasant, with its shining white collar glistening in the sunshine against the vivid green of the wheat, remain sharply etched in his memory. Whenever he relives that day, he experiences anew the presence of God and a supernatural sense of contentment.

All around us are awesome reminders of a big God who created everything in a matter of days. Isn't it great to know the Artist firsthand?

❧

When God makes His presence felt through us, we are like the burning bush; Moses never took any heed what sort of bush it was—he only saw the brightness of the Lord.

Wake-Up Call

Awake to righteousness, and sin not.
1 CORINTHIANS 15:34 KJV

How CAN
I PREPARE
MYSELF FOR
HARD TIMES
AHEAD?

Boot camp was a rude awakening for a young man who entered the Army to get away from his parents' rules. He knew boot camp would be tough, but he was certain he could handle it. Besides, boot camp only lasted for six weeks. After that he would be free!

Upon waking that first morning to his sergeant's yells, the young soldier came face-to-face with the reality that Mom, Dad, and all his teachers clumped together couldn't compare to what he was about to face. His six weeks loomed as an eternity. He regularly wrote his family and included the first thank-you notes his parents had ever received from their son. He even expressed thanks for what his teachers had done for him.

This young soldier found out quickly how to handle what could attack a soldier in war. He was faced with a reason to wake up and a reason to be prepared. The sergeant trained the young recruits to anticipate the enemy's strategy, making certain they knew the enemy was lurking and ready to attack without warning. He taught them that the enemy is extremely cunning and watches and waits to attack during their weakest, most vulnerable times.

The Bible tells us to awake to righteousness and to prepare ourselves, so we will not sin. God has provided the right armor and training required to defeat the enemy. We become soldiers for Christ when we join His family.

God shall be my hope, my stand,
my guide, and lantern to my feet.

Good Morning, Lord

*In the morning, O LORD, Thou wilt hear
my voice; In the morning I will order
my prayer to Thee and eagerly watch.*
PSALM 5:3 NASB

I find

MY BEST

OPPORTUNITY

TO PRAY . . .

There is something extraordinarily special about early morning devotions. Before the hectic day begins with its noise and numerous distractions, there is usually a calm that is uncommon to any other time of the day, a peaceful prerequisite for entering into the prayer closet with Christ. Christ set an example for us when He rose up early and prayed.

Morning is a wonderfully private time where intimate conversation and gentle responses can take place between God and His children. This is a time to listen to the very heart of God.

Oswald Chambers said, "Get an inner chamber in which to pray where no one knows you are praying, shut the door, and talk to God in secret. Have no other motive than to know your Father in heaven. It is impossible to conduct your life as a disciple without definite times of secret prayer."

Between Midnight and Morning

You that have faith to look with fearless eyes
Beyond the tragedy of a world of strife,
And trust that out of night and death shall rise
The dawn of ampler life;
Rejoice, whatever anguish rend your heart,
That God has given you, for a priceless dower,
To live in these great times and have your part
In Freedom's crowning hour;
That we may tell your sons who see the light
High in heaven—their heritage to take—
"I saw the powers of darkness put to flight!
I saw the morning break!"

—Owen Seaman

*I can tell you that God is alive because
I talked with Him this morning.*

The Art of Caring

*Now these three remain: faith, hope and love.
But the greatest of these is love.*

1 CORINTHIANS 13:13

Who

NEEDS MY

ENCOURAGE-

MENT TODAY?

This was the first meeting of a support group for middle school youngsters who had suffered significant losses in their lives. The group leader was unsure of what to expect, so the question really caught him by surprise.

"Why does God kill babies?"

The question hung in the air for an eternity, and two young faces stared intently at the group counselor, waiting for an answer. He gazed at the two brothers' faces as he contemplated how to respond. He wished to reassure them that God does not kill babies, yet, for the moment, the answer to the question seemed far less important than what prompted it.

"Something really sad must have happened for you guys to ask such a question," he finally responded.

The two brothers shared the sad story of how their entire family had hoped for a new baby. The boys wanted to become uncles in the worst way. Finally, their older sister became pregnant, but the baby was stillborn. They could not understand why this would happen.

With careful encouragement and much listening, the counselor found a way for the two brothers to come to grips with the loss of their niece. Although they eventually understood that the loss of their niece was not a direct act of God, they still struggled with why it happened.

As the other group members shared their own stories of loss and sadness, a kinship developed among the group that lifted the sadness.

Take time to care every chance you get!

❧

*The capacity to care gives life
its deepest significance.*

Just the Facts

*He that is void of wisdom despiseth his neighbour:
but a man of understanding holdeth his peace.*
PROVERBS 11:12 KJV

What TIME
HAVE I JUDGED
ANOTHER, TO
FIND LATER
THAT I WAS
WRONG?

There was once a man that John Wesley thought of as miserly; therefore, he had little respect for him. He felt so strongly about this man that, on an occasion when the man gave only a small gift to a worthy charity, Wesley openly criticized him.

Not long after, the gentleman paid a visit to Wesley. He was surprised to hear that this man—someone whom he assumed was simply greedy—had actually been living on parsnips and water for several weeks. The man told him that, in his past, he had amassed a great deal of debt. But since his conversion, he had made a choice to pay off all of his creditors and, therefore, was buying nothing for himself and spending as little as possible elsewhere in order to do so.

"Christ has made me an honest man," he said, "and so with all these debts to pay, I can give only a few offerings above my tithe. I must settle up with my worldly neighbors and show them what the grace of God can do in the heart of a man who was once dishonest."

Wesley then apologized to the man and asked his forgiveness.[104]

It's easy to find fault with others when we don't know their circumstances or the reasons for their actions. It's also amazing how a few facts can forever alter our perceptions. When we feel compelled to judge, it's a good time to ask God for wisdom and patience to understand the facts.

*Every man should have a
fair sized cemetery in which to
bury the faults of his friends.*

As Time Goes By

This is the day which the Lord has made;
we will rejoice and be glad in it.
PSALM 118:24 NKJV

Today, I
SHOULD TAKE
TIME TO . . .

"Where does the time go?" we ask. Here it is—a new day on the horizon—and we can't remember how it arrived so quickly. Why, last week seems like yesterday, and last year flew by like a video in fast-forward.

And worse, it's hard to remember what we spent it on.

Shouldn't I have more great memories? we wonder. *What did I accomplish?*

Singer Jim Croce mused in his hit song "Time in a Bottle" that "there never seems to be enough time to do the things you want to do, once you find them." We search so hard for happiness. But often, we don't understand that happiness is not a goal to be won, but a by-product of a life well spent.

This "Old English Prayer" offers simple instruction for enjoying the day that the Lord has made:

Take time to work, it is the price of success.
Take time to think, it is the source of power.
Take time to play, it is the secret of perpetual
    youth.
Take time to read, it is the foundation of wisdom.
Take time to be friendly, it is the road to happiness.
Take time to dream, it is hitching your wagon
    to a star.
Take time to love and be loved, it is the privi-
    lege of the gods.
Take time to look around, it is too short a day
    to be selfish.
Take time to laugh, it is the music of the soul.

True happiness comes from
the job of deeds well done,
the zest of creating things new.

A New Song

He put a new song in my mouth,
a hymn of praise to our God.
PSALM 40:3

What NEW
SONG DOES HE
WANT TO PUT
IN YOUR
HEART TODAY?

Singer and songwriter Bobby Michaels tells how one summer he sensed a growing hunger to come up with a new song, but he could not find it within him. As he was visiting his publishing company to discuss a new album, he met a young man working as an intern. The young man mentioned that he wrote songs, and Bobby found himself pouring his heart out to the young man.

"Forget what might be appealing or what might sell," said the young man. "Just tell me what you think God wants you to sing about." Bobby's story inspired the young man to write a beautiful song that uncannily communicated Bobby's heart. The name of the song is "My Redeemer Is Faithful and True." It is an unpretentious and simple prayer of thanksgiving to our Creator.

The sales staff and editors did not believe that it would sell. "Too slow," they said. "Too redundant." But Bobby remained adamant that this song was directly from God and that it was anointed of God.

Guess what? Bobby was right. God has used the song to bless countless numbers of individuals, and the testimony he gives at his concerts prior to singing the song makes thousands of hearts sing right along with him. And the young man who wrote the song was Steven Curtis Chapman, winner of numerous Dove and Grammy awards.

Isn't God simply amazing!

A bird doesn't sing because
he has an answer—he sings
because he has a song.

A Reason to Rise

Arise, shine, for your light has come,
And the glory of the Lord has risen upon you.
ISAIAH 60:1 NASB

A memory
I CHERISH
IS . . .

While camping deep in the woods, the first sense to attract our attention each morning is smell. The aromatic whiffs of food cooked over an open flame are a wonderful treat to awakening senses. The savory aroma of bacon, sausage, and especially a fresh pot of coffee, gently moves through the forest and rests overhead just long enough to rouse the sleeping camper and produce a memory like no other. Years later campers talk about that experience as if they were reliving it, almost capable of smelling the coffee right then. It's a wake-up call campers fondly cherish.

Each of us has moments like these that provide a platform for memories past that are special to us. These classic times of pleasure linger in our minds, much like the smells of a delicious breakfast on a long-ago camping trip. The first call of the morning brings us into the new day and helps to set the pace and tone for the tasks ahead.

Could it be that as followers of Christ, we experience wake-up calls in our lives that are for more than just reminiscing? Our wake-up calls, lessons learned, and "deserts crossed" with God's help and presence, can turn these experiences into opportunities that allow God's loving plans for our lives to shine through us to a lost and depraved world.

Isaiah shouted, "Arise, shine!" Share the joy of knowing Christ with others.

A candle loses nothing
by lighting another candle.

Strangers and Pilgrims

*There will be no more death or mourning
or crying or pain, for the old order of things
has passed away.*
REVELATION 21:4

I envision
MY FINAL
DESTINATION
AS A PLACE
OF . . .

Day in and day out, the details of everyday life can cause our attention to be focused on only the here and now. When change comes—the birth of a child, the first day of school, a new job, the death of a parent—it can be exciting, bittersweet, or even sad.

The first line of a hymn written by Albert E. Brumley gives us the perspective we should have toward the time we spend on this planet. "This world is not my home, I'm just a passing through."

In his book *Strangers and Pilgrims,* W. R. Matthews describes how we should see ourselves. While he doesn't recommend a total detachment from the life that swirls around us, he advises:

We should live in this world as if we did not wholly belong to it. It is wise to remind ourselves that even our most cherished ambitions and interests are passing; the soul will grow out of them or at least must leave them behind.

To the pilgrim these passages should not be wholly sad. He may feel regret, but not desolation; they do not cause him to rebel. These phases of life are incidents of the journey, but it is the way that matters, not the accidents of the road. The time has come to move on? Then break up the camp with a good heart; it is only one more stage on the journey home![105]

*By heaven we understand
a state of happiness infinite in degree
and endless in duration.*

What's the Problem?

I can do all things through Christ who strengthens me.
PHILIPPIANS 4:13 NKJV

When PROBLEMS LOOM LARGE OVER ME, I CAN . . .

Ever had a difficulty that gives you "2:00 A.M. wake-up calls"? It could be a project at work, a committee you've suddenly ended up chairing, or simply the challenge of trying to figure out how to get everything done with only two hands. Whatever the issue, it ruins your sleep and saps your energy for the upcoming day.

The developer of a popular series of business training films describes the phenomenon of discovering your problem-solving skills are going nowhere:

You start thinking, *I'm uncomfortable. I'm anxious. I can't do this. I should never have started to try. I'm not creative. I was never creative in school. I'm a complete failure. I'm going to be fired, and that means my spouse will leave me and*—in other words, you start enjoying a real, good, old-fashioned panic attack.[106]

Problems can feel ten times as large in the middle of the night. But in reality—and by daylight—solutions might not be as distant as they seem.

Inventor Charles Kettering had a unique problem-solving method. He would divide each problem into the smallest possible pieces, then research the pieces to determine which ones had already been solved. He often found that what looked like a huge problem was already 98 percent solved by others. Then he tackled what was left.

In bite-sized pieces, problems become more manageable. Remember that, with God, all things are possible. He can give us peace in our darkest nights and bring wisdom with the morning.

❦

Obstacles in the pathway of the weak become stepping-stones in the pathway of the strong.

Like a Newborn Babe

I will give you a new heart and put a new spirit within you; I will take the heart of stone out of your flesh and give you a heart of flesh.
EZEKIEL 36:26 NKJV

I enjoy
BEING UNIQUE
IN THE AREA
OF . . .

In 1994, Jim Gleason underwent a life-saving heart transplant at age fifty-one. After he survived one of the most extreme surgeries imaginable, many asked how it felt to live with a new heart. His analogy was "like being born again, but with fifty years of memories and experiences built in."

He tells of coming home just ten days after his transplant. He wanted to go for a short walk around the yard. Accompanied by his daughter, he gazed in wonder at the green grass—so brilliant after weeks of drab hospital-room walls. He recalls:

I stopped walking. "Look at that!" I exclaimed to Mary. I was pointing to our small maple tree, so vibrant with the colors of that crisp, clear fall day. Then I spied a grasshopper and, like the young child, exclaimed in glee, "Look at that! A grasshopper!!"

Her response, in disbelief at my reaction, was an almost sarcastic, "Well, if that's exciting, look here—a lady bug!"

After four years with his new heart, Jim still cherishes life's simple pleasures. And when is the danger of losing that gift greatest? "As friends and family wish you would return to being 'normal,'" he reflects. "I struggle to never become 'normal' in that sense again."[107]

With God's help, we, too, can walk in newness of life—no surgery required. Give thanks that we don't have to be "normal."

*Think not on what you lack
as much as on what you have.*

Double Blessing

*In your godliness, brotherly kindness,
and in your brotherly kindness, love.*

2 PETER 1:7 NASB

What ACT
IF KINDNESS
CAN I COMMIT
TODAY?

British statesman and financier Cecil Rhodes, whose fortune acquired from diamond mining in Africa endowed the world-famous Rhodes Scholarships, was known as a stickler for correct dress—but not at the expense of someone else's feelings.

Once it was told that Rhodes invited a young man to an elegant dinner at his home. The guest had to travel a great distance by train and arrived in town only in time to go directly to Rhodes' home in his travel-stained clothes. Once there, he was distressed to find that dinner was ready to begin and the other guests were gathered in their finest evening clothes. But Rhodes was nowhere to be seen. Moments later, he appeared in a shabby old blue suit. The young man later learned that his host had been dressed in evening clothes but put on the old suit when he heard of his guest's embarrassment.[108]

Rabbi Samuel Holdenson captured the spirit behind Rhodes' gesture, saying:

Kindness is the inability to remain at ease in the presence of another person who is ill at ease, the inability to remain comfortable in the presence of another who is uncomfortable, the inability to have peace of mind when one's neighbor is troubled.

The simplest act of kindness not only affects the receiver in profound ways, but brings blessings to the giver as well. It makes us feel good to make others feel good. So do something nice for yourself today—commit a random act of kindness!

*You cannot do a kindness too soon
because you never know
how soon it will be too late.*

Beauty for Ashes

God has sent me to bestow on them a crown of beauty instead of ashes, the oil of gladness instead of mourning, and a garment of praise instead of a spirit of despair.

ISAIAH 61:3

What TALENT HAVE I NEGLECTED AND WHY?

The gray December day reminded Sharon of a similar day when she was in seventh grade. She could still see her teacher standing at the chalkboard, asking the class to write a poem.

Aware that Christmas was at the doorstep, she began writing. Her poem, so different from those of her classmates, was about the birth of the Christ Child. She took it home and rewrote it until the poem shone as though it were the star of Bethlehem itself.

"This is wonderful," the teacher said the next day. "Did you do this all by yourself?"

Beaming, Sharon said, "Yes, ma'am." Then the teacher read the poem to the entire class. She was beside herself with joy that day.

A couple of days later, however, the teacher asked to speak with her in the hall. There, after talking to another teacher, she accused her of stealing the poem from a book. Brokenhearted, Sharon refused to write another poem—until twenty-five years later.

By then, Sharon was a woman who had returned to writing as a form of therapy during some difficult trials. One day, with Christmas again approaching, she wrote several Christmas poems. She sent them off to a publisher, expecting a rejection. Later, she received a letter indicating that two of her poems had been accepted.

Are you neglecting your talents because someone criticized you in the past? Don't let your gifts become ashes; turn them into a crown of beauty for God.

He who neglects the present moment throws away all he has.

Fix Your Focus

"I know the plans I have for you," declares the Lord,
"plans to prosper you and not to harm you,
plans to give you hope and a future."
JEREMIAH 29:11

Danish philosopher Sören Kierkegaard addresses the nature of true humility by suggesting we think of an arrow soaring on its course toward its target. Suddenly, the swift-moving arrow halts in mid-flight to see how far it has come, how high it has soared, how its speed compares with another arrow, or to apprehend the grace and ease with which it flies. Right at the moment when it turns to focus on itself, the arrow falls to the ground.

Preoccupation with self is counterproductive to reaching our goals. It is the opposite of humility, which is preoccupation with the Lord.

How many times do we compare ourselves to others and measure our success or failure according to someone else's life? The Bible says this is not wise. (See 2 Corinthians 10:12.) The reason God tells us that comparing ourselves to others is not wise is because His plan for our life is totally unique. If we have a question about our life, we should look only to Him.

Whether we are examining our hearts or using the gifts and talents God gave us, our focus is always on the Lord. Our motivation is to please Him, draw closer to Him, and serve those He leads us to serve.

The irony of the Christian life is that when we give our lives to God and to others, we receive true joy and fulfillment. Take your mind off yourself and concentrate on your loving Heavenly Father. Ask Him about His plan for your life.

Trust the past to the mercy of God,
the present to his love, and
the future to his providence.

Today,
I WANT TO
TRULY GIVE OF
MYSELF BY . . .

In Jesus' Name

My purpose is that they may be encouraged in heart and united in love, so that they may have the full riches of complete understanding, in order that they may know the mystery of God, namely, Christ, in whom are hidden all the treasures of wisdom and knowledge.
COLOSSIANS 2:2-3

People WILL
SEE JESUS IN
ME WHEN I . . .

Thirty-seven-year-old Joyce Girgenti, a Christian artist, shares her faith by painting the name of Jesus into her inspirational paintings.

In the fall of 1994, Joyce was approached by an organization to raise money for a local boys' club. They wanted her to donate a Christmas card scene. Her first effort, a fireplace scene complete with a Christmas tree and nativity, was turned down. Undaunted, she replaced the scene with another, and it was accepted. Later, she realized why her original scene was rejected—God had other plans.

Joyce had used a photo of her own fireplace to paint the original scene. Working from the top of the canvas, she painted the Christmas tree, the nativity on the mantel, the roaring fire, and the stones that formed the fireplace. As she began to paint the bottom of the fireplace, she turned to her daughter. "Wouldn't it be neat to hide something in the fireplace that refers to Christmas?" she asked.

Before her daughter could answer, Joyce said, "What better than Jesus? He's why we celebrate Christmas." She then arranged the fireplace stones to spell out the name of Jesus.

It's a mystery trying to find Jesus' name so well hidden in Joyce's paintings, but the real mystery is not His name—it is Jesus himself. Only when Jesus is revealed are we able to discern His hidden treasure for us—His gift of salvation.

Salvation is a gift you can ask for.

Yule Log

Thy name, O Lord, is everlasting,
Thy remembrance, O Lord,
throughout all generations.
PSALM 135:13 NASB

It took place around the second week of December every year. Mother would open her cedar chest and gingerly begin to sort through her most prized material possessions. She took such care as she reached inside and one by one removed items that held great meaning to her. Bubble lights, ornaments, tinsel, and many things shiny and fragrant renewed the season year after year.

One special item was always placed on the mantel, transforming the home. It was a Yule log, covered in artificial hyssop and man-made holly berries. It had a place in the center for a candle. A bright red satin ribbon was attached with a metal staple on the end to enhance its beauty.

Each year, the family had a tradition of discussing the yule log and remembering what each part of the decoration meant. The log signified a celebration, the birth of Christ. Hyssop, a fragrant herb, was used in ancient Hebrew sacrifices. The lovely red satin ribbon signified the blood of Christ that was shed for our sins. The holly berries represented growth, a bountiful supply. And the candle glowed as a loving reminder that Christ is the Light of the World.

Sometimes in the ordinary, sometimes in our traditions, sometimes in our celebrations, we can find the foundation of our faith. Here, a plain log, a few faded green leaves, some old berries, and a tattered ribbon tell the ageless story of God's infinite love.

God's love for us is proclaimed
with each sunrise.

If MY FAMILY COULD POSSESS SUCH AN OBJECT OF TRADITIONAL MEANING, WHAT WOULD IT BE?

Hearing God's Voice

Be still, and know that I am God; I will be exalted among the nations, I will be exalted in the earth.
PSALM 46:10

The AREA I
NEED TO
TRUST GOD
IN IS . . .

The last time Allison saw her sister, they had had a difference of opinion and decided to go their separate ways. She later learned her sister had turned her back on God.

As the years passed, Allison missed her younger sister and unsuccessfully tried to find her. For a long time, she pleaded with God to help her find Beth. Finally, she stopped begging God to answer her prayers and placed the request in His hands to do what pleased Him. The days, months, and years passed, and it seemed as though her prayers would remain unanswered.

But God had heard her prayers. Two weeks before Christmas in 1998, Allison took a batch of cards from the mailbox. All of the envelopes, except one, had return addresses. Curious, she turned it over and opened it.

"Please forgive me, Sis," it read. "I apologize for not getting in touch sooner. I hope we can talk." Allison looked at the enclosed photos, and tears sprang to her eyes. Fifteen years was a long time.

When the sisters finally spoke to each other, Allison was surprised to learn that her once-wayward sister was now a believer. "I still have the Bible you gave me when I was six," Beth said. "It's still in the original box, and not only that, I use it."

To Allison's surprise, God had shared His love gift of Jesus with her sister. How awesome is our God when we put our full trust in Him!

The more we depend on God,
the more dependable we find He is.

What Should We Do?

> *"I tell you the truth, whatever you did for one of the least of these brothers of mine, you did for me."*
>
> MATTHEW 25:40

You see them on the streets of every major city—the homeless. They live in a culture of their own in modern America, existing day-to-day in a world of handouts and hand-me-downs. Their presence is a source of heated debates in many cities, and no one seems to want them in "my neighborhood."

Where do they come from, and what should be done about them?

One answer can be found in the life of P. W. Alexander and her essay "Christmas at Home," where she reflects on her dedication to community service—much of which involves caring for the homeless. She writes, "As a child I did not look forward to the holidays. It began with Halloween. In the morning we went to church and in the evening we collected for UNICEF. Thanksgiving and Christmas were equally painful. My mother would sign us all up to work at the soup kitchen." [109]

Thus, she was raised in the art of serving, and as she grew older she began to understand better the reasons why her mother insisted that they care for others during the holidays. In fact, the closing words of her essay demonstrate the impact of her mother's actions: "I do this not out of a sense of duty or obligation; I do it because it is my family tradition." [110]

What neat family traditions are you creating for your children?

Dedicate some of your life to others. Your dedication will not be a sacrifice; it will be an exhilarating experience.

I cherish
MY FAMILY'S
TRADITIONS
BECAUSE . . .

Guess What?

Let them ever shout for joy.
PSALM 5:11 KJV

Father,

FATHER.

GUESS

WHAT—I . . .

"Mom, Mom, guess what, guess what!" she screamed as she bounded into the room and jumped into her mother's lap.

"What? What?" she responded with equal vigor and enthusiasm.

One of the greatest joys of Jean's life was seeing her seven-year-old daughter, Crystal's, contagious love of life. In fact, she seemed to attack life with a voracious appetite for discovery Jean had not seen in any other child.

Before she could respond, she remembered a similar time two years earlier when Crystal came home from school with a brochure that described the coral reefs found in the Florida Keys. At that time she could not read yet, but her teacher had read the brochure to the class, and she remembered it nearly word-for-word. A couple of weeks later, on a glass-bottom boat ride over the reefs, Crystal delighted everyone on board by identifying the types of coral even before the guide could point them out to the group.

Shaking Jean from her reverie, Crystal announced with glee, "My picture won first place in the County Art Fair!" Jean was so proud of her and so glad that God had blessed her life through Crystal.

God the Father also takes great joy in our accomplishments. Wouldn't it be neat to rush into His presence, jump onto His lap, and scream, "Guess what, guess what!" whenever we achieve a life goal?

Joy is the echo of God's life within us.

Grace Tickets

"The one who comes to Me I will certainly not cast out."
JOHN 6:37 NASB

God WAS
GRACIOUS
TO ME
WHEN HE . . .

A Bible teacher once talked about God's "Grace Tickets." She said God makes himself available to us no matter how many times we reach out for an extra Grace Ticket. His grace is available to us in liberal amounts. She even prayed that she would have the wisdom to know when to reach out and take another.

When the alarm goes off at 5:30 A.M., it is all too easy to slip a hand from under the covers and push that snooze button to allow for ten more minutes of sleep. You might repeat the same involuntary movement every ten minutes until 6 A.M., when the clock radio is programmed to come on.

The minute the announcer's voice is heard, you are immediately jolted from bed, realizing you have overslept and must do in twenty minutes what would normally take fifty.

We all need several of God's Grace Tickets for times in our lives when we attempt to put God and His timing on hold. Yet God has made himself available to us every minute of the day. We are privileged to call out to Him no matter how severe or minuscule our situation. His grace is sufficient for each of us—at all times. He never runs out. It is up to us to open our eyes each morning and reach out to the Giver of all Grace Tickets.

Grace comes into the soul as the morning sun into the world: first a dawning, then a light; and at last the sun in his full and excellent brightness.

A Photographic Memory

If we confess our sins, He is faithful and just to forgive us our sins and to cleanse us from all unrighteousness.
1 JOHN 1:9 NKJV

I can MAKE THE WORLD A MORE BEAUTIFUL PLACE BY . . .

Famed photographer and conservationist Ansel Adams was known for his visionary photos of western landscapes, inspired by a boyhood trip to Yosemite National Park. His love of nature's raw perfection is apparent in his stark, mysterious, black-and-white wilderness photos.

In 1944, he shot a beautiful scene, later entitled "Winter Sunrise: The Sierra Nevada, from Lone Pine, California." It portrays the craggy Sierra Mountains in the bright morning sunlight, a small dark horse appearing in the foothills.

But the story is later told that, as Adams developed the negative, he noticed an "LP" carved in the hillside. Apparently, some local high school teenagers had etched their initials on the mountain.

Intent on recapturing nature's original, he took a brush and ink and carefully removed the initials from his negative. The man who gave the Sierra Club its look believed in preserving, even perfecting, nature in life as well as in photography.[111]

Ansel Adams probably never gave a second thought to the unsightly scar on the mountain in his photo creation. In his mind's eye, he saw the beauty of the original and took steps to bring that beauty back into focus.

Someone once observed that "the purpose of the Cross is to repair the irreparable." Through the blood of Christ, we know that our sins have been forgiven—our scars erased—and that once removed, our sins are forgotten. When we are willing to confess our sins, He takes joy in restoring us to our original beauty.

The cross is rough, and it is deadly, but it is effective.

Saved by the Weeds

> *"While you are pulling the weeds,*
> *you may root up the wheat with them. '*
> *Let both grow together until the harvest.'"*
>
> MATTHEW 13:29-30

Farming, like other high-risk occupations, requires a great deal of faith, dependence, and trust in God's timing and goodness.

One year a potato farmer encountered some problems due to hot weather. Because potatoes are a very temperamental crop and must be in the ground a certain period of time, the farmer was concerned that the planting be done according to schedule.

The weather broke, however, and he planted the potatoes only five days late. As the cultivation program began, everything looked good except for two plots where weeds began to grow out of control two weeks before the harvest. It was too late to destroy the weeds. The farmer had to let them keep growing.

Another problem emerged when a truck strike interfered with the targeted harvest date. The farmer knew that leaving his potatoes too long in the Arizona summer heat would destroy the crop. In the meantime, the "carpet weeds" continued to flourish and provided an almost blanket-like protection over the potatoes, while taller weeds gave additional shade. Later as the harvesters examined the fields, they discovered that wherever the weeds had grown up, there was no spoilage of potatoes. In weed-free areas, the potatoes were ruined because of the heat.

God often uses seemingly adverse circumstances to shield and shade us from "spoilage" in our lives. The very "weeds" we chafe about—petty irritations, chronic interruptions, irregular people—are often the means He uses to enhance our ultimate growth and develop a harvest of Godly character in us.

Strength and growth come only through
continuous effort and struggle.

A negative THAT GOD USED FOR GOOD IN MY LIFE WAS . . .

Get Understanding

*Incline your ear to wisdom, and apply
your heart to understanding.*
PROVERBS 2:2 NKJV

What
ADVENTURE
WOULD BE
WORTH THE
RISK TO ME?

In a sociological study, fifty people over the age of ninety-five were asked the question: If you could live your life over again, what would you do differently? Three general responses emerged from the questionnaire.

If I had it to do over again . . .

- I would reflect more.
- I would risk more.
- I would do more things that would live on after I am dead.[112]

An elderly woman wrote this about how she would live her life if she had it to live over again:

I'd make more mistakes next time; I'd relax; I would limber up; I would be sillier than I have been this trip; I would take fewer things seriously; I would take more chances; I would climb more mountains and swim more rivers; I would eat more ice cream and less beans; I would perhaps have more actual troubles, but I'd have fewer imaginary ones.

You see, I'm one of those people who lives sensibly and sanely hour after hour, day after day. Oh, I've had my moments, and if I had it to do over again, I'd have more of them. In fact, I'd try to do nothing else, just moments, one after the other instead of living so many years ahead of time.[113]

Listen and learn! Life cannot be all work and no play, and yet you want your life to be meaningful to God, to your loved ones who follow you, and to yourself.

Knowledge comes, but wisdom lingers.

Acknowledgements

Jewish Proverb (9, 12, 65, 268), Robert Seymour Bridges (10, 33), Indian Proverb (11), Saint Bernard (13), Charles Dickens (14, 264), Author Unknown (15, 16, 31, 38, 55, 56, 70, 89, 90, 98, 100, 112, 122, 123, 124, 129, 132, 163, 165, 176, 181, 194, 205, 217, 253, 257, 267, 280, 292, 308, 309, 311, 316, 318, 323, 324, 325, 329, 366, 367), Meister Eckhart (17), Elie Wiesel (18), Bernard Meltzer (19), Mary Gardiner Brainard (20), Lord Chesterfield (21, 120), Plutarch (22), Thales (23), C. S. Lewis (24, 25, 255), English Proverb (26, 40, 99, 157, 159, 238), Danish Proverb (27, 28, 97), Daniel Louis Rottinghans (29), Lin Yutang (30), Thomas Heywood (32), Robert Bridges (33), Douglas Jerrold (34), Samuel Taylor Coleridge (35, 68, 114, 142, 314), Oswald Chambers (36, 126, 155, 250, 263, 289) John Dryden (37), Herbert Hoover (39), Walt Whitman (41), German Proverb (42), Arthur Helps (43), Barbara J. Winter (44) Miguel de Cervantes (45, 102), Oswald C. Hoffmann (46), Samuel Wilberforce (47), Robert Browning (48, 82, 118), Chinese Proverb (49, 94, 214), Jospeh Addison (50), Horace Bushnell (51), Theodore Roosevelt (52), Christina Rossetti (53), Saint Augustine of Hippo (54, 104, 365), Ella Wheeler Wilcox (55), Robert Harold Schuller (58, 295), Nicholas Grimald (59), Henry Drummond (60, 235, 305, 345), Washington Irving (61), Thomas Jefferson (62, 286), Ralph Waldo Emerson (63, 77, 106, 111, 128, 212, 269, 363), Margaret Sangster (64), John Flavel (66), Benjamin Franklin (67, 151, 192, 201, 213, 360), Aristotle (69, 79), E. C. Rayburn (71), Robert Burns (72), Henry David Thoreau (73, 143, 215, 259, 330), George Herbert (74, 335), George E. Rees (75), OVID (76, 349), Epictetus (78), Italian Proverb (81), Frances J. Roberts (83, 167, 188), Saint Basil (83, 336), Thomas Carlyle (84, 361), Richard Owen Roberts (85), Erwin W. Lutzer (86, 342), Amelia C. Welby (87), Phillips Brooks (88), John White (89), William Bernard Ullathorne (91), Dorothy Bernard (94), Inscription over Mantel of Hinds Head Hotel, England (95), Francis Bacon (96), Thomas à Kempis (100, 142, 297), Victor Hugo (104), Colin Urquhart (106), French Proverb (107, 137), Orison Swett Marden (108, 182), James Dobson (109, 113, 211, 216), Gabrielle Coco Chanel (111), Johann Kaspar Lavater (115), Henry Ward Beecher (116, 186, 319, 356), Walter Rauschenbusch (118, 307), François Fénelon (119), Andrew Murray (121), Thomas Tusser (125), Charles (127, 170), Sir Lohn Lubbock (130), Dean Hole (131), Charles Wesley (133), Edgar W. Work (134), Henry Van Dyke (136), Vance Havner (135, 296), Robert Green Ingersoll (138), William Shakespeare (139, 223, 234, 353), John Heywood (140), Marcus Tullius Cicero (141, 225, 331), Robert Hall (144), William Wordsworth (145, 153), Persian Proverb (146), Saint Francis de Sales (147), Erasmus (148), John Sheffield, Duke of Buckingham and Normandy (149), Maltbie D. Babcock (150, 300), Albert Pine (152), Julia A. Fletcher Carney (154, 196), A.W. Tozer (156, 204, 287, 298, 317, 372), Joshua Loth Liebman (158), Thomas Adams (160), Sidney Greenberg (160), Paul E. Scherer (161), James Martineau (162), F. B. Meyer (164, 256), David Belasco (166), Martin Luther (168, 189), *Book of Wisdom* (169), Traditional Amish Prayer (171), Brother Lawrence of the Resurrection (173), Ian Maclaren (173), George Horne (174), Dante Alighieri (175), Johann Wolfgang von Goethe (177), Hugh Walpole (178), Samuel Smiles (179, 333), John Oxenham (180), William Cowper (183), Edward Rowland Sill (184), Demosthenes (185), Sir William Temple (187), Motto from an Amish School (190), Robert Louis Stevenson (191), Alexander Pope (193), Roberta S. Culley (195), Mahatma Gandhi (197), Lucy Larcom (198), Sir James M. Barrie (199), Henry Ford (200, 239), George Eliot (202, 352), Fred Beck (203), Henry Wadsworth Longfellow (206), Saint Vincent de Paul (207), Pearl S. Buck (208), Elbert Hubbard (209), Charles R. Swindoll (210, 242), Helen Steiner Rice (218), Johann Tauler (219), Jakob Bohme (220), Rainer Maria Rilke (221), Milo H. Gates (222), James Douglas (224), Canon Henry Ellacombe (226), George M. Adams (227), B. C. Forbes (228), John Powell (229), Philip James Bailey (230, 261), William Frederick Halsey Jr.(231), Martin Luther King Jr. (232, 283) Charles G. Finney (233), Jean-Pierre Camus (236), Hammer William Webb-Peploe (237), Katharine Tynan Hinkson (240), Norman Vincent Peale (241), Elton Trueblood (243), Terence (244), John Ruskin (245), Saint John

Chrysostom (246), Daniel Bliss (247), Rev. J. M. Gibbon (248), Prentice Mulford (249), Robert Montgomery (251), Dwight Lyman Moody (252), Thomas Benton Brooks (254), Abraham Lincoln (258), Erich Fromm (260), Paul Tillich (262), W. D. Gough (265), Bill Gothard (266), John Henry Jowett (270), Josh Billing (271), Sir William Osler (272), Johann Tauler (273), George MacDonald (274, 339), Elbert Hubbard (275), Harold S. Hulbert (276), John Kendricks Bangs (277), Ralph Washington Sockman (278, 290, 292, 312), Parks Cousins (279), Corrie ten Boom (281), Roy L. Smith (282), Giambattista Giraldi (284), Mark Twain (285), Frederick William Faber (288), William Penn (291), John R. MacDuff (293, 294), James Russell Lowell (299), Angelus Silesius (301), Isaac Penington (302), John Milton (303), Henry Rische (304), William Mountford (306), Frederick James Woodbridge (310), Charles E. Jefferson (313), Lawrence Pearsall Jacks (315), John Greenleaf Whittier (320), Alfred Lord Tennyson (321, 374), Father Andrew (322), Martha Collier Graham (326), James Kok (327), Charles Fillmore (328), Evan Esar (332), William Hawthorden Drummond (334), Robert Herrick (337), Sir William Gurney Benham (338), Thomas Huxley (340), Hebrew Proverb (341), Amish Saying (343), Saint Thomas Aquinas (344), Don Basham (346), Donald Hankey (347), Pope John XXIII (348), Josiah Gilbert Holland (350), Blaise Pascal (351), Billy Graham (354), Pablo Casals (355), Antoine de Saint-Exupéry (357), Joan Anglund (358), Proverb (359), Greek Proverb (362), Johann Friedrich Von Schiller (364), Cliff Richards (368), Thomas Dooley (369), Joseph Columba Marmion (370), Thomas Adams (371), Napoleon Hill (373).

ENDNOTES

1 Craig B. Larson, *Illustrations for Preaching & Teaching* (Grand Rapids, MI: Baker Book House, 1993) p. 106.

2 *Reader's Digest* (October 1991) pp. 59-62.

3 *Reader's Digest* (March 1991) pp. 128-132.

4 *Reader's Digest* (December 1992) pp. 101-104.

5 Craig B. Larson, *Illustrations for Preaching & Teaching* (Grand Rapids, MI: Baker Book House, 1993) p. 106.

6 Kenneth W. Osbeck, *Amazing Grace* (Grand Rapids, MI: Kregel Publications, 1990) p. 38.

7 Anne Frank, *The Diary of a Young Girl* (NY: Doubleday, 1952).

8 Ibid.

9 Ruth Youngdahl Nelson, *God's Song in My Heart* (Philadelphia: Fortress Press, 1957) pp. 248-249.

10 *Reader's Digest* (March 1999) p. 117.

11 Linda J. Vogel, *Teaching and Learning in Communities of Faith* (San Francisco: Jossey-Bass Publishers, 1991) p. 124.

12 *A Moment a Day*, Mary Beckwith and Kathi Milled, eds. (Ventura, CA: Regal Books, 1988) p. 37.

13 Meryle Secrest, *Leonard Bernstein: A Life* (Knopf, 1995).

14 Ibid.

15 The Misheard Lyrics Website, *www.kissthisguy.com*.

16 *Today in the Word* (September 2, 1992).

17 Maya Angelou, *Wouldn't Take Nothin' for My Journey Now* (NY: Random House, 1993) p. 62.

18 Judy Seymour, "The Freeway Not Taken: Lake Route Worth the Slower Pace," *Minneapolis Star Tribune* (May 12, 1997) p. 15A.

19 "Words of Love By Mother Teresa," *Education for Democracy*, Benjamin R. Barber and Richard M. Battistoni, eds. (Dubuque: Kendall / Hunt Publishing Company, 1993).

20 Ibid.

21 *Masterpieces of Religious Verse*, James Dalton Morrison, ed. (NY: Harper & Brothers Publishers, 1948).

22 Jean Shepherd, *The Endless Streetcar Ride into the Night, and the Tinfoil Noose*, in *The Riverside Reader*, Vol. 1, p. 17.

23 Patricia D. Brown, *365 Affirmations for Hopeful Living* (August 17).

24 Aubrey Franklin, *Teatime by the Tea Ambassador* (NY: Frederick Fell Publishers, Inc., 1981) pp. xi-xii.

25 Paul Lee Tan, *Encyclopedia of 7700 Illustrations* (Garland, TX: Bible Communications Inc., 1979) p. 1477.

26 Aubrey Franklin, *Teatime by the Tea Ambassador* (NY: Frederick Fell Publishers, Inc., 1981) p. 62.

27 Joni Eareckson Tada, *Diamonds in the Dust* (Grand Rapids, MI: Zondervan, 1993) February 17 entry.

28 San Francisco Chronicle (February 4, 1996) p. 4.

[29] Charlie W. Shedd, *Brush of an Angel's Wings* (Ann Arbor, MI: Servant Publications, 1994).

[30] Irene Harrell, *Ordinary Days with an Extraordinary God* (1971).

[31] Author unknown.

[32] Walter B. Knight, *Knight's Master Book of 4,000 Illustrations* (Grand Rapids, MI: Eerdmans Publishing Co., 1956) p. 448.

[33] Ibid.

[34] Paul Lee Tan, *Encyclopedia of 7,700 Illustrations* (Garland, TX: Bible Communications Inc., 1979) p. 1387.

[35] *Newsweek* (January 22, 1996) p. 14.

[36] *Webster's New World Dictionary of the American Language* (NY: World Publishing Co., 1968) p. 1258.

[37] *Today in the Word* (February 1991) p. 10.

[38] *The Forbes Scrapbook of Thoughts on the Business of Life* (Chicago: Triumph Books, 1992) p. 111.

[39] *San Luis Obispo Telegram/Tribune* (March 9, 1996) p. C8.

[40] Helen Simpson, *The London Ritz Book of Afternoon Tea* (NY: Arbor House, 1986) pp. 6-7.

[41] *Treasury of Christian Faith,* Stanley I. Stuber and Thomas Curtis Clark, eds. (NY: Association Press, 1949) p. 806.

[42] W. Phillip Keller, *Songs of My Soul,* Al Bryant, ed. (Dallas, TX: Word Publishing, 1989) pp. 100-101,158.

[43] Kelly McHugh, "The Upper Room" (January 9, 1999).

[44] Marion Bond West, *Look Out Fear, Here Comes Faith!* (Ann Arbor, MI: Servant Publications, 1991) pp. 155-158.

[45] Nanette Thorsen-Snipes, *Georgia Magazine* (1999, to be published).

[46] Nanette Thorsen-Snipes, *Southern Lifestyles* (Summer 1996) p. 38.

[47] Catherine Marshall, *Beyond Our Selves* (NY: McGraw-Hill, 1961) pp. 87-88.

[48] *The New Dictionary of Thoughts,* Tryon Edwards, ed. (NY: Standard Book Company, 1963) p. 506.

[49] Richard Blanchard, "Fill My Cup, Lord," *Chorus Book* (Dallas: Word, Inc., 1971).

[50] *Encyclopedia of 7700 Illustrations,* Paul Lee Tan (Garland, TX: Bible Communications, Inc., 1979) pp.1477-1479

[51] Nanette Thorsen-Snipes, *After the Storm: Learning to Abide* (Star Books, 1990).

[52] Helen Keller, *The Open Door* (NY: Doubleday & Co., 1957) pp. 12-13.

[53] Swindoll, *Hand Me Another Brick* (Thomas Nelson, 1978) pp. 82, 88.

[54] Lloyd John Ogilvie, *Silent Strength for My Life* (Eugene, OR: Harvest House Publishers, 1990) p. 32.

[55] Reuben P. Job and Norman Shawchuck, *A Guide to Prayer* (Nashville, TN: The Upper Room, 1983) p. 234.

[56] *San Luis Obispo Telegraph-Tribune* (January 31, 1996) B-3.

[57] Donald S. Whitney, *Spiritual Disciplines for the Christian Life* (Colorado Springs: NavPress, 1991) p. 37

[58] Denis Waitley and Reni Witt, *The Joy of Working* (NY: Dodd Mead and Company, 1985) p. 253.

⁵⁹ *Pacific Discovery* (Summer 1990) pp. 23-24.

⁶⁰ Walter B. Knight, *Knight's Master Book of 4,000 Illustrations* (Grand Rapids, MI: William B. Eerdmans Publishing Co., 1956) p. 93.

⁶¹ Denis Waitley and Reni L. Witt, *The Joy of Working* (NY: Dodd, Mead and Company, 1985) pp. 23-24.

⁶² *The Message,* Eugene H. Peterson, ed. (Colorado Springs: Navpress, 1993, 1994, 1995) pp. 722-723.

⁶³ Gary Johnson, *Reader's Digest* (September 1991) pp. 164-165.

⁶⁴ *The Methodist Reporter* (November/December 1995) editorial section.

⁶⁵ Charles R. Swindoll, *The Finishing Touch* (Dallas: Word Publishing, 1994) pp. 186-187.

⁶⁶ *Reader's Digest* (December 1991) pp. 96-100.

⁶⁷ Marjorie Holmes, *Lord, Let Me Love* (NY: Doubleday) pp. 104-105.

⁶⁸ Author unknown.

⁶⁹ Mike Nichols, "Self-Esteem," *The Complete Book of Everyday Christianity,* Robert Banks and R. Paul Stevens, eds. (Downers Grove, IL: Intervarsity Press, 1997) p. 872.

⁷⁰ *Christianity Today* (December 9, 1996) Vol. 40, No. 14, p. 80.

⁷¹ Swindoll, *Hand Me Another Brick* (Thomas Nelson, 1978) pp. 82, 88.

⁷² *Today in the Word,* Moody Bible Institute (January 1992) p. 8.

⁷³ Bill Cosby, *Fatherhood* (New York; Berkley Books, 1986).

⁷⁴ George Sweeting, *Who Said That?* (Chicago: Moody Press, 1995).

⁷⁵ Barbara Hatcher, *Vital Speeches* (March 1, 1987).

⁷⁶ *Treasury of the Christian Faith,* Stanley Stuber and Thomas Clark, eds. (NY: Association Press, 1949) p. 355.

⁷⁷ *Health* (March/April 1995) pp. 48-49.

⁷⁸ Ginger Galloway, *Guideposts* (August 1997).

⁷⁹ Hannah Whitall Smith, *The Christian's Secret of a Happy Life* pp. 38-40.

⁸⁰ Billy Graham, *Unto the Hills: A Devotional Treasury* (Waco, TX: Word Books, 1986) p. 158.

⁸¹ Ibid. p. 223.

⁸² *A Moment a Day,* Mary Beckwith and Kathi Mills, eds. (Ventura, CA: Regal Books, 1988) p. 25.

⁸³ Ibid. p. 174.

⁸⁴ Ibid. p. 184.

⁸⁵ Herman W. Gockel, *Give Your Life a Lift* (St. Louis: Concordia Publishing House, 1968) pp. 38-39.

⁸⁶ Ibid. pp. 56.

⁸⁷ Prevention (March 1996) pp. 25- 26.

⁸⁸ *The Treasury of Inspirational Quotations & Illustrations,* E. Paul Hovey, ed. (Grand Rapids, MI: Baker Books, 1994) p. 168.

⁸⁹ *The Treasure Chest,* Brian Culhane, ed. (San Francisco: HarperCollins, 1995) p. 92.

⁹⁰ Ibid. p. 94.

⁹¹ Ibid. p. 146.

⁹² *The Upper Room* (May-June 1996) p. 15.

⁹³ Patricia Gentry, *Teatime Collections* (San Ramon, CA: Chevron Chemical Co., 1988) p. 5.

[94] *A Guide to Prayer for All God's People,* Rueben P. Job and Norman Shawchuck, eds. (Nashville: Upper Room Books, 1990) pp. 255-256.

[95] *Encyclopedia Judaica,* Prof. Cecil Roth and Dr. Geoffrey Wigoder, eds. (Jerusalem: Kefer Publishing House, 1972) Vol. 4, pp. 142-143.

[96] Doris Donnelly, *Spiritual Fitness* (San Francisco: Harper, 1993) pp. 111-124.

[97] "Leisure," *The Family Book of Best Loved Poems,* David L. George, ed. (Garden City, NY: Doubleday & Co., 1952) p. 261.

[98] *The Treasure Chest,* Brian Culhane, ed. (San Francisco: Harper, 1995) p. 162.

[99] Craig B. Larson, *Illustrations for Preaching & Teaching* (Grand Rapids, MI: Baker Book House, 1993) p. 190.

[100] *The Treasure Chest,* Brian Culhane, ed. (San Francisco: Harper, 1995) p. 171.

[101] Ibid.

[102] Walter B. Knight, *Knight's Master Book of 4,000 Illustrations* (Grand Rapids, MI: William B. Eerdmans Publishing Co., 1956) p. 615.

[103] JAMA (January 10, 1996) p. 99.

[104] Arden Autry.

[105] *Daily Bread* (July 20, 1992).

[106] John Baillie, *A Diary of Readings* (Collier Books, Macmillan Publishing Co., NY, 1955) Day 182.

[107] *Newsweek* (February 15, 1999) p. 47.

[108] Jim Gleason (Transplant Recipient Support List: trnsplnt@wuvmd.wustl.edu).

[109] *Today in the Word* (February 1991) p. 10.

[110] P. W. Alexander, "Christmas at Home," *Writing for Change: A Community Reader* (San Francisco, CA: McGraw-Hill, Inc., 1995) pp. 100-101.

[111] Ibid. p. 102.

[112] Ansel Adams, *Morning Edition* 11-24-97 (National Public Radio).

[113] Tony Campolo, "Who Switched the Price Tags?" *The Inspirational Study Bible,* Max Lucado, ed., (Dallas, TX: Word Publishing, 1995) p. 402.

[114] *Illustrations Unlimited,* James W. Hewett, ed. (Wheaton, IL: Tyndale House, 1988) pp. 25-26.

Additional Copies of *Quiet Moments with God Devotional Journal for Women*
and other titles from Honor Books
are available from your local bookstore.

Check out these great titles:

Quiet Moments with God
Quiet Moments with God for Couples
Quiet Moments with God for Mothers
Quiet Moments with God for Teens
Quiet Moments with God Devotional Journal for Teens
Quiet Moments with God for Women

If you have enjoyed this book,
or if it has impacted your life,
we would like to hear from you.

Please contact us at:

Honor Books
An Imprint of Cook Communications Ministries
4050 Lee Vance View
Colorado Springs, CO 80918
www.cookministries.com